DATE DUE

BEING SKILLED

BEING SKILLED

The socializations of learning to read

STUART McNAUGHTON

METHUEN
London and New York

First published in 1987 by
Methuen & Co. Ltd
11 New Fetter Lane, London EC4P 4EE

Published in the USA by
Methuen & Co.
in association with Methuen Inc.
29 West 35th Street, New York, NY 10001

© 1987 Stuart McNaughton

Typeset by Boldface Typesetters, London EC1
Printed in Great Britain by T.J. Press (Padstow) Ltd, Padstow, Cornwall.

British Library Cataloguing in Publication Data

McNaughton, Stuart
Being skilled: the socializations of learning to read.
1. Reading, Psychology of
I. Title
428.4'01'9   LB1139.R4

ISBN 0-416-01622-7
ISBN 0-416-05302-5 Pbk

Library of Congress Cataloging-in-Publication Data

McNaughton, S. (Stuart)
  Being skilled

  Bibliography: p.
  Includes index.
    1. Reading.   2. Socialization.   3. Learning,
  Psychology of.
  I. Title.
LB1050.M.38   1987   372.4   87–11198

ISBN 0-416-01622-7
ISBN 0-416-05302-5 (pbk.)

Contents

vi Being Skilled

Acknowledgements

My special thanks to Trudie, Sam and Talia McNaughton who have all provided profound support. I am indebted to them for their understanding and contribution.

Many of the ideas contained in the book have grown from experiences with teachers and colleagues. Marie Clay and Ted Glynn are both, and I deeply appreciate their stimulating friendship. The book has benefited from other discussions with Margaret Clark, Richard Cowan, Joe Delquadri, Hazel Francis, Jim Marshall, Vance Hall, Colin Lankshear, Rod Maliphant, Todd Risley, Viviane Robinson, Kevin Wheldall and many of my students at the University of Auckland

Parts of the book were written while on Research and Study Leave from the University of Auckland. This opportunity provided by the University of Auckland, the generous financial and other practical support of the Nuffield Foundation and the stimulating hospitality of the University of London, Institute of Education (Department of Child Development) are much appreciated.

My own research reported in the book has been funded from a variety of sources. Principally research funds have been provided by the New Zealand Department of Education, the Children's Health Research Foundation, the University of Auckland Research Committee and the Juniper Gardens Children's Project.

Typing of this book has been a difficult and frustrating task. Special thanks to Paula Nicholson and Judith Hampson for their expertise, and to the editors at Methuen for their special skills.

Finally, my thanks to my parents Dick and Beryl McNaughton and Don and Oreti Pert for their encouragement and faith.

Introduction: another account of learning to read?

How a child learns to read holds a special fascination for psychological researchers. Over the last hundred years there must have been more books written about reading than any other single human skill. This is as it should be. Becoming literate is a major task which most contemporary societies deliberately set their children. So deliberate is this concern that the place and time for learning to read is legislated for, and providing instruction has become the prerogative of a professional élite.

The exact benefits that reading bestows on the user are controversial. For example one can find radically different claims about the effects that learning to read might have on political behaviour and decision-making. One American educator has argued that an important function of teaching reading is to ensure that a population is susceptible to political and social regulation (Postman, 1970). But Third World educators such as Paulo Freire see a different, more positive reality. Freire claims that becoming literate can be a cultural act for political freedom (Freire, 1972). Both writers would agree that being literate grants an expertise that alters the way in which a person can function in a society. Learning to read has psychological, social and political significance. This is why the attempts by psychological researchers to describe and explain the processes of that learning are tremendously important.

But what does this book hope to add to the extensive literature that is already available? The specific focus of this book is the early stages of learning to read: the acquisition of early oral and silent reading abilities. The overriding aim is to account for children's learning in homes and in classrooms. It is not an analysis of how children might learn to read. Rather it is a description and explanation of how children do learn to read and, in particular, how those children who learn easily and quickly are able so to do. Taking this approach certainly allows us to make claims about more ideal environments for children's learning, and how to avoid making children fail at school. But these claims will follow from the primary focus on how children actually learn to read within the environments in which they develop.

The explanations for how children learn to read which are offered in this book are based on a theory which has the following key features. It conceptualizes reading as a skill. Thus the way in which reading develops is partly determined by its structural properties as a skill. It is also a social practice determined by the activities of particular learners experiencing particular environments. The learner is seen as a problem-solver. When solving, the novice engages in directed learning activities. The effectiveness of these activities depends on how much the learner intends to learn and how much he or she actively controls that learning. In turn, environments are conceptualized as composed of variables which determine the learners' intentions to learn and the characteristics of the learning activities in which they are engaged.

The theoretical approach draws heavily on the work of writers such as Marie Clay (1979) and Frank Smith (1978) who also view reading as a skill. Similarly it draws on concepts of learning processes which examine how environments directly and indirectly influence learning. In addition, this account uses developmental views of social environments which provide an analysis of the contextual determinant on development.

Out of these different and often separate views of development and learning comes an integrated theory. What follows in successive chapters is a systematic presentation of this integrated account. However, before details are examined the need for a more comprehensive theory should be demonstrated. While there are many phenomena associated with learning to read which are discussed throughout the book there are three which are particularly compelling. These observations highlight the limitations of current understanding. They also illustrate the sorts of questions a theory of learning to read which deals with naturally occurring phenomena would need to address.

In search of explanations: three features of learning to read

Inventive conformity

Rebecca Barr has provided the basic observations that make up the first phenomenon. They come from her comparisons of the reading behaviours of children from different programmes of instruction. Two such programmes have been studied by Barr. There are those based on a systematic training of letter-sound associations (phonics programmes) and those which concentrate on teaching a carefully controlled set of basic words (sight word programmes).

Her 1972 observations describe the patterns of word recognition errors made by pre-readers taught a controlled set of words under experimental conditions by the two methods.[1] When children taught with a phonics programme were faced with a difficulty they tended, more so than the sight word programme children, not to respond. If they did respond, and it was an error response, it was far more likely to be a nonsense word (27 per cent of their response errors were of this sort compared with just 6 per cent for the sight word readers). Conversely, the sight word programme children were likely to substitute a real word. Also, the phonic programme children's errors were much more likely to contain the sound equivalent of the first letter in the target word (19 per cent of the response errors were so constrained whereas none of the whole word programme readers' substitutions were). With such data Barr demonstrated that different instructional methods influence patterns of word recognition errors in different ways. The patterns reflect different styles of approaching the task of reading.

A second study in 1974 took the observations out of an experimental setting and followed two groups of children over their first year of instruction with either a phonics or a sight word programme. Patterns of responding, this time after a year of exposure in classrooms, again differed according to the instructional programme. In addition, however, she found individual variation within programmes, especially at the beginning of the year. Some children, possibly due to preschool experiences, initially tended to respond with a pattern that was not consistent with the programme of instruction. But they had mostly changed to the requisite pattern by the end of the first year. Related to this individual variation in style of responding *within* programmes was an important outcome. Those children who were responding with the appropriate pattern after several months of instruction were the children who had made the greatest progress after the first year, as measured by standardized achievement measures of word recognition and comprehension tests.

Barr's observations and those which add to them may seem little more than a truism: simply that children learn what they are required to learn. But her data contain two significant implications. The first is that there are alternative developmental routes to acquiring reading skill. The second is that progress depends on adapting to the reading tasks that are set in classrooms.

Children develop different reading abilities in a sequence that is peculiar to a particular instructional milieu. The sequence is a product of that instructional milieu. Barr has described two alternative developmental routes, and there are other sequences which are different again from these.

These different sequences are, to some extent, viable alternatives. Reviewers of reading research find it very difficult to show any one programme as being markedly superior to another. This is so especially in the first years of school when comparisons are made of classroom achievements. So while it is often said that children learn despite teachers there is a more appropriate phrasing in the context of the present discussion: children can learn despite programmes.

This point does raise an interesting issue concerning the nature of 'developmental' phenomena. There are developmental theorists (Wolwhill, 1970) who have argued that reading isn't a true developmental phenomenon because it is a task which society imposes and deliberately instructs. Most societies need to set up special conditions for learning the 'unnatural' skill of reading. The state of affairs is often contrasted with a 'natural' developmental phenomenon such as learning to talk which doesn't need formal tuition. It may be currently the case that many children would find it difficult if not almost impossible to learn to read if they didn't go to school. But research which is reviewed in this book suggests formal tuition (that is schooling) is not a necessary condition for learning to read. Moreover, the argument that oral language does not need to be deliberately instructed does not exclude the possibility that language is *learned*. Indeed this would be a fair representation of the status of current language acquisition research.

Children learn to talk, which has as its corollary that there are conditions or contexts which can be conceived of as providing input for learning. Children learn to talk because their caregivers, siblings, peers and others provide conditions in naturally occurring interactions which are 'instructive'. Furthermore, it can be argued that different developmental sequences can be detected in how children learn language (e.g. Nelson, 1972; Snow, 1983). Even in sensorimotor development, often regarded as the most fixed and most fundamental of developmental phenomena one can find clear demonstrations of alternative sequences as well as rates of development, which are related to socially mediated conditions of learning (Zelazo, Zelazo and Kolb, 1971).

So there are alternative developmental routes for reading. But there is a second implication in the descriptions that researchers like Barr have supplied. Irrespective of the particular instructional programme, the behaviour of high progress readers is quite consistent in one major respect. Rapid acquisition is marked by the development of adaptive behaviours which meet the requirements of the reading tasks set by the programme. Successful learning is characterized by children capitalizing on what the programme offers. They develop abilities which are both efficient and expedient for the demands placed on them.

Again, this is not merely stating the obvious, mainly because the phenomenon involves more than a passive reception of instruction. What is 'efficient' and 'expedient' responding is often not specified in the instruction received, nor could it be except under extremely unusual circumstances. The active and potentially inventive nature of this conformity to the programme's demands can be demonstrated with observations from a third type of instructional programme.

In 'natural language' programmes beginning readers are faced with early reading books which are very different from those used by the programmes described by Barr. Sentences have been deliberately designed to approximate both the syntax and the experiences or knowledge encoded in a typical beginning reader's oral language. High progress readers in such a programme, faced with such a book, are exceptionally sensitive to syntactic structure and the meanings contained in the book. For example they use their oral language expertise to capitalize on the redundant sources of information in sentences to predict characteristics of text portions yet to be met. In concert with their developing knowledge of letters and associated sounds they use these redundancies in the syntax and meaning of a sentence to identify words.

This utilization is revealed in the errors high progress readers make in their first year of instruction. Clay's (1968) data on 100 readers over their first year at school showed that for a reader in the top 25 per cent of the sample (judged in terms of standardized tests of word recognition after the first year) about eight errors in ten were grammatically acceptable substitutions for the text word that was misread. The equivalent proportion for a reader in the bottom 25 per cent was closer to six errors in ten. Specifying the rules to follow in producing these acceptable substitutions would be a very difficult linguistic task. Certainly teachers in the programmes do not attempt to specify what readers need to do in order to anticipate words or word classes for syntactic and semantic cues. What they do provide, however, is an instructional environment that accentuates the predictability of the language in the texts which are used. As will be argued in Chapter 7 they achieve this through their use of conversation, their emphasis on the development of writing skills, and other events.

These data supply behavioural evidence of what could be termed inventive adaptation to the instructional programme. There are other examples. High progress children systematically taught with a well-structured phonics programme were found by Calfee and Piontkowski (1981) to have well-developed sensitivity to letter-sound associations early in their instruction. This knowledge enabled them both to decode accurately and to write nonsense words. Yet the 'words' themselves and the experimental tasks which tested this expertise were presumably not part of their normal instructional programme.

Going beyond the teaching received

From such observations high progress readers can be characterized as taking advantage of the idiosyncratic resources that a programme offers. So effective is this that the forms which much of this adaptive responding may ordinarily take could not have been directly taught. But this is only one facet of high progress reading. There are other facets of their behaviour which make it even more obvious that the learning which high progress readers engage in is anything but passive or slavish.

The second phenomenon which challenges our understanding of learning to read is hinted at in one of Barr's studies (1974). It indicated that effective adaptation to a phonics programme, revealed by patterns of responding in word identification predicted high achievement by the end of the first year of instruction. Achievement was measured not only in terms of word identification but also in an aspect of reading skill which had not been emphasized: comprehension.

This feature can be called going beyond the teaching received. High progress readers, irrespective of their instructional milieu, go *beyond* the direct teaching they receive. They discover those elements that would have been directly taught had they been in a different programme. These discoveries are of just those elements that guarantee more general proficiency.

There are two sets of studies of early reading behaviour which have systematically observed this feature. One is of children learning in a highly regular 'code emphasis' or phonics programme, and the other is of children in a 'natural language' programme. Both observed children over the first year of instruction and could describe the growth in knowledge, and strategic use of that knowledge when reading texts.

Children learning in the phonics programme were observed by Cohen (1975) under two conditions. They read texts on which they received instruction (example: 'We hear Pete read. Neal sees three weeds. He feels the leaf.'), and they read non-instructional texts. These were the texts that might be found in a different programme. They were less phonically controlled and had the form of familiar stories (example: 'Mr Green and Mr Kanya look for a chimp. They want a chimp to go to the moon.'). Of particular interest are the error patterns on the non-instructional text.

Graph 1 in Figure 1 shows the percentages of word substitution errors which were grammatically 'acceptable' over eight months of schooling. An error was judged 'acceptable' on a rather simple criterion, whether or not the sentence where the

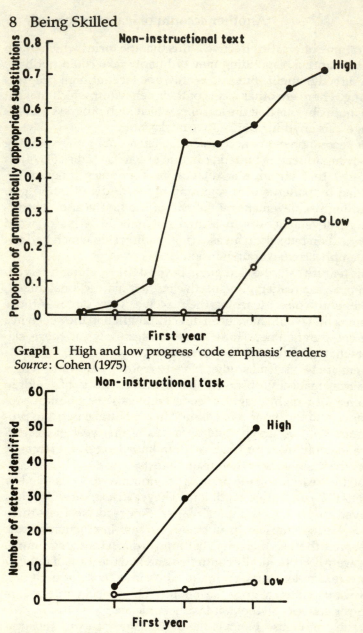

Graph 1   High and low progress 'code emphasis' readers
Source: Cohen (1975)

Graph 2   High and low progress 'natural language' readers
Source: Clay (1966)

Figure 1   Reading behaviour of first-year children in two programmes

substitution occurred could be completed in any sensible way. The thirteen best readers of the sample (the top quartile) show increasingly higher percentages of word substitutions which were grammatically acceptable on the more story-like non-instructional text. They were considerably advanced compared with the thirteen worst readers.

Without further data this observation could legitimately be condemned as circular. After all, the selection of best and worst readers was partly made from the average number of words identified accurately on both texts over the year. But with further analyses of error patterns it can be seen that the best readers developed two styles of text reading to produce accurate identification of words on the two different texts. On the phonically regular texts the good readers approached the task of accurate reading by paying very close attention to letters and thereby attempted to decode each word (about nine word substitutions in ten contained at least half the letters of the text word). On the non-instructional texts they were less likely to attempt an accurate sound approximation of a word (fewer than two-thirds of their substitutions had half of the letters of the text word). But they were somewhat more sensitive to grammatical cues and they were much more likely to self-correct errors (17 per cent of errors were self-corrected on the instructional texts compared with 30 per cent on the non-instructional texts). Their error patterns and self-corrections show that they were developing the ability to make use of extra information. This extra information was available from syntactic and semantic information in the texts.

The response patterns represent a strategic adaptation to both the demands made and the pay off available, in the two types of texts. Choosing to decode each word carefully versus attempting words with less immediate accuracy and fixing up mistakes via self-corrections seem eminently reasonable styles for accomplishing the tasks 'accurately' and thereby gaining the different types of meaning available in each. But it must be emphasized that the components of the style adopted for the non-instructional texts were not directly taught in the programme.

This example can be reversed. There are studies (e.g. Clay, 1966) which yield equivalent data for children in a 'natural language' programme. Graph 2 in Figure 1 shows the development in knowledge over the first year of instruction that readers gained about the letters of the alphabet and their sound equivalents. Readers were required to identify letters, either by providing alphabetic names, sound equivalents or by supplying a word beginning with the letter. The twenty-five high progress readers (top quartile of a representative sample) on first entering school could give one of the responses to only four letters.

After one year, the average was fifty letters able to be accurately responded to (out of fifty-four letter forms commonly used in English orthography). The identification could be made flexibly, not only with alphabetic names but also with sound associations and with words having the letter in the initial position. In contrast, the twenty-five low progress readers could give acceptable responses to only six letters after one year of instruction.

The knowledge gained by the high progress group went beyond the teaching elements of the programme. Little if any time is usually spent directly focused on teaching letters or letter-sound associations as shown by systematic observations of the tasks teachers and children engage in during reading instruction (B. Watson, 1980). The measure of progress in Clay's study is based on a standardized achievement test of word identification so these initial observations which associate letter knowledge with high progress are less susceptible to the criticism of circularity than the equivalent observations of Cohen's.

To match Cohen's observations further there are also Ng's (1979) descriptions of high progress readers from the 'natural language' programmes after one year of instruction reading both instructional and non-instructional texts. In this case the instructional texts are those which are designed to be highly interesting stories in their own right and the non-instructional texts have a decoding emphasis, being based on controlled exposure to letter-sound correspondences.

Again, strategic adaptation to the demands of the texts was clearly observable as high progress readers read selections of instructional and non-instructional texts. With the more meaningful stories these readers attempted to produce contextually appropriate word substitutions (nine out of ten errors were acceptable either in terms of the sentence portion preceding the error, or the portion following the error, or the whole sentence). The likelihood of an error being self-corrected was also high (60 per cent of errors were self-corrected). But the readers' word substitutions suggest they were attempting to make meaningful responses rather than accurate responses in terms of letter-sound associations (only two errors in ten had half the letters of the text word).

However, with phonically regular texts the high progress readers read more like their peers learning via a phonics emphasis. Considerably more attention was paid to producing an accurate sound representation of text words than the other texts (more than four errors in ten contained half the letters of the text word). Responses were somewhat less likely to be contextually appropriate and only 10 per cent of errors were self-corrected. A different style of responding was adopted. But it yielded relatively high accuracy for these texts even though they were judged by the children to be very odd. These readers, like their high progress phonics peers, had acquired knowledge and could use that knowledge to advantage even though they had not received explicit instruction.

Clay's data about letter identification in the natural language programme indicate that the extent of knowledge after one year of instruction is highly correlated with progress at two and three years. The correlations were higher than those for the general variables of tested intelligence and reading readiness which she examined.

In stark contrast, she found in a different study that this time knowledge about books and story reading was the variable that was most associated with reading progress for children. Why was there a difference? These were different children learning in a phonics programme (see Clay, 1979).

For these children developing knowledge about what constitutes a book and the knowledge of some of the conventions of written language, rather than the specific focus of their programme (learning to associate letters and sounds) was most associated with high progress. Her conclusion from these comparisons summarizes this feature of learning to read:

> Those children who make good progress are those who gain that skill in spite of, or in addition to what they are taught.
>
> (Clay, 1979, p. 249)

Never schooled and yet learned[2]

The final set of observations focuses on the unschooled learner, in particular those children who have learned to read before school. There are two major group studies of American and English early readers conducted in the 1960s and early 1970s (Clark, 1976; Durkin, 1966). These studies are discussed further in Chapter 10. Their conclusions about such precocious learning can be introduced here with a dramatic example which comes from a fictionalized account of one child's learning.

Oskar, the diminutive hero of Günter Grass's novel *The Tin Drum*, is thrown out of school on his first day for a number of atypical acts, including shattering the teacher's spectacles with a high-pitched scream. Although denied schooling he decides he still needs to learn to read, because reading and writing are valued and used to advantage by grown-ups. Oskar had refused to grow physically beyond his third birthday. As a 6-year-old, in order to learn to read, he systematically capitalizes on his physical appeal as a toddler and behaves as one. He develops an enduring relationship with one person who reads stories to him. He chooses the stories, two in particular, and appealingly demands of his chosen tutor that they be read repeatedly.

Oskar shows intense sustained interest during these story-reading sessions which he initiates and controls. On occasions, however, he throws a tantrum, in the process of which he manages to rip pages out of books and conceal them under his shirt. Later, in the quiet of his own bedroom, he smoothes the pages out and matches the written words against the remembered oral reading. By systematically matching patterns and creating new patterns (novel combinations of pages) he learns 'quickly and regularly without much effort'.

In the general case of the precocious reader truth mimics Günther Grass's fiction, albeit with less malevolence. An estimated three-quarters of the children classified as early readers learn without deliberate or planned help from older persons. Like Oskar most early readers have set out to learn to read rather than being systematically intentionally taught. Indeed, a characteristic response of the parents in the two major group studies is that they were embarrassed and a little worried by the initiative taken by the children.

The question of what variables are associated with this precocity is the subject of a later chapter. It is more relevant to the present point to note those variables that are not found to be related to precocity. The learning is achieved without it being necessary for the child to come from a 'high' social class or from a family of a particular size or composition. Nor is it necessary to have parents of a certain age or level of education. More importantly, perhaps, it is not necessary for the child to have high tested intelligence.

Although many of the precocious readers that have been studied are above average in measured intelligence there are significant numbers of average and even below average intelligence readers in the group of precocious readers. This indicates that a child does not have to show exceptional learning across a broad range of skills. The factors that influence learning can be relatively specific to literacy skills and they are certainly of a different kind from the usual variables such as 'class' studied by psychologists concerned with conditions of socialization.

The available studies do indicate the specific attributes of environments that are associated with precocity. A theory of learning to read needs to explain why these environmental variables operating in home settings provide conditions for learning. But the challenge of this phenomenon is not simply one of establishing principles which explain the relationship between aspects of the child's behaviour such as an intention to learn, and aspects of the immediate *home* environment such as reading as a salient family activity (see Table 19, p. 189). There is a more general requirement. The concepts which might explain socialization of literacy at home need to be applicable to the realities of classroom learning and vice versa.

If a theory of learning to read is to explain everyday learning phenomena it must deal both with the precocious readers' development and the processes of acquisition at school. Although the course of learning may differ in major respects, ideally a generalized theory which accounts for what can happen in both settings is required. Such a theory would be able to compare and contrast the dimensions of different socialization experiences at home and at school.

It turns out that very few writers attempt to do this. Most accounts of learning to read focus exclusively on classroom experiences. There are assumptions made about and in some cases descriptions of the variability between children in terms of their reading abilities on reaching school. But the account is focused on how the skill then develops within the deliberate environments constructed by schools. Conversely most studies of preschool readers do not explicitly attempt to conceptualize learning and the conditions of development in a framework that would include activities in classroom contexts.

What sort of explanation?

Taken individually, contemporary explanations of the processes of learning to read do not deal easily with the challenge set by these phenomena. The need for a more comprehensive or more integrated theory can be underlined in two ways.

Is and ought: predictions about how reading should be taught

Claims about how reading ought to be taught abound in psychological theories of reading. These predictions are usually unequivocal in specifying a best and, explicitly or by implication, a wrong way of teaching reading. Protagonists can be lined up against each other.

Frank Smith's (1978) understanding of reading has led him to list twelve ways to make learning to read difficult. These add up to a concerted attack on code emphasis (phonic) programmes. His particularly *bête noir* is one which might use procedures such as extrinsic reinforcement coupled with discrimination or concept learning tasks which are presented in isolation from a meaningful context. There are such programmes and their theoreticians in turn offer predictions of what an ineffective instructional programme would look like. They criticize environments which do not specifically produce knowledge of letter and letter-sound associations at the outset of teaching and are so loosely structured that learners make numbers of errors early in their learning (e.g. Becker and Engelmann, 1978).

There are of course instructional programmes which have the characteristics which these latter theorists predict would be less than effective. For example a central feature in the 'natural language' programmes described earlier is that errors be allowed to occur and to be corrected by learners.

Such predictions and the accounts that they are based on are inadequate. The existence of alternative developmental routes which do not appear to confer on their separate students, at least within the first few years of instruction, any advantage in classroom achievement undermine their believability. The creative and inventive characteristics of high progress learners in any programme further call into question the adequacy of a unilateral theory of instruction. Finally, theories of learning to read which can be operationalized only in terms of controlled instruction in classroom environments fail totally to account for children who are 'learned but not yet schooled'.

A construction model: active learner and active environment

Theories of learning to read can be roughly grouped into two types. First, there are those which take the child as the major focus of analysis. Some of these view the child as an information processor whose processing mechanisms and knowledge structure determine what is learned. Others of these adopt a less formal model but nevertheless conceptualize the child as controlling learning via structures for perceiving and acquiring information. These structures provide the bases for operating on the sources of information available in the environment.

Within this assorted group of theories there are other differences. For example some adopt a very mechanical model of information processing in contrast with ones of a more active information gatherer. But they each have in common a tradition of downgrading or ignoring the significance of environmental conditions in determining what is learned. What is learned is determined by the child. Environments make it easy or hard by providing clear or noisy information. The environments are not the source of motivation to learn. The processing of information is fueled by systems of internal regulation, and external motivating systems are at best redundant, at worst interfering.

But environmental conditions have more of an effect, either positively or negatively, than such theories explicitly allow. The forms that learning takes over time, as shown by the conformity *and* invention phenomena, are very closely determined by the structures of the environment. It is not simply a matter of acquiring information more slowly or more quickly. The style of learning and the features of what is learned are intimately connected with environments. The phenomenon of precocious readers who are not necessarily generally precocious nor generally skilled also strongly suggests environments are active determiners of how learning processes occur.

Contrasted with these child-oriented perspectives are the various types of learning theory. Again the grouping is a simplification because they vary along several dimensions such as the degree of determinism assumed in the theory or the degree to which the theory admits reciprocal processes of influence. But again they have a commonality. That is a tendency to view the child as an organism with repertoires of behaviours which do not, however, have structural properties. Behaviours involved in reading are assumed to have the same formal properties as any other behavioural system, and behavioural change is controlled and therefore explained by deliberate modifications of environmental events.

But the function of environmental events can easily be demonstrated to be determined by activities that children engage in. For example precocious readers evidently often learn to read in spite of there being no deliberate modification of environments that would systematically teach them. Perhaps the more compelling phenomena, however, are those showing creativity and invention. While it is possible to train children to be creative and inventive, and it is possible to view the activities which might produce them in behavioural terms, their 'spontaneous' and generative nature makes any ordinary learning theory suspect. The children can contribute too much to their learning in the absence of deliberate contingencies to make typical learning theory accounts viable.

Both approaches appear incomplete, yet each appears to offer some analysis of phenomena that the other lacks. The solution is not obvious. They cannot easily be integrated because the concepts of one cannot simply be translated into the concepts of the other framework. How is a traditional behavioural framework to incorporate a concept of processing mechanisms and still retain the general commitment to treating reading in terms of a response system? And how can an information-processing model adapt to concepts of control over responding by contingencies?

Admittedly these approaches are not immediately compatible. But a new theory which incorporates some features of both is possible. The first characteristic of such a theory is that it sees reading skill as constructed by a process that is both transactional and interactional. Learning occurs through the actions of the learners as they are guided, directed or constrained by attributes of environments. How the actions occur and what the actions achieve are jointly determined by a dynamic relationship between learner and the environments within which the learner exists.

There is no learner without a set of experiences, and events are not experiences without a learner. Furthermore, the learner's activities in learning are not either on or off, operative or dormant. There are degrees and varieties of action. Conversely the experiences for learning are potentially multifaceted.

This is a construction model of learning. In the following chapters children learning to read are viewed as engaged, with varying degrees of involvement, in solving the learning tasks presented to them by active, malleable and changing environments. It will be claimed that effective learning arises from actively performing the skill. But viewing both learners and environments as potentially active agents in a construction that is based on performance demands a special description of what is constructed, what it is to read. Reading and changes in how one reads need to be described in a way which allows for potentially active learning within active environments.

The only description of the performance of reading which is consistent with a construction model of learning is that of reading as a skill. Showing why this is so will be the task of the next two chapters.

This book

The purpose then of the book is to explain how effective learners actually learn to read. It describes real environments and explains their effects. It takes reading phenomena from home and school settings and, using concepts which are applicable to both settings, explains how they occur. It does this by examining reading as a skill and then by showing how learning activities arise from the problems which readers face. It presents an analysis of how multifaceted environments can influence learning activities and applies these concepts to the available descriptions of home and school environments.

Part 1

An orchestrated performance: reading as a skill

1 Strategies and feedback

To claim that reading is best viewed as a skill is to claim that it has certain properties in common with other so-called skills. These properties are suggested in Bruner's description of skilful action.

> In broad outline, skilled action requires recognizing the features of a task, its goal, and means appropriate for its attainment; a means of converting this information into appropriate action, and a means of getting feedback that compares the objective sought with present state attained. . . . When we learn something like a skill, it is in the very nature of the case that we master a wide variety of possible ways for attaining an objective – many ways to skin a cat. For we learn ways of constructing many responses that fit our grasp of what is appropriate to an objective.
>
> (Bruner, 1971, p. 112)

Components of skills

Bruner refers to several general properties of a skill. The most obvious of these is the performance itself, which has the general property of being strategic. But this property is dependent on two other components of skilled behaviour. Skilful performance derives from knowledge, knowledge of the goals, functions and expressions of the skill. And this knowledge supplies the basis for the third component, that of self-regulatory activities apparent in the way performances are directed and controlled.

While these properties are referred to as components they are, in reality, inseparable. They are interdependent parts in the skilled act, parts of an orchestrated whole. However, examining them as components is useful because the description is made easier, and because their development can, to some extent, be analysed separately.

Performance strategies

The act of reading, whether by a novice or an expert, has a strategic quality. This quality can be seen even in early reading as shown in a series of studies of high progress readers in a 'natural language' reading programme (McNaughton, 1981a, 1983a, 1983b, 1984). The aim was to describe how 6-year-old readers deal with unfamiliar words in books which they were reading by themselves for the first time.

The children were given passages out of unfamiliar books which contained target words. These words had not been encountered previously and the readers were demonstrably unable to recognize them in isolation. Successive encounters which the readers had with these previously unknown words were monitored. Their encounters had two major characteristics. With some words reading remained fluent. The rate of reading did not alter and without hesitation the readers made a response and kept reading. Even on that first encounter the readers had a high chance of being correct.

With other words the readers stopped before any attempt was made. Within about five seconds, usually with no easily observable additional activity other than fixating on the difficult word, a response typically occurred. If not correct it was often a very close approximation in terms of grammatical and semantic (meaning) characteristics of the text word. Apparently cues within the sentence provided a strong source of information. But because sounds corresponding to initial and final letters in the difficult word also were often found in the readers' responses it could be concluded that some systematic sampling of letter (graphemic) cues was also occurring.

The first route to solving words in context might be termed fluent guessing. In contrast, the second involved deliberate checking. The data from one of the studies, which involved twenty-seven high progress readers (aged 5:6 to 6:6), illustrate these general features.

With this group of readers an average of 37 per cent of the target unknown words were checked in some way and the remaining six words in ten were read without any interruption. The characteristics of their deliberate checking are shown in Table 1. More than three-quarters of the unknown words were checked before a response was attempted (77 per cent per reader). Checking of words mostly took the form of a pause in which the reader focused on the word, with no other easily observable behaviour such as sounding out word components, or looking at illustrations (context use) or asking for help. These latter activities occurred relatively infrequently. Given that checking did occur the most probable outcome was a response (in 53 per cent of these checks). In the absence of a response the readers sometimes stopped for up to ten seconds at which time they were asked to keep reading. Occasionally they left the word out and kept reading.

In what way can the readers' behaviour solving words be said to be strategic; what does this description entail? Common to all

Table 1 Checking unknown words in context by high progress 6-year-olds

Characteristics of checking	Proportion of encounters
Sequence	
Check first	0.77
Response then check	0.23
Behaviour	
Pause	0.66
Sounding out	0.18
Context use	0.09
Seek help	0.07
Checking outcome	**Probability of outcome**
Check → respond	0.53
Check → stop	0.33
Check → leave out	0.14

Source: McNaughton (1983b)

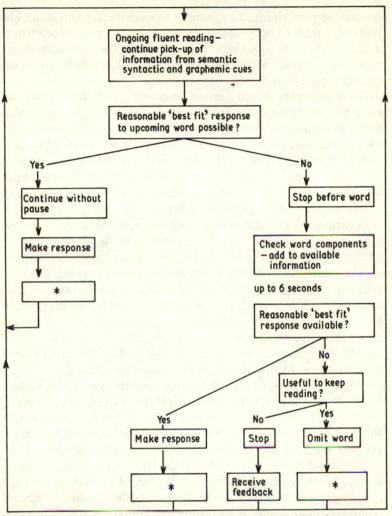

Figure 2   Idealized word-solving strategy for 6-year-old high progress readers in a natural language programme

Note: *Regulatory activities occur throughout the sequence and
include checking and evaluation after responses are made.

definitions of strategic behaviour are two complementary attributes. They are captured in David Wood's enviably succinct definition of a strategy as a 'programmatic assembly of operations aimed at a common goal' (1978). The first attribute is the appearance of consistent patterning, a regularity in performing the skill. The pattern is made of up a flexible sequence of acts which conform to a rule an observer could infer from watching the performance. In turn this implies that there is some potential for choice in routes to obtaining a goal.

The 6-year-olds' behaviour when reading unfamiliar texts can be described in terms of specific rules. At one level these rules detail the sequence and conditions for alternative routes in solving difficult words. A simple idealized representation of this strategy is shown in Figure 2. It is assumed that choices are made in some way, at various points. For example the 'first' choice for different 'solving' routes is assumed to depend on whether a good response can be made in the course of normal fluent performance.

According to Wood it is necessary to show that the word solving consistently conforms to a rule and in some way choices are made. Evidence for the former has been found in several studies which show a consistent pattern in the checking route. The consistency of pausing and the characteristics of how information is sampled, which sets this style of solving apart from other potential styles, is compelling. Choice is suggested in the finding that the readers apparently do different things with different sorts of words. And they appear to know before they try some words that they have to stop and systematically check them.

Wood's definition also refers to a common goal. The second attribute of strategic behaviour is that the sequence of observed acts has a specific function or goal; indeed, the rule is only fully sensible with reference to the state of affairs defined by a goal. For the 6:0-year-old readers who have been described, their strategies reflect knowledge about the tasks presented to them as they learn to read, particularly the types of texts used and the goals of the skill as defined by their experiences in the natural language programme. For example unfamiliar words, those that have not previously been encountered, are likely to be very predictable from context and solvable when informative graphemes are checked.

What is implied here is that this relationship between strategy and knowledge is constructed out of socialization experiences. Indeed, when children are observed in different programmes or at different points in the development of their skill the social roots of this relationship become apparent. In this respect, Barr's comparisons between children in different programmes which were discussed in the introduction provide a classic demonstration of strategies varying with knowledge.

So learning to read involves learning to perform strategically. It also involves self-regulation. But before this second component of skilled action is examined two possible confusions need to be clarified. The first is what counts as a performance strategy in reading? The illustrative data and their representation in Figure 2 identify a strategy for 'solving' unknown words met in context. It is possible to identify the two tactics or routes used within this strategy as strategies themselves. Alternatively, it is possible to embed the word-solving performance within a more general oral reading performance strategy.

In other words, the identification of a strategy might be made at different levels of reading performance. A definition such as Wood's allows different levels of anlaysis given that 'goals' and flexible 'operations' can be identified. It is apparent that different authors writing about reading as a skill have highlighted the strategic quality of performance, but at differing levels of analysis.

The second potential confusion is also definitional. The term strategy as used here has been qualified by the word performance. The strategies which mark skilled action are strategies of performance. In the case of word solving in context the strategy is very obviously problem-oriented. It may also result in a solution which is related to acquiring more knowledge of words, or indeed how to use that knowledge in performance. But the strategies to which reference has been made do not of themselves produce changes in performance and knowledge. With additional activities carried out by the reader they become primary *vehicles* for learning, but they are not the source.

Other writers who have analysed strategies in problem-solving and concept-learning have used terms such as 'learning strategy' or 'strategy of acquisition'. It would seem they are referring to similar phenomena as in reading, strategies of performance which enable a goal to be met. In the process of achieving that goal some learning may eventuate but the cause of the learning is in other activities. Given our later concern to examine those learning activities in which novices engage that produce changes in performance and knowledge, it would be confusing to use such terms here.[1]

Regulatory activities

Among the descriptions which are commonly applied to skilled behaviour are references to the automatic and fluid nature of performance; to flexibility and adaptability in the face of altered environmental demands; to purposefulness in initiation and performance of the act; and, even when fully proficient, to the potential for a creative modification in the deployment of the skill. Collectively these descriptions reflect the important psychological feature of regulation.

A skilled act is a result of constant control by the performer. The automatic quality of responding may sometimes interfere with the appreciation of this regulation but successful performance depends upon continued regulation. Regulation is achieved in three ways: via feedback, intention and intervention. Because of its significance in learning to read the rest of this chapter and much of the next is devoted to these characteristics of regulation.

Regulatory phenomena in early reading

An extensive body of reading research has demonstrated the presence of regulation in early oral reading. Self-correction of oral reading errors is a pervasive feature of early reading in such programmes described as 'look and say', 'natural language' and 'whole-word' programmes.[2] Independent of external prompting a normal progress child, that is a child who is learning the requirements of the particular programme at an average rate, will correct around one in three incorrect attempts when reading texts at an appropriate level of difficulty. A typical example provided by Clay is taken from the protocols of a first year reader.

(1)   TEXT: You went to the shop for the bread.
        CHILD: 'You want . . . won't . . . went to the shop for bread.'

As noted above, self-corrections during oral reading are limited to specific programmes. Indeed, in some programmes they may be explicitly defined and acted on by tutors as unacceptable, being seen as unnecessary dysfluencies. If the argument made in succeeding chapters is correct these programmes may have inappropriate outcomes. They restrict opportunities to regulate with potential difficulties over time for the general development of the skill *if* no other opportunities to practise and regulate are available.

The attributes of texts which are related to the occurrence of self-corrrection have been investigated. Semantic and syntactic dissonance brought about by an error is a good predictor of self-correction, especially for high progress children. That is if the error results in a response which is syntactically unacceptable or it produces a gross distortion in meaning then a self-correction is highly probable. Example (1) illustrates these conditions.

Dissonance and self-correction can occur prospectively as an error jars with sentence portions which follow the response. Self-corrections also are associated with dissonance that occurs retrospectively as an error breaks linguistic constraints already established prior to the production of the error.

But semantic and syntactic dissonance are not the only sources of dissonance associated with self-correction. Dissonance is also created by mismatch between the graphemes and associated phonemic representation of the textual stimulus and the phonemes and associated graphemic representation of the reader's error response. Such mismatches can be also associated with self-correction, even in the absence of syntactic and semantic confusion. Here is another example from Clay:

(2) TEXT: The teacher said, 'Hullo Timothy'
     READER: 'The teacher said *to* . . . Hullo Timothy'

A note about how errors occur is appropriate at this point. The error a reader makes provides an insight into the reader's attention to sources of textual information when making the response. Lack of attention or misrepresentation of stimuli may produce an error. To avoid the connotations of both unfortunate psychological and pedagogical theorizing various writers have adopted the term 'miscue' to replace that of 'error'. This certainly captures the concept of problematic selective attention. It tends, however, to remove the phenomenon from an important area of psychological research, that of error behaviour and corrective feedback in complex learning. The term error is retained here in order that connections between error phenomena in oral reading and other areas of complex learning be maintained.

Errors of the sort contained in the examples given above can be said to reflect incomplete use of the information available from graphemic cues, syntactic cues and semantic cues to form an accurate integrated response. Correction of these errors involves the redeployment of selective attention. In the face of dissonance readers will act to increase the salience of informative cues. They must re-examine stimuli from which information has already been picked up. Or they may search for cues that were previously unattended.

One final set of data on self-corrections is pertinent to this discussion about regulation in reading. Developmental changes in self-corrections, suggested in cross-sectional data and revealed in longitudinal research, show the sources of dissonance associated with self-correction change with increasing proficiency. At 5:3 a mismatch between number of spoken words and written words in a familiar sentence on a page may cue self-correciton. But older children's self-corrections are related to subtle inconsistencies at the level of interword syntactic and semantic stimuli and intraword graphemic stimuli. Furthermore, overt self-correction may become less frequent after the first years. This is not only associated with generalized high accuracy and automatic responding but also as the perceived need to provide an oral (that is public demonstration of) self-correction changes.

Lest these data on self-correction appear unequivocal it should be noted that there are substantial issues in the interpretation of some aspects. An often-quoted finding for readers in natural language programmes is that between 5:0 and 6:0 years high progress readers self-correct a high *ratio* of errors (for example around one self-correction to three errors) compared with low progress readers (fewer than one self-correction to five errors). In the original research such as Clay's the ratios were found to be highly correlated with progress over the first year of instruction, more so than reading readiness or intelligence test measures. Clay's data in Table 2 show the correlations between each of three measures, self-correction rates, reading readiness scores and intelligence test scores, and a test of reading achievement at the end of the first and second years of instruction.

Recently, however, Thompson (1981) has pointed out that in the computation of a self-correction ratio the number of errors made critically affects the ratio.[3] The ratio can change dramatically even though the number of self-corrections remains the

Table 2   Correlates of reading progress in Clay's longitudinal study

| | Reading progress [1] | |
	6:0	7:0
Self-correction rates (means 5:0 to 6:0)	0.67	0.61
Reading readiness (at 5:0)	0.55	0.49
General intelligence (at 5:0)	0.55	0.54

Source: Clay (1979)
Note: [1] Progress of 100 children measured by word tests.

same. He recalculated the total error rates of progress groups in Clay's original research reports and found two things. The low progress groups were making more errors but they were producing an equivalent *number* of self-corrections. The net effect was to produce low *ratios* for low progress groups. Other researchers also have found similar numbers produced by low and high progress groups, especially when reading books that are experienced at the same level of difficulty for each group.

Thompson has questioned the theoretical and predictive status of self-corrections given that frequency does not distinguish progress groups. But arguing on these grounds that self-corrections may be epiphenomena is not convincing. In response it can be argued first that the presence of self-correction in all progress groups is an indication of its central importance in development. Like other skills learned under conditions where children can monitor their success or failure self-correction is an integral part of the act. Second, self-corrections may have different functions or outcomes for different readers. For example the studies suggest that self-correcting for different progress groups can be associated with different cues. For normal and high progress readers a function of self-correction is to maintain a meaningful context for effective decoding strategies, so that ongoing accuracy within and across stories is effected (Goodman and Burke, 1973; McNaughton, 1981c; Weber, 1970). It appears that self-correcting is not as functional for low progress readers.

Feedback in self-regulation

These data on self-correction illustrate the processes involved in the regulation of a skill. They first of all show that readers monitor their behaviour and evaluate their performance. In analyses of skilled activity such activities are conceptualized in terms of feedback control and they have been examined both behaviourally, as in the descriptions of self-correcting, or neurophysiologically.

Across skills feedback has the same general features. The behaviours making up the performance strategy are continually monitored, evaluated and corrected in terms of how they fit into the overall performance. There is constant comparison of intended action with feedback from action already accomplished (Bruner, 1973; Kaye, 1979).

Modes of feedback: performance-directed and other-directed   There are two modes of feedback which can operate in the regulation of skilled behaviour. One involves a feedback loop which arises from the performance of the skill. This can be called a performance-directed feedback loop and it makes performance-directed regulation possible. In reading, such loops are exemplified by a completely independent self-contained cycle of performance, ongoing monitoring, evaluations and correction.

A reader making adequate progress monitors performance checking for dissonance in the pursuit of an accurate representation of the author's intended messages. Under appropriate circumstances checking the adequacy of performance and modifying that performance on the basis of feedback can be the sole prerogative of even the most unskilled novice. Rudimentary forms of self-correction have been observed in children who have barely started formal instruction in a natural language programme. Examples come from children reading picture books with repetitive sentence frames (for example, 'Here is a cow', 'Here is a horse', and so on). Novices are able to check that the right message has been obtained when reading a caption. They do it by comparing the oral sentence response, which is minimally based on a systematic identification of words, with general cues such as the picture or the number of words in the sentence caption.

Similar acts of self-correcting have been documented in other skills. For example there are observations of self-correction by infants, preschool and school age children learning language and in the development of the sensorimotor skill of reaching and grasping. In the latter case infants closely monitor their hands and the object to be grasped, with correction following incomplete or erroneous reach.[4]

Some skills allow substantial opportunities for performance-based regulation from the beginning. From the beginnings of reaching and grasping infants can perceive, at least in general terms, the task and its goal, and hence what is needed to solve the task. Others, particularly the symbolic (social) skills such as reading require a more elaborate knowledge base to be gained. Children need to learn the arbitrary symbols and social conventions associated with the skill. This does not mean that environments for reading cannot be encountered which allow for rudimentary forms of performance-directed regulation. But it does mean that regulation is tempered by the need to gain conventionalized information from a more skilled person.

Performance-directed regulation is still possible in the early stages but often may be able to proceed only as far as registering that one's performance is inadequate. The monitoring and evaluation phases of regulation may occur in the absence of being able to do anything about a problem because of insufficient knowledge or an immature performance strategy. Being aware but not fully capable is arguably the point at which enhanced feedback from someone else is most effective. This condition arises from a 'near miss'. It is the reality behind such catchy pedagogical phrases as the 'teachable moment', and is the object of direct manipulation in a Socratic dialogue. However, children may confront situations in which the potential for feedback that is inherent in performing the task is reduced to a minimum. For example, the task may be presented in such a way that its meaning is not directly perceivable, nor is the adequacy of one's performance directly perceivable. A beginning reader attempting to read a text which is beyond his or her level of skill does not have a performance strategy which will generate usable response-produced feedback.

When situations are confronted in which performance-directed feedback is not possible, where the task is literally meaningless, then the meaning of the task and the goals for performance come to reside in the behaviour of another. That is regulation either has to be initiated by a 'tutor' and monitoring and evaluating activities are undertaken by that person (the child is performing blindly as it were), or the child's regulatory activities are centred on the mismatch between performance and the behaviour of the tutor (the child is still blind to what a response 'means' in terms of the skill). Response-produced feedback is extrinsic, existing in statements such as 'No', 'Wrong', 'Yes', 'Right', and so on.

This is the second mode of feedback in the regulation of skilled behaviour. In contrast to the first mode of feedback it arises outside the performance. It is the condition of not directly having, or not being able to pick up immediately perceivable information about the adequacy of one's performance of the skill. It occurs where the meaning of performance is added by the behaviour of a tutor.

The significance of performance-directed feedback   Feedback in some form is critical to skilled behaviour. The psychological reality of this general claim is clear and examples can be drawn from many areas of research. At one extreme are the neurophysiological studies of people who are unable to pick up response-produced information because normal pathways have been interfered with. For example Luria (1973) describes a condition of kinaesthetic apraxia where disturbance of fine movements results from missing incoming impulses.

Performance of a symbolic skill such as reading is as dependent on response-produced feedback as the motor skills studied by Luria. Although the phenomena of most practical interest involve feedback at a behavioural level and interference which is social in origin, the consequences can be just as dramatic as those produced by neural damage.

This is demonstrated by a study of normal progress 6:0-year-olds in a 'natural language' programme (McNaughton and Glynn, 1981). As the children read texts, tutors corrected errors whenever they occurred, using two different procedures. With delayed correction the tutors waited for at least five seconds if a reader paused after an error, or until the end of a sentence if the reader kept on reading. Under a second procedure the identical feedback was given immediately, within five seconds of an error having occurred.

The latter condition interfered with response-produced feedback and performance-based regulation. There was little opportunity to monitor and evaluate the consequences of errors either through systematic checking when making the response, or checking the response made against information (that is syntactic and semantic cues) available in the sentence portion following the error.

Not surprisingly this interference, consistently applied with each error, considerably reduced self-corrected errors compared with the delay condition. And self-corrected errors continued to be infrequent when the children were given a second set of texts immediately after tutoring with immediate error corrections. These texts were slightly more difficult but were read without any help, even that available in error correction.

The self-correction data are shown on page 34. Two groups of children received both immediate and delayed correction in counterbalanced sequence of four phases each of which lasted eight days. Results for the days for each phase have been averaged to produce the phase means shown in the graphs. It is clear that the percentages of errors self-corrected were depressed during the immediate error correction phases. And they continued to be depressed when new books were read independently (shown in the right-hand graphs).

Thus the graphs suggest a generalized interference with self-monitoring and checking. When the children read under delayed correction they self-corrected higher percentages of error and continued to do so in texts read independently after this tutoring.

What is of most importance to this discussion is what happened when performance-directed regulation was turned on and off. Simply the children's performance suffered when self-produced feedback was interfered with. Their initial identification of words in the books was consistently less accurate especially on the difficult texts read independently as shown in the set of graphs reproduced on page 35.

It was not the case that they simply did not try as hard when regulation was interfered with, although the motivational consequences of such a procedure would be significant over time. Indeed, just as infants do not like to be forced to solve a problem by being physically led through it these children voiced their discomfort and displeasure with the immediate correction procedure.

However, it appears motivation was not the critical cause of lowered accuracy. Rather, regulation was critical to how they

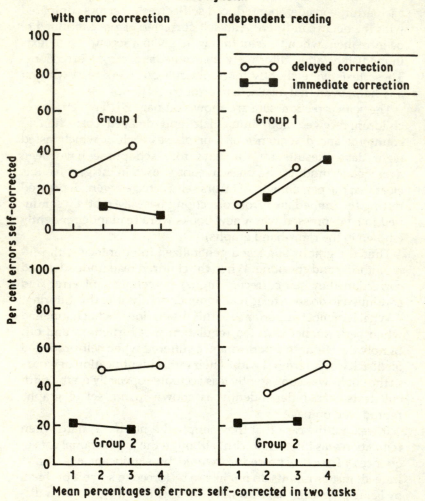

Figure 3   Interference with performance-directed feedback during oral reading

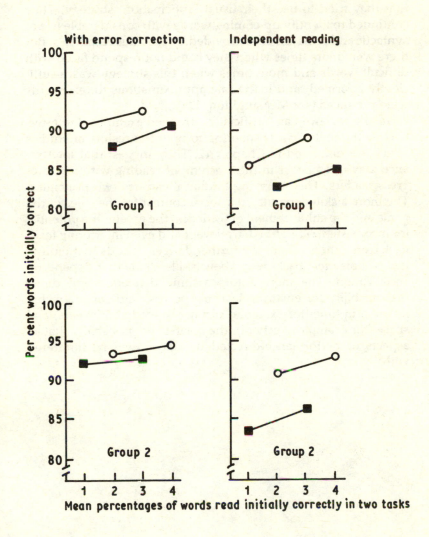

With error correction   Independent reading

Group 1   Group 1

Group 2   Group 2

Per cent words initially correct

Mean percentages of words read initially correctly in two tasks

Source: McNaughton and Glynn (1981)

could perform. Without it performance could not be finely tuned. There was more ambiguity in the bases for performing because contexts built up by sequences of responses were not able to be adjusted. Measures of the readers' ongoing behaviour showed that they tried to use their usual 'anticipation' strategy. They continued to identify up-coming words with considerable use of syntactic and semantic cues provided by previous responses. But there were more times when they could not respond faced with difficult words and more times when this strategy was insufficiently informed, and inaccurate approximations to text words were produced (see McNaughton, 1981c).

Having reviewed an 'artificially' arranged example of interference with feedback it is sobering to note the results of studies which are discussed in Chapter 12. They suggest that interference may often occur in the teaching of reading with low progress readers. This worrying finding illustrates two principles. The more a skill depends on a social context for the rules of the game and the enhancement of feedback, the greater the potential for inconsistent, ill-defined, irrelevant and even interfering feedback from others. There is a further danger. It adds to the problem of noisy feedback in symbolic skills, skills that depend on socialization. The more tutors assume deliberate and direct responsibility for ensuring learning occurs, and constrain that learning in time (for example learning to read at 6:0 years) and space (for example at school), the greater the probability that all aspects of performance-directed regulation will be interfered with.

2   Intending and knowing

One aspect of regulation was discussed in Chapter 1. But the description of skilful action with which that chapter was introduced refers to other attributes of regulating performance. In this chapter the intention to act is discussed in concert with the third major component of skilled action – knowledge.

Intention in regulation

Intentions are also involved in the regulation of a skill. Intention is claimed by Bruner to precede, direct and provide a criterion for terminating an act. In his account there are two ways in which intention enters regulation. There is the general case in performance when the performer already has begun to learn components of the skill. There is also a developmental perspective: an intention to be skilled. Initial reactions to compelling circumstances which provide a basis for skill development.

The concept of intention has long plagued psychological theorizing. In using the concept there are obvious dangers. Saying someone performed a skill because they intended to can tend to circular explanations. Nevertheless, it can be claimed that on logical as well as empirical grounds intention must be significant in a skill. The philosopher Searle (1980) argues that the personal experience of intending to do something which leads to action is undeniable. Analysing the concept further he says the content of intention is the experience of action. But one could not experience without knowing what would satisfy the conditions of acting appropriately. Concepts such as trying, succeeding or failing are applicable to these conditions. In this way Searle argues that intention is logically significant to action.

Intention in performance

The argument for intention as a significant psychological variable must rest on demonstrations of its significance in skilled behaviour. The demonstration can be made in several ways. However, before these demonstrations are described, intention as a psychological concept must be clearly specified together with the implications which this concept has for action.

Intention in the regulation of a skill involves a plan of and for action or performance (Kelso and Wallace, 1978; K.M. Newell, 1978). The characteristics of this plan depend on the developmental status of the act, that is how skilled it is, and the environment which is to be acted on. For a child learning a skill like reading there are three outcomes of an anticipation of performance. The intention serves as a standard for monitoring and evaluating information. It thereby sensitizes the actor to attend to selectively and pick up specific sources of information related to the standard. Thirdly, it maintains action in pursuit of the goal.

It follows that feedback is critically dependent on intention and, as in the case of feedback, that intention is a critical component of skilled behaviour. Without appropriate intention skilful performance is impaired. Put another way, reduced volition depresses performance. This claim can be illustrated in many areas of psychological research.

Descriptions of the psychological processes are closely related to neurophysiological models of intention. In these models neurophysiological events are taken to be consequences of intention.[1] Intention involves an internal discharge in the nervous system. This not only has an effect on the neural areas underlying the action but also transmits signals activating related sensory and co-ordination areas. It thereby prepares these areas to pick up certain kinds of information.

The significance of neurophysiological events has been examined in studies of patients with brain lesions. When the connections underlying this preparedness for motor acts are severed certain behavioural disturbances follow. In general there is a lowering of tone in the performance of the act. This is marked by slow reaction times and even psychological problems such as depression and indifference (Luria, 1973).

Such outcomes of anatomical interference are paralleled by studies of interference which are social in origin. Kelso and Wallace's (1978) studies of the 'preselection affect' in voluntary movements show that greater accuracy in reproducing an act occurs when a person chooses to act, that is intentionally behaves, compared with when a person is passively led through the same action.

The authors interpret the general affect as being based on a 'corollary discharge' mechanism. Superior pick-up of incoming information occurs during the course of first performing the action due to preparedness of the action-system. Superior reproduction of performance occurs because the plan of the action serves as a better referent or context for feedback-controlled performance.

The basis of the 'preselection' effect is anticipation of the availability or presence of certain kinds of information, and preparedness to pick up that information. This same effect is apparent in studies of perception and cognition, if the environment and tasks are structurally predictable (Bransford, 1979; Neisser, 1976). It also occurs in learning to read.

Reading with intent

A reader can intend to gain meaning. This in itself may be a source of significant difference between readers. Such an intention is a product of particular knowledge of the functions and goals of the skill which in turn is constructed within particular socialization experiences. With this intention readers can be sensitive to the sources of meaning in a text (Clay, 1979; Wildman and Kling, 1979).

Under appropriate conditions it leads in early reading to a general performance strategy of anticipation from semantic and syntactic cues. Integrated responses are made using those cues together with selected information from graphemic cues; responses are then checked for appropriateness. Because of this intention, errors which do occur are usually highly appropriate to the context provided by syntactic and semantic cues within the

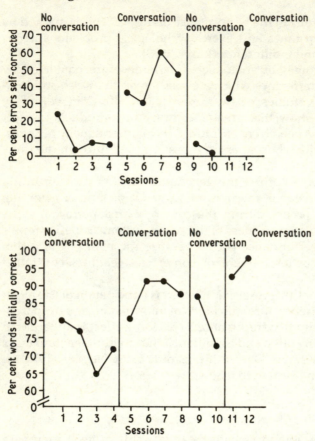

Figure 4   Reading with and without a conversation by a low progress reader
Source: Wong and McNaughton (1981)

sentence and even earlier ones. Those that are not have a high probability of being corrected. In Searle's terms one of the 'conditions of satisfaction' of the act of reading is that it continues to make sense.

Intention is grounded in knowledge. The success of a performance strategy is dependent on the appropriateness of that knowledge base for the task at hand. Thus, when a child's knowledge of syntax and meanings is not congruent with those contained in a text, the psychological processes of intention are restricted.

Padmini Wong demonstrated this interdependence in a case study of a low progress 7:6-year-old reader.

The boy was given books to read which would have been appropriate for normal progress after two and a half years at school. These books were very difficult for this reader to read by himself as he could read accurately only texts appropriate to the first year of instruction. Repeated measures of reading successive passages showed an error rate of three errors in every ten words. The errors were often inappropriate to the context supplied by the sentence and were seldom self-corrected ((fewer than one error in ten self-corrected). These characteristics of 'baseline' responding are shown in the four sessions making up the first phase of the two graphs in Figure 4.

But the pattern of responding without effective anticipation and self-correction was altered by a simple manipulation. Before reading a new passage the previously passive observer would discuss with the boy the story about to be read. Some concepts, events, actions and vocabulary were highlighted in the conversation (for example, 'What would be a good thing to do if you couldn't keep warm in a cave?') which lasted less than five minutes. Words in the text were not identified.

In the next four sessions, where this conversation preceded reading, the reader produced only one error in every ten words read. Many of his errors were accurate anticipations and he often self-corrected errors (one in every two errors were self-corrected), particularly the ones that were inappropriate to the context. Given that returning to the baseline conditions in the third phase also produced a return to ineffective responding, and that with conversations restored again (in the fourth phase) proficiency returned, then the effects of this variable were clearly demonstrated.

Two features of this reader's performance specifically demonstrate a greater preparedness to pick up meanings and grammatical forms which would carry those meanings. The first is the patterning of self-corrections. There was an increased sensitivity to errors which were inconsistent with semantic and syntactic cues. In the baseline phases the percentage of these errors which were self-corrected was 11 per cent; it was 47 per cent with conversations. Second, the increase in initial accuracy of identifying words suggests a general enhancement of word recognition due to the increased salience of contextual cues.

The vehicle for this enhanced intention to pick up information was knowledge that was socially constructed. Regulation from both intentional processes and feedback processes is based on knowledge. Performance, regulation and knowledge are inter-dependent. This knowledge base is the third component of skilled action regulation, but before it is described further another sense of intention needs to be noted.

The arousal of intention

Earlier it was noted that in Bruner's account of skilled behaviour there were two perspectives on intention. The first has been des-cribed. The second, a developmental perspective, concerns the initial reaction to stimulation which provides a basis for skill development.

Intention is at the very roots of the development of competence in infancy, because rudimentary activities which are evoked enable performance-directed regulation to occur. For example in the reach and grasp skills that Bruner has studied there are pre-paratory responses which can be observed. They are induced by those objects which have particularly compelling features such as sharp contours, and easily detected differences. The early res-ponses involve some movement of the arms, the opening and closing of hands, and even working of the mouth. These rudi-mentary activities are the precursors of fluid reaching which is under the precise visual control of the infant. When they are acti-vated the infant is able to receive performance-directed feedback. In turn, this increases the knowledge of how to reach which can be used in subsequent reaching.

This obervation of arousal of intention at the beginnings of development is particularly significant to the arguments in this book. When this is added to the research reviewed in the next chapter a fundamental principle of learning is suggested. The arousal of a primitive intention to act on the world provides a set of conditions for very effective learning. It does so because it allows for performance-directed regulation and, as a conse-quence, learning activities.

The foundations of learning to read can be like the elicitation of primitive reach and grasp responses. At the roots of learning to read a child can have a strong intention to act and acquire competence. Admittedly the glimmerings of literacy may not involve the same reflex-like response to a class of stimuli that characterizes the rudimentary reach and grasp response. But the research reviewed in Chapter 10 on precocious readers suggests that parallels between sensorimotor skills such as reach and grasp and a complex symbolic skill such as reading can exist at the roots of development. In the accounts of children learning to read and write before school it is often reported that the initial movement, the intentional curiosity about literacy skill, was at the child's initiative. While the eliciting stimuli are much more socially defined and dependent on socialization practices the parallels are unmistakable. An implication of this claim is that although learning to read is often initiated and controlled substantially by others, the intention to be literate does not have to be so deliberately, and for some children laboriously, transmitted from others.

Knowledge

There is a famous saying attributed to the Greek poet Archilocus which runs 'The fox knows many things: the hedgehog knows one big thing (Berlin, 1953). It has been used to describe how different species became specialized in the course of evolution and adjusted to particular ecological niches. Hedgehogs, it is argued, are handicapped by knowing one big thing because they are not flexible.

In adapting to societal demonstrations about becoming, or demands to become literate, children become knowledgeable. It is to their advantage in learning to be literate that they have different sorts of knowledge, some of it general. Being like *both* foxes and hedgehogs guarantees adaptability. But it will be argued that general knowledge about literacy is critical for children in their adaptation. It enables them quickly and easily to adapt to the varied environments that make up classrooms.

Knowledge of the 'big things'

Children acquire knowledge in several domains. Knowledge in some of these has been referred to by Downing and Leong (1982) as 'cognitive clarity'. It involves knowledge of the purposes and functions of reading, and understanding the technical concepts of reading. To these areas can be added knowledge of how the skill can be learned, and making sense of how environments provide information about reading.

These domains of knowledge might be termed knowledge *that* reading is a skill. There is also knowledge of *how* it is performed. That is readers also acquire information about the performing of different reading acts. Not all of this knowledge may be accessible in a form that permits the child to articulate it verbally. Together knowlege on how to read and knowledge that reading is a skill constitute a base for acts of reading by a learner. At whatever level of expertise the performance of an act of reading is a realization of this knowledge.

Children differ considerably in the knowledge of reading that they bring to instruction. Since the early empirical work by Reid (1966) and Downing (1970) it has become increasingly apparent that children entering school vary remarkably in what technical concepts they are familiar with and what they know of the purposes and uses of written language. Their variety in the latter area is captured in a recent intensive study of children starting at the same London school by Hazel Francis (1982).

For one child, reading was a task to be learned because the school and now his parents defined it as important, but he was not at all sure any benefits derived to him other than in meeting their demands. Reading as such was an end in itself and not a tool. At the other extreme was a child on entry to school who was aware of the direct communicative significance of written language. This boy knew he would get information to direct his other activities from such mundane things as shopping lists and shop signs to the immeasurably more significant information in the *TV Times*.

We might incorrectly define the first child's knowledge as inferior, deficient or unclear. But that assumes the fault, if there be fault, is somehow in the child's means for acquiring knowledge. But this knowledge is a result of socialization and reflects social realities as indicated in the interview data reported in that study. Perhaps it would be more accurate to say his knowledge was different, and possibly an appropriate representation of his immediate past social experiences with literacy skills. On this view it was representative of current but not necessarily potential social realities.

To some children in this study the classroom tasks were literally incomprehensible, they did not know what was expected of them. Their intention in action was largely to match models provided by teachers and peers, and identify or reproduce specific stimuli when called upon to do so. From the general descriptions provided it is apparent that their strategies of performance and their pattern of development were affected. These children were the slow learners *until* they gained a schema of the functions of the activities itself. Not anticipating meaning, they did not find any. Negative correlates of this state are reported in the study, notably dislike of or a withdrawal from the classroom activities relating to reading.

Technical concepts

It turns out that much more empirical work has been directed toward describing children's knowledge of technical concepts than knowledge of functions and processes of instruction. That is there is considerable information about children's knowledge of such terms as 'sound', 'letter', 'word' and 'sentence', and concepts about print such as directionality, orientation and correspondence. The data are extensive, and provide both developmental and cross-cultural information.

A recent study by Schmidt illustrates the general findings. Schmidt (1981) randomly selected ten boys and ten girls at each of four age levels (5:0, 6:0, 7:0 and 8:0) in Denmark and a matched sample in the USA. She then administered a test of the children's concepts about print. In the test a small paperback story was read to a child and at specific points the person reading the book paused and asked the cild about book orientation, about where the story was coming from (text or pictures), about directionality, and about other concepts and technical terms numbering twenty-four in all.

The resulting average number of questions about concepts for Danish and American children at each age level is shown in Figure 5. At first glance it appears that while the children were knowledgeable to about the same extent at 5:0 years, children in the USA acquired much more knowledge over the ensuing two years. But then by 8:0 the Danish children had caught up.

The trends reflect two characteristics of the growth of this

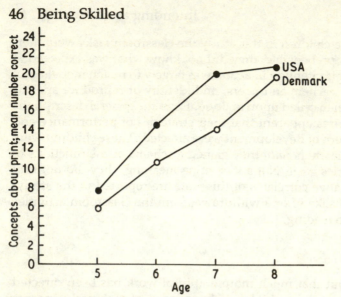

Figure 5   Average scores of 5, 6, 7 and 8-year-old boys and girls from the USA and Denmark on a knowledge of reading test
Source: Schmidt (1981)

knowledge. There is the obvious point that knowledge increases over time. There is also a less obvious point. The onset of schooling is associated with increased knowledge. The 5-year-olds in the USA were all in kindergartens, some of which were explicitly providing instruction in reading, and this formal instruction began in earnest on entry to school at 6:0 years. In contrast only some Danish children were in kindergarten at 5:0 years and formal instruction did not occur until entry to school at 7:0 years. These events explain the significant differences found between children in the USA and Denmark at 6:0 and 7:0 years which were not present at 5:0 and 8:0 years.

So conceptual knowledge increases with formal schooling in the skill. But a question arises as to the significance of this knowledge for general achievement in learning how to read. This is a theoretical issue concerning the interrelatedness of knowledge and skilful performance and match with reading programme.

There appears to be a very strong correlation between the extent of this knowledge and reading progress. Studies in several countries show high positive correlations between knowledge at the start of schooling and progress after one or two years (e.g. Clay, 1979). Correlations decline after this time but this is to be expected. If school reading programmes were guaranteeing mastery of the basic concepts and reducing some of the variability between readers on this measure correlations would decline.

Both predictive and concurrent correlations, which are positive and high at least at the beginning stages of instruction, are consistent with our skill model of reading. The model assumes that knowledge and the development of performance capabilities are interdependent. But the model does not assume a static unidirectional relationship between knowledge and performance capabilities. For example it is argued in the next chapter that knowledge may set the occasion for some learning of the skill.

Nor should it be assumed at this early stage in our analysis that 'cognitive clarity' in technical concepts needs to be directly trained as a necessary prerequisite to formal instruction. It is apparent from studies such as Schmidt's that for many children some of that specific knowledge is constructed outside the instructional settings provided by the school. The extent of that construction goes hand in hand with general progress. Thus the correlational data that are available indicate that extensive knowledge of technical concepts on entry to school predicts general achievement in the school. But for some children those concepts are easily and quickly acquired after entry to school and this is also associated with high progress.

It is possible that the more specific of the technical concepts such as the identification of letters may contribute very little by themselves to the generativeness of a knowledge base. But the more general of the technical concepts, such as knowledge of what constitutes a book and where the messages are located, coupled with knowledge of the purposes and functions of reading, may do so. The data reviewed in the next chapter would suggest that even in rudimentary form such knowledge could supply a critical framework for performance-directed regulation to operate and thereby support learning activities. Armed with a knowledge of 'big' things children are able to learn the specific technical concepts required by formal instruction.

Part 2
The acts of learning

3 Being perturbed: Learning from problems

In the previous chapter skills were described in terms of their components. There is another perspective which highlights different properties of the skill in development. The second perspective is not in conflict with the first, it simply analyses different dimensions of the skill, although there are points at which the two accounts do overlap.

This second perspective examines the structural properties, focusing on how the structures of behavioural events change with developing skill. From this perspective developmentl processes involved in structural change can be described. It is necessary to introduce concepts from this perspective into our model of reading as a skill in order to understand what children do when they learn. Their learning activities, which are the subject of the next three chapters, are closely bound to developmental changes in the structure of their skill.

Developing melodies

Skilful behaviour has an impressive structure which Luria's description of a 'kinetic melody' captures so well. Skilful performance is fast, fluid and flexible. A proficient 7-year-old reading aloud can be a delight to observe and every bit as compelling as the descriptions of athletes which have tended to capture the attention of theorists of skill.

A general structural theory of skill, equally applicable to the proficient reach and grasp of a 6-month-old and the professional pugilist, stresses two characteristics. First, the acts that make up the performance are interchangeable and combinations are modified in the face of demands of each new instance. This 'systemic' structure is seen in the shifting between uses of different sources of information in a text as a 7-year-old decodes to gain meaning. For example at beginnings of sentences when the predictability of word classes is low, greater use may need to be made of graphemic and phonemic information than may occur following the verb in a simple subject-verb-object sentence.

A second characteristic is the unitary nature of the performance. Although systemic it is also melodious. Each performance of discrete motor acts such as playing a stroke or catching a ball is in part novel. Yet these components are integrated and blend into one another. This has provided a continuing theoretical problem for structural theorists. Pianists, punchers and other skilled persons can execute a complete sequence of their skill more rapidly than it would take them to perform each component of that sequence separately.

The phenomenon is explained in terms of how the performances are controlled. From a structural perspective the behavioural acts are seen as being controlled through hierarchical organization and monitoring. That is individual components are chunked together and run off as single acts. What were previously separate acts become embedded in a more general single representation in which increasingly larger units of a complex sequential action are encompassed.

The reference to representation and control here is a point of contact with the previous description of skill. These are the features previously conceptualized as a knowledge base and intentional control. More sophisticated schema require less activity to control performance because much is anticipated.

The general concept of embeddedness and hierarchical control is primarily associated with sequences of motor acts. But in early accounts the concept was not limited solely to simple motor skills. Lashley analysed piano playing, and the symbolic skill of reading yields similar phenomena; indeed the phenomena can be found at all levels of activity when reading.[1]

More expert treatments of the structure of skills are available elsewhere (e.g. Bruner, 1973). What is important to this discussion are the descriptions from the structural perspective of how a skill develops over time. What structural processes occur in the achievement of the flexible melody? Drawing on the previous accounts we can distinguish three such processes in the development of a skill: modularization, integration and differentiation.

Structures in development

Modularization occurs as a discrete act becomes 'automatic, less variable, and achieves a predictable spatio-temporal patterning' (Bruner, 1973, p. 252). When an act is modularized it becomes capable of structural reorganization, either by 'integration' or 'differentiated elaboration'. Integration, as the term suggests, is the production of new performances by the inclusion of the newly modularized acts into a more general act with other acts.

In contrast, differentiated elaboration is a process of decomposition and reconstitution. What was previously a whole, indivisible act becomes separable into discrete elements. These discrete components become acts able to be combined in different ways. The structures resulting from integration and differentiated elaboration then go through the process of modularization, becoming automatic.

There are examples of these processes in the development of other skills such as early sensorimotor acts. It is possible to illustrate them in the development of early reading but often the resulting singular descriptions are somewhat artificial because developments may not be as linear nor acts as unitary as those which are described in accounts of sensorimotor acts. However, there is an amusing account of differentiated elaboration in one theorist's own development:

> I can remember at the age of 4 or 5, long after I had learned to say the alphabet, my surprise at discovering that 'elemeno' was not one letter between K and P but actually four letters.
>
> (Kaye, 1979, p. 47)

More complex examples of the same process occur as directional behaviour, moving from left to right across the page in the case of written English, differentiates into one-to-one correspondence, the matching of isolatable configurations of words with single spoken words in the transverse of the line. A parallel is afforded by the differentiation of identifiable words into recombinable components (for example letters or letter clusters) within a teaching programme which stresses the learning of whole words.

Integration operates as words which have become able to be automatically recognized in one context are generalized to other contexts as happens when the identity of a previously unfamiliar word is solved during the reading of a passage and is identified fluently on successive encounters, irrespective of context.

Modularization and control

This diversion into accounts of structural development is necessary for one major reason. Modularization can be described in performance terms. Changes occur in the spatio-temporal qualities of behaviour as for example in the recognition time for a specific word. But the changes in performance are accompanied by changes in regulatory activities, which have profound theoretical significance.

In the account of regulation provided earlier the psychological phenomena have been described behaviourally. The description has been in terms of activities which are both internal and overt. In the analysis of structural change performances are also seen as controlled. Control over the sequence of acts which make up the performance, its orchestration, is exercised via selective attention. This concept of selective attention enables theorists of structural change to explain what happens when performance becomes nearly automatic yet it still appears to be regulated.

A favourite example of such theorists is that of driving a car. With proficiency a driver can not only drive carefully and flexibly but also be, among other things, a skilful conversationalist. This is not possible with impunity for the novice. It is quite clear that when performing an act the expert is not as perceptually bound to the task.

There are different theories of selective attention. In traditional theories attention is seen as a distinct and separate mechanism operating in a processing system. Changes in what a proficient driver can do are said to reflect changes in 'attentional capacity' and shifts from one mode of attention (for example 'controlled processing') to another (for example 'automatic processing'). In the early stages of a skill the capacity of the attentional mechanism is all used in regulating the activity. With proficiency only a small amount is necessary, and parallel processing becomes possible (e.g. Shiffrin and Dumais, 1981).

There are alternatives to this view. Attention is argued by other theorists to be an attribute or quality of perceptions. Performance becomes nearly automatic and deliberate regulation minimal. But the limitations on selective attention, the manner in which events are perceived, are due to the potential incompatibilities between the activities and skills involved. There are some things that you can not do at the same time because they involve the same behavioural systems (Neisser, 1976).

Both approaches claim, however, that what changes in regulatory activity or attention are the aspects of performance which are selectively attended to. The schema associated with performance strategies specify different levels of information at different stages of development. They become increasingly generalized in terms of what can be anticipated as more specific information is acquired about the skill and conditions of performance. The performance comes to rely on fewer disembedded acts, and regulation involves fewer discrete events.

With modularization, either from integration or differentiation of component behaviours, the monitoring of performance changes. In perceptual terms this can be described as economy and efficiency of information in perceptual learning, or more generally as the elimination of step-by-step controls.

There is considerable similarity between the concepts of attentional control and the regulatory activities discussed previously. Present in both perspectives on development is the possibility of control yielding opportunities to evaluate performance. A fundamental claim follows: learning activities arise out of regulatory activities.

Also present in both perspectives is the view that action and its regulation are dependent on a knowledge base. An illustration of this interdependency is contained in the following account of perception. It could equally apply to skill and indeed the author of the quote, Ulric Neisser, has drawn similarities between his model of perception and skilled action.

> Anticipatory schemata . . . prepare the perceiver to accept certain kinds of information than others and thus control the activity of looking. . . . At each moment the perceiver is constructing

anticipations of certain kinds of information that enable him to accept it as it becomes available. Often he must actively explore the optic array to make it available, by moving his eyes or his head or his body. These explorations are directed by the anticipatory schemata which are plans for perceptual action as well as readiness for particular kinds of optical structure . . . optical information can specify objects and events at various levels of abstraction and meaning, and a schema organised on one level need not be sensitive to the others.

(1976, pp. 20–1)

The bases of learning

A child, 2 years 6 months old, looks at her father reading the paper. She points to the title (*The Star*) and spontaneously offers the observation, 'Look, S for Sally'. She is recognizing a component of her own name which she had often seen written, and which she had attempted to copy on several occasions. This was the first time she had made an observation about S outside the context of her own name. It was unsolicited.[2]

This act of recognizing a component in what had previously been an undifferentiated whole reflects the process of differentiation. The concept provides a useful generalization about the development of skills. It summarizes one aspect of *what* happens to the structures of behaviour in the development of a skill. But it is not an explanation of *how* transformations occur. That requires an analysis of the processes of learning that produced the change.

A complete account of how structural change occurs requires an analysis of both learners *and* their environments. In this section we take the former and examine the 'child's contribution' to the process of learning; what the child in the above observation might have done in the course of differentiating / S / from the familiar context of 'Sally'.

Modes of regulation

The term performance-directed was introduced in Chapter 1 to describe a major form of regulation in the performance of a skill. Performance-directed regulation occurs when the performance is under the intentional control of the learner who utilizes feedback inherent in performing the skill. Such regulation is not limited to experts; it can occur at the very roots of the skill.

One dimension of this concept needs to be elaborated here. Performance-directed regulation occurs given a performance which is initiated and maintained by the learner even though someone else enhances the feedback, as illustrated by further information about Sally, the subject of our earlier example. On previous occasions she has with delight recognized her name saying, 'Look, that word says Sally'. Her parents had responded to her observations which drew on previous interactions not only with the confirmation, 'Yes, that does say Sally . . .', but also with the additional information ' . . . see the S at the beginning'.

Thus the defining characteristics of performance-directed regulation can be seen to be that a child intends to perform the skill, is sensitive to some task-relevant attributes of performance, and actively endeavours to monitor and check that performance. Feedback from others under these conditions can be meaningful to the child because the child has some plan of action. From that knowledge base the child knows something about the adequacy of performance. More importantly that child has some appreciation of what better performance would require. Performance-directed regulation can be contrasted with performance that is externally controlled. The latter occurs when performance is not initiated and maintained by the learner. This may eventuate because conditions are encountered which restrict knowledge of the intrinsic goals and functions of the skill. It may also occur where the timing and mode of feedback is usurped by someone else. Under these conditions that person acts as the external regulator of performance by providing information about the adequacy of performance. It may be that this information is well matched to the child's performance. But whatever the usefulness of this information the critical distinction is that the timing, contingency and content of that information is initiated and controlled by another in a manner which excludes performance-directed regulation. Thus other-directed and performance-directed regulation represent two extremes in the conditions of performing a skill which usually lead to different outcomes of learning activities. We first examine learning via performance-related regulation.

Learning outcomes

'Outcomes' is a term deserving some clarification. In order to say that learning has occurred one must show three things. First, there must be an interactional process involving the learner and a functional environment. Second, there must be an identifiable change in performance which, lastly, is demonstrably a consequence of the process. The outcomes then are detectable physical and/or spatio-temporal changes in the characteristics of a person's performance which are relatively long lasting and transferable across time and settings. Because symbolic skill learning does not occur in an all-or-nothing manner, the phenomena of concern are the degree of detectability, transferability or 'decontextualization' the performance has (see Bransford, 1979; Donaldson, 1978).

The most immediately impressive performance changes are those involving new behavioural components. But there are equally significant outcomes of learning: gradual changes in behaviour. Currently these latter changes enjoy descriptions such as 'tuning' and 'automaticity'. The more general concept of modularization which has already been discussed subsumes these attributes of change in the smoothness and rapidity of performance. The referents of these terms are exemplified in a child's haltingly careful identification of a word which changes to a smooth and nearly automatic response.

Learning from performance-directed regulation

Learning activities can arise out of performance-directed regulation. One dramatic example in early reading shows that learning can be initiated by beginning readers and can proceed in a self-contained fashion, relatively independently of any intermediary.

The data come from several studies of problem-solving in early reading which were referred to in Chapter 1. In these studies readers, after one year of instruction, were given difficult books to read containing words which had not been encountered previously in classrooms. In practice this meant they were given books from the classroom reading series considerably in advance of where they were currently receiving instruction. They were required to read them without any help from the observers.

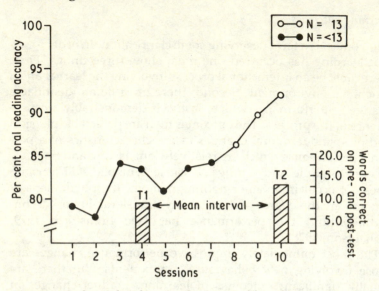

Figure 6 Independent learning by 6-year-old readers
Source: McNaughton (1983a)

Becoming accurate in reading these, initially very difficult, texts posed problems. The texts contained new initially unidentifable words. After several sessions the readers were retested on their ability to identfy words which they had previously not been able to identify in isolation.

These average to high progress readers attempted to solve the unknown words with a strategy described in the last chapter. The significance of this solving is shown in one of the studies involving thirteen readers, who were faced with books which they could initially read with very low accuracy (all thirteen read between 80 and 85 per cent words correct). It took them on average six sessions to achieve a predetermined criterion for high accuracy, twice reading at above 90 per cent words correct. They read consecutive passages in the books. The changes in accuracy over three sessions a week reading 200-word passages are shown in Figure 6. The data are presented in the form of a backward learning curve. The last data point is the average accuracy for all thirteen readers on the session in which they met the criterion. The immediately preceding data point is the average accuracy on the second to last session. As some readers took only three sessions to reach the criterion the fourth to last data point is an average of fewer than thirteen readers. One reader took ten sessions.

The curve represents considerable learning. The readers were able to identify words in context which they couldn't previously identify in isolation, and having identified them once they continued to do so across successive encounters in different sentence contexts. More and more words were identified correctly and highly accurate reading was achieved. Through their independently controlled performance they were able to teach themselves how to read the difficult books.

Their solving in context is an impressive display of independence by relative novices. But it had a further significance for learning. After an average of six sessions the readers were able to identify, in isolation, three to four of the previously unidentifiable words. Those words which were read in context correctly had a high probability of also being identified in isolation. So something had been learned in the course of solving. This learning was accomplished without any *formal* requirements in the experiment to learn or remember anything. The children were simply told to read as well as they could and that the observers were interested in how well they could read.

Under very difficult conditions, that is reading hard passages and encountering unknown words infrequently over a few short sessions, the thirteen readers could learn about one new word per 200-word passage. Thus by themselves and incidentally these readers could add five new words a week to their sight vocabulary given daily passages of 200 words.[3]

The learning arose out of strategic problem-solving which was initiated and controlled entirely by the learner. It illustrates the characteristics of learning via performance-directed regulation. The impetus for such learning is provided by knowledge of a perturbation in performance. A perturbation exists when a learner becomes aware of a problem. When learning to read, a performance which is inaccurate or inexact poses specific problems. In addition readers can recognize a more general problem when they are aware that current skill levels are inadequate.

In both cases the structural analyses of skills supplied in the previous chapter provide an explanation for how a problem comes to be recognized as such. Regulatory processes link performance with a knowledge base which provides a plan for action.

Comparisons of performance with the knowledge base proceed until an error or an incompleteness in performance is detected.

Specific difficulties and the general problem posed by modularization represent quite distinct occasions where a more skilful person might provide input, even to the extent of increasing the salience of the perturbation. They may lead to different interactions having different functions. Accordingly the discussion will follow this distinction, beginning with learning which happens following the perception of a specific problem.

When learning is occasioned by a specific problem

Becoming aware of a specific problem such as an unfamiliar word in a sentence to be read provides an immediate occasion for learning. When that awareness has come about from performance-directed regulation the learning which eventuates during problem-solving is self-initiated. To the extent that the solving proceeds with the learner actively regulating the ongoing performance then learning continues to be self-initiated.

This is not to say that the conditions of learning may not be deliberately structured or even that someone else might not enter into the ongoing solving. The course that the learning episode takes may very well be influenced by instructional input. But the essential characteristics of learning from performance-directed regulation are these. The learning activities are rooted in the child's own performance of the skill and the performance is acted upon by the learner who continues to judge performance in terms of knowledge of the skill.

Some general features of learning via problem-solving The earlier descriptions of how a group of beginning readers solved specific problems show learning from performance-directed regulation in a relatively 'pure' form. The learning was independent of any direct instruction from someone else prior to or following the solving. However the solving and the consequent learning did take place within the general framework of a particular reading programme. What can be said more generally about problem-solving, for example, by children in different programmes?

When the descriptions available from different studies are examined two major characteristics of problem-solving emerge.

The first is demonstrated with data from the studies referred to in the introduction by Rebecca Barr. Barr compared children learning to read under two distinct programmes, those using a word study method and those using a phonics method.

Table 3 Beginning readers' strategies for identifying unfamiliar words in two different instructional programmes

Instructional	Mean number non-words	Mean % programme words	Readers with strategy, reflecting instruction
Phonics method (N = 16)	1.9	33.5	13
Sight-word method (N = 16)	0.1	84.9	12

Source: Barr (1974, Table 2 – test word data)
Reprinted with permission of Rebecca Barr and the International Reading Association

In Table 3 the manner in which after six months of instruction thirty two first graders solved unfamiliar words in texts and in lists is described by Barr through an analysis of their substitution errors. Two types of mistaken solutions were used to judge the presence of a solving strategy. The first was the production of non-words, which were approximations based on a synthetic blending of phonemes corresponding to the letters in the text word, but which nevertheless were not a recognizable word. The others were substitutions of a word from the set of reading words already introduced into the instructional materials.

A phonics strategy was identified when a reader tended to produce non-words when in error (at least one per reader) and not real words which had already been learned. That is the reader attempted to solve a word by relying on accurately identifying components irrespective of the meaningfulness of the resultant attempt. The reverse criterion was applied for judging a sight-word method; no non-words and a majority of the substitution errors being made up of familiar words already introduced in the programme. Readers using this strategy would rely on known words to overcome a difficulty.

Out of the sixteen readers from each programme studied, thirteen phonics method and twelve sight-word method readers met the criteria for using the strategy reflecting the method of instruction. Barr's data illustrated in Table 3 demonstrate that children from different programmes solve problems in different ways. Her observations are made even stronger with data showing that although some children started school employing an incipient strategy at odds with the programme emphasis, the majority of these children had altered their strategy after six months of instruction to match the programme emphasis.

So the solving strategy reflects the method of instruction. Another feature of problem-solving is that it develops. The evidence in Figure 7 comes from observations by Murray Wilson of readers after several months in a 'natural language' programme. It will be recalled from Chapter 1 that a major characteristic of

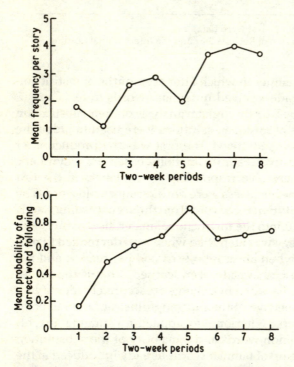

Figure 7.   Changes in pausing by 6-year-olds during oral reading
Source: Wilson and McNaughton (1983)

deliberate solving by children in such programmes is pausing. The average frequency of self-initiated pausing per story is shown in the top graph. The data were collected during daily oral reading interactions between the teacher and each reader. A major change over sixteen weeks of classroom instruction occurred: the readers went from pausing about twice per story to about four times per story. Furthermore, the outcomes of this activity changed as indicated in the bottom graph. The likelihood of an attempt following a pause being correct became greater; 80 per cent of the pauses produced correct words at the end of the sixteen weeks whereas 20 per cent had done so at the start.

Thus the characteristics of solving differ between programmes, and change occurs over time. Variety in problem-solving strategies is a constant research finding even on highly constrained laboratory tasks. It is therefore not surprising to find inter- and intra-individual differences in problem-solving when learning to read. The implication is that the strategies deployed in overcoming and learning from a specific problem are learned; for example it takes, among other things, knowledge of the redundant information afforded by English orthography as well as knowledge of possible grapheme-to-phoneme correspondences to search effectively for the information to solve a difficult word.

It may seem an unnecessarily obvious point to make, that it takes acquired knowledge to develop problem-solving strategies that have learning outcomes, but the point has implications for the analysis of how learning occurs. When learning occurs as a consequence of overcoming a specific problem it does so within the vehicle of a solving strategy, which can incorporate basic learning activities. These activities (to be defined in Chapter 5) find local expression in the solving routine; to the extent that the activities occur, the solving strategy becomes a learning strategy.

So the data discussed thus far also introduce the possibility of differences in learning, in at least two ways. The manner of solving may give rise to different degrees of learning. Certainly the studies of word-solving by children in natural language programmes suggest this. While solving a word in context predicted generalized learning, some words which were solved were *not* able to be identified out of context. Such a situation would be consistent with the wider literature on learning from problem-solving. There is a yet more general possibility, that the basic learning activities, or at least their potential for expression, are modified and developed through use; again this would be consistent with arguments made by other theorists. [4]

Further examples of self-initiated problem-solving: using others
Although early on in learning to read children are capable of completely self-contained learning, they may not often engage in it. Moreover, they may not like to depend on it. In the first few years of insruction a reader's task environment often includes the resources of a tutor and peers.

The use of others to aid in overcoming a problem can arise from performance-directed regulation. However, in contrast to completely independent learning the learner seeks out, or avails him or herself of information which comes from outside the performance. The initiation and maintenance of the seeking comes from the child as a result of performing the skill. In the event of not having sufficient skills to learn directly from task performance, or in the event of it being inefficient to do so, the child goes elsewhere (e.g. Francis, 1982; McNaughton, 1981a).

Going elsewhere can be achieved in a number of ways. An obvious strategy is to ask the available resources for help in overcoming a problem. When asked what they do to solve unknown words in classroom instruction beginning readers often say they use the resources of teachers and peers. These self-observations are matched by systematic classroom observations.

It appears that children ask others about difficult words, and they also seek corroboration of their own independent attempts. High progress readers report asking others to be a favoured strategy within classrooms. Obviously then it can be a productive strategy, perhaps because it is simply sometimes more efficient than relying on one's own more limited knowledge base. But in terms of its effectiveness for learning, any outcomes would depend on the learning activities deployed in the strategy.

A less direct form of approaching others occurs when teachers and peers are imitated. Children learning to read have been observed as they themselves observed and imitated other children; these same studies suggest that a teacher's behaviour when independently occupied may be observed and used as a basis for developing knowledge of the functions of a skill.

There is yet another major strategy for using outside information, which occurs during instruction as attempts are made and tutors' reactions become available as feedback. The general strategy of utilizing information from feedback is sometimes described in a way that suggests a deliberate or conscious attempt to obtain feedback. A word-learning strategy during early language development has been described in this way. It is claimed that children deliberately talk a lot and test out concepts of words and sentences against their acceptance by the environment (Nelson, 1972).

It is unlikely that readers often consciously attempt to obtain feedback. What is more likely is that they respond with the general expectation of utilizable feedback becoming available if needed. Nevertheless, early readers have been shown to differ in their willingness to attempt a difficult word perhaps reflecting differences in how environments support their learning (Barr, 1974; Goodman and Golasch, 1981).

As in the case of self-contained learning, the behaviours that a child engages in to go elsewhere to gain information can be conceptualized in strategy terms. They are task-specific strategies which are local expressions of basic learning activities. Again certain implications follow, such as the possibility of such strategies being learned and differential effectiveness.

The relationship between problem and solution   Thus far the topic has been how self-initiated learning occurs when a child is confronted by a perturbation. Descriptions have been provided of task-specific strategies which can also function to acquire new skill components in the course of overcoming a problem during reading. So perturbation provides the cue and solving strategies the mechanisms, but what attributes of the learner's relationship to the specific problem guarantee a productive application?

When a problem is picked up from performance-directed regulation three classes of information are potentially available to the child, because the child's current knowledge base has been violated. Performance as specified by the current action plan is wanting. Having monitored performance a child first has knowledge of *where* the problem occurred. In reading, a mismatch between an oral response and the textual stimuli provides the basis for fixing the general locus of the problem, even given an eye–voice span whereby the child is fixating several words in advance of the spoken word.

Following a perturbation a child also knows *what* attributes of performance were associated with the perturbation. Having registered a difficulty there must be awareness that skills are inexact or faulty. Given that the performance strategies are being monitored in accord with the knowledge base *and* that the locus of the problem is able to be fixed, some relatively specific sources of inadequacy can be isolated.

In the following example lack of agreement between noun and verb when reading a sentence specifies the locus of the problem and the aspect of performance associated with the mismatch:

TEXT: The cats were cold.
CHILD: 'The cat were . . . '

Monitoring the mismatch the child can 'know' generally that the relationship between number and verb is violated. The child may also know that some textual information has not been fully utilized in the performance strategy.

As a consequence of having these sources of information, knowledge can also be gained of how performance might be modified, or what needs to be known or done in order to overcome the particular problem, and possibly the class of problems. This is the third source of information, and with this deliberate solving strategies can be employed which produce learning, when they include learning activities. Whether or not the learner is completely self-sufficient depends on such things as efficiency, pay-off knowledge and what the environment offers.

There is, however, a potential contradiction here. How can a child know what he or she needs to know, if they do not already know it? The contradiction is resolved if one conceptualizes the child as generally knowing that something needs to be learned. If learning is completely self-contained then the child has creatively used already existing knowledge to produce a novel skill component as illustrated in the phenomena of 'insight' learning or inventiveness (Kohler, 1927; Resnick, 1980).

The solving strategies which are the vehicle for learning activities can produce insights depending on one limiting factor. This factor is captured in a series of studies by Siegler on problem-solving. He refers to this factor in an 'encoding' hypothesis

which is used to explain why older children can learn from negative (corrective) feedback better than younger children (Siegler,
1981; Siegler and Klahr, 1982). In a typical experiment children
are faced with a balance scale problem. Their task is to say what
will happen to the balance when given problems which alter
position and number of weights on either side of the fulcrum.
Will the scale balance or will it go down – and if so on what side?
Siegler can describe four discrete rules children might use which
have sequential developmental characteristics. Early rules are
successful only with some problems while later rules deal with a
variety of problems. Individual children can be reliably categorized as using one of these rules exclusively. Not only can Siegler
specify what characterizes further expertise, that is learning, but
also he can carefully select problems which are geared as solvable
by a child operating one level (one rule) above the level at which
they are currently operating.

That is children could solve these problems by advancing to the
next rule. For example a child using Rule I considers only a single
dimension, number of counters, that is the amount or weight on
each side. These children can be given problems which keep the
amount the same on either side of the fulcrum and constant across
problems. Only distance from the fulcrum is manipulated. Solving these problems demands Rule II, which considers distance.

Siegler examined how children of differing ages but at the same
level of expertise responded to feedback. Feedback trials simply
involved being shown the behaviour of the balance subsequent
to their prediction which was then either confirmed or unconfir-
med: 5-year-olds and 8-year-olds were given problems and feedback either one level (e.g. Rule II) or more (e.g. Rule III) above
their current level of functioning. Following feedback on problems one level in advance both younger and older children shifted
to the next level. But the surprising result was that the older
children also learned from more difficult problems which enabled
them to shift more than one level. In contrast, the younger children
were not able to learn any more from the more difficult problems.
Indeed their learning was interfered with; they did not even
acquire the greater expertise represented by the next level (that is
Rule II) when they were given the very difficult tasks.

Siegler's explanation for why children learn anything at all
from corrective feedback, and specifically why older children

may be able to learn more, is contained in his detailed concept of encoding. Encodings are said to be the ways in which events and objects are represented in memory. Representation is used here to mean the state of the knowledge base of events and relationships pertinent to the task at hand. Operationally encoding is measured by a reconstruction paradigm whereby children see a specific example of a problem and are asked to recreate it. The accuracy of their reconstructions shows what information they are picking up about the various elements.

Measurements of encoding demonstrated under rigorous scrutiny that children who learn from feedback have encoded aspects of the dimensions as yet not appropriately used in their performance. Thus even though 8-year-olds were not using information about distance in their performance based on Rule I, they were shown to be picking up information about weight *and* distance. The 5-year-olds were not, as shown by their inability to reconstruct accurately the distance elements of problems, whereas they could do this for weight.

The encoding hypothesis then states that children's learning will be restricted if they have limited encoding of component dimensions. An encoding deficit can be overcome, as Siegler has shown, by manipulations which change either knowledge of the previously unattended dimension's importance, or the perceptual salience of the dimension, or the ability to maintain attention to various sources of information. An interesting point to note is that Siegler claims that with age children systematically pick up more information about features and relations in tasks than are fully used in their performance routines. This information is then 'used' given awareness of a perturbation. The suggestion is that a major difference between older and younger learners is their knowledge base.

But Siegler not only refers to learning being dependent on encodings, but also realizes he has to include basic learning mechanisms in the process. These are referred to in as yet undeveloped concepts of 'production systems for learning'. That is he says that given encoded information children do things with that information following corrective feedback to overcome the problem and acquire greater competence. These production systems are formally equivalent to the learning activities referred to in this chapter.

This brings us back to the discussion about the conditions for self-initiated learning. Such learning is seen to be possible because performance-directed regulation provides the learner with focuses for learning activities. Siegler's encoding hypothesis can be rephrased. Completely independent learning can occur only if the child's knowledge base is sufficient to provide elements for a creative construction. The learner acts on information available from the task and task performance, and their relationships with a knowledge base. This may provide the potential for new response capabilities.

There are parallels between the graded problems Siegler's children confront and children learning to read at school and even at home. The similarity is this: children also learn this skill in specially constructed environments that control the degrees of freedom, that is the complexity of the task, which match the levels of the child's competence. The task of identifying a word such as 'horse' becomes in many reading programmes a problem which is presented with more or less structure depending on the level of the child. When encountered in a picture book with repetitive sentence frames ('Here is a . . . '), the picture of a horse plus the repetitive frame provide considerable structure. The degrees of freedom are considerably reduced. A problem of greater complexity, at a different level, is confronted within a story which has a picture of a farm and one of the several sentences relating to the picture states, 'There was a horse in the paddock'.

Contexts for learning language can be described in a similar way. For example the task of learning lexical items often occurs in a structured environment. Successive encounters with words occur in contexts where both the linguistic and social dimensions of environments reduce variability and are modified to match the child's skill.

What Siegler's work adds to the present analysis is an experimental demonstration of the effect of an elaborated or relatively extensive knowledge base on learning. Therefore it provides support for the claims made about the child's contribution to the learning process. The strategies children use to solve specific problems can be vehicles for learning activities. Learning occurs given that a knowledge base exists which provides potentially usable information when actively attempting to solve problems. The extent of learning is dependent both on how elaborate the knowledge base is and on the activities that are engaged in to solve problems.

Thus both regulation of the skill and learning from the skill are intimately related to the knowledge the child has of the skill. In performance-directed regulation there exists a heightened activation of a plan for action which sensitizes the performer to pick up certain sorts of information. Learning activities also operate with this action plan using existing knowledge in concert with the information derived from current solving. Thus the more elaborated the knowledge base, or the more relevant it is in terms of the task environment, the more able a child is both to engage in performance-directed regulation and learn from solving performance problems.

4 Overcoming the general problem: Practice making perfect

Ulric Neisser has an impressive demonstration of the conditions under which a learner solves general problems. In a series of studies he has examined the ability of subjects to look selectively at visual displays and pick up one sort of information rather than another. He has, for example, studied adults watching two superimposed ball games on a television set. With practice the observers are not confused, and become able to follow either of the games. When first exposed to some of the more difficult varieties of these tasks Neisser has superimposed a third moving image. In one such study this was a woman with an umbrella who appeared to walk across the two games. Surprisingly the observers did not notice this third image until several trials had elapsed. Summarizing these results Neisser says:

> people fail to notice unexpected events when they are deeply engaged in a task they believe to be difficult. The easier the task becomes, or seems to become, the more likely they are to notice other things.
>
> (1976, p. 216)

Learning via modularization

The case of noticing the woman with the umbrella provides a useful illustration of what modularization in the development of a skill enables a child to do. In the course of performing more automatically and fluently a child becomes able to perform other activities.

Given appropriate circumstances these activities occur and changes in behaviour follow.

The phenomenon and its explanation

Like learning which arises from problem-solving, learning via modularization can be completely self-contained. An especially fine-grained description in reading comes from Soderbergh's case study which involved her 3-year-old daughter (1971).

Soderbergh taught her daughter to read, initially within the structure of playing a word game, usually conducted before going to bed. She used a highly controlled but meaningful 'look and say' programme, built around words and sentence forms from the child's oral language. The sequence over the first three months involved introducing a new word printed on a card and the mother saying the word. Over this time there was no deliberate instruction in letters or components of words.

Soderbergh's observations are rich with instances of spontaneous analysis of components and comparisons between words made by the child when becoming fluent in recognizing a new word. For example in the third month (the girl was 2:7) she recorded the child as saying:

> 'precis liknar pappa' ['precis is like pappa', pointing at the p in precis] 'men i papp e de tre stycken' ['but in pappa there are three of them'].

> (p. 32)

Another observation made during this time is particularly pertinent. The girl in learning to recognize 'det' [it] made the comment:

> 'det liknar dem, ta fram dem sa far vi likna' [det is like dem, show dem to me and let us compare]

> (p. 33)

Shortly before this incident Soderberg had attempted to provide instruction for what had earlier proved to be a difficult task, that of learning 'functors' (words without concrete referents and having important grammatical functions). So she introduced two functors which were minimally different -nar (when) and -dar (there); one after another and then both simultaneously. The child had imitated this arrangement. She spontaneously adopted it as a strategy for comparing and analysing when she next learned another functor, the word 'det'. Soderbergh's observation provides data which illustrate not only the use, but also the acquisition of task-specific learning strategies.

It could be argued that these observations coming from notes taken by an involved parent may be unreliable. They are, however, matched by descriptions taken from studies of children learning to read without formal tuition before school. Furthermore such learning has been observed in studies of children in the early stages of learning to read at school (Francis, 1982; Torrey, 1979). Similarly the studies of word-solving in context described earlier provide experimentally controlled descriptions which suggest learning following modularization.

In those studies two routes were followed in correctly reading previously unknown words in context. Deliberate problem-solving accounted for some words but another route was obvious. Some words were never hesitated over or checked; they were read fluently both initially and in succeeding encounters. Many of these words were subsequently able to be identified in isolation although this had not occurred previously. Given that something about the components of these words was learned sufficiently to enable them to be identified over successive contexts and out of context, then, it appears a process akin to rapid modularization occurred. The readers did something more than fluently 'guess' in the enriched context.

It appears that with the response in context being nearly automatic readers were able to pick up information in a way similar to being able to attend to the woman with the umbrella in Neisser's task. Given Soderbergh's observations, the arguments which were used when discussing the immediate problem-solving route are equally applicable here. That is the effective learning, reflected in decontextualized identification, arose from strategic behaviour. This behaviour again could be described as task-specific solving strategies which were vehicles for learning activities. [1]

The need to learn

Modularization results in a potential for learning. But it is *not* a sufficient condition for acquiring more expertise. Given an environment in which it is not immediately useful to learn anything more it is unlikely that further information will be picked up. Hale (1979) has shown this in laboratory studies of children who are required to learn the spatial position of stimuli in a display. Each stimulus has two dimensions, and the children need to use only one to solve the task. For example the stimuli may systematically differ in terms of both shape and colour. The children are required to identify the position of different stimuli on test cards. Responses to test cards which present one dimension of each stimulus indicate what dimension children chose to use. Only information about one component dimension which is sufficient to solve the task is typically learned.

Even with extra training which ensures nearly automatic responding there is no increase in the amount of information picked up about the second dimension. There is, however, a gradual developmental trend to acquire such information. From this Hale argues that children of different ages pick up different amounts of information due to general developmental changes in their selective attention.

Undoubtedly general developmental changes in the *conduct* of perceptual learning occur. But this conduct can be seen in terms of strategic activity which is a reflection of the learner's knowledge base or plan for action (Gibson and Rader, 1979; Neisser, 1976). It might therefore be the case that older children bring a different knowledge base to the laboratory environment specially created by Hale. One such aspect of their knowledge might be to assume they need to know or learn more than the experimenter's questions seem to require of them. Indeed, this is one aspect of the argument which Siegler used for the superior learning of older children in his studies of the balance beam problem.

Hale's own studies show the significance of task environments and how children interpret them. In further research Hale changed the task so that only one dimension was explicitly and experimentally defined for the child as relevant. No developmental increase in amount of further learning was observed. Alternatively when 5-year-olds were instructed also to attend to the dimension about which they ordinarily would not pick up information, they performed like older children.

This discussion throws light on recent research findings on reading behaviour and their translation into statements about how reading should be taught. Ehri and Wilce (1979) and others have carried out research which suggests beginning readers may learn more about word components when they learn these words in isolation compared with learning words in a context. These writers find that in the context of a sentence children rely on additional sources of information when learning to recognize words. Given this finding the suggestion for teaching practice is that children should first learn words in isolation and then use context to practise and provide conditions for generalization.

There are problems in the interpretation of these studies. For example the data, which are further discussed in Chapter 7, show high progress readers learn as much about components of words whether or not they meet them in isolation or context. This suggests the issue is really one of what activities children engage in when encountering words, and conditions which give rise to appropriate activities.

There are also empirical issues. Because of their strategic use of context the children in the context conditions learned to identify their words more quickly. Given the criteria used in the experimental design this means they received less feedback. It is misleading to compare how much different groups have learned when they have received different amounts of instruction.

Finally, such studies say nothing about the developmental significance of learning under either condition. For example they do not examine the degree of stimulus and response generalization from different conditions of learning and the motivation to engage in further learning and gain greater competence. A short-term laboratory study does not provide that sort of information. Later chapters will argue that judgements about the appropriate conditions for learning require more than this; they require a developmental socialization perspective.

A range of strategies

The argument thus far has been that even beginning readers can capitalize on incipient proficiency to learn about the components of that proficiency. But the comments made earlier about the occurrence of completely self-contained learning and the likelihood of children engaging in this when their skills are limited and when other resources are available are equally applicable here. In most task environments learning cued by modularization will some-times be self-contained and at other times be mediated by others.

This interplay between different modes of learning within per-formance-directed regulation is suggested in Soderbergh's case study. The major characteristic of the child's learning in the early period appears to have been commenting out loud about her com-parisons and analyses. Some of these comments were prefaced by inviting her mother to participate in the observation ('Mother, mage is like "oga" ',p. 32). Given the mother's responsiveness and the playful interaction described in the report, it is highly likely these comments resulted in some response. Thus the com-ments may have elicited information from the other person, although the resultant feedback was not recorded by Soderbergh.

Soderbergh's case study is not the only description of learning following modularization. Hazel Francis (1982) studied forty-eight inner London school children prior to their receiving any deliberate phonics instruction. The 'look and say' programme concentrated on words with sentences and books carefully designed to support a developing word vocabulary.

Despite the early programme emphasis on whole words, over the first few months the children showed increasing know-ledge of spelling. This included general positional and sequential probabilities of letters which could be used when decoding words. In one school after one year the majority of the children's errors contained two or three of the letters also contained in the text word. Moreover, this developing knowledge enabled them to identify words which had not been previously seen or trained.

They had learned aspects of English orthography. But it was not entirely independently achieved. Some of that information was supplied to them. Although the teachers did not systematic-ally attempt to teach phonics or phonic analysis strategies at times they did draw their children's attention to letter structures, and some letter naming occurred.

Even so Francis's observations suggest that some self-contained learning occurred. This can be assumed because the children could do things that were unlikely to have been system-atically taught. Her observations, like Soderbergh's, contain instances of spontaneous pattern matching. At 5:9 one child when sounding out g-e-t-t-i-n-g points to the text word and says, 'That's *tin* and that's "ing" ' (1982, p 62).

Modularization and learning from a perturbation

Several points made earlier can be reiterated here. The impetus for Soderbergh's daughter to ask questions could be called an awareness of a difficulty, just as much as it could be seen to be an outcome of modularization. She faced a general, albeit rather diffuse problem. She became aware that her well-learned words were composed of elements and that knowing these elements and their combined properties supplies some of the rules of the game. But it may not have been immediately apparent to her that facility with this knowledge held the key to efficiently learning more words.

The learning that occurs via modularization is a special case of being cued by a perturbation. As before the question can be asked, what attributes of a child's increasing sophistication with a skill component guarantee the productive application of learning activities? The same three sources are available in the special case. Knowing a problem exists, a child also has knowledge of what attributes of performance are currently successful, and what circumstances require more sophisticated skills. Given a knowledge base which provides guidelines for strategies then learning is possible. Thus a child can differentiate components of a new modularized skill.

The sufficiency of a knowledge base is to be gauged in reading by the extent of a child's linguistic insight or knowledge of the acts of reading and writing. Even a simple concept that words do indeed break up into letters could guide the search for patterns. But although modularization provides the basis for perceiving a problem and analysing elements, the learning activities occur only if there is a need to engage in them.

The need to go beyond present expertise can be both generally perceived, or specifically cued as indicated by Hale's and Siegler's research. The general case is captured in the observation that age correlates with an increasing tendency to apply learning activities and differentiate aspects of an acquired skill. It was suggested that the correlation may often occur in laboratory tasks because older children assume that sometime in the future more may be required of them than is initially apparent.

Specific needs arise from a task environment when even modularized skills are found to be incomplete or not fully effective. An interesting developmental question to ask in future research would be what experiences provide conditions for children to want to analyse tasks and skills beyond the immediate requirements of the task environment.

Integration and generalization

Differentiation is but one of two structural changes that occur in skills. The twin structural change made possible in modularization is integration. Integration refers to the use of a newly modularized aspect of a skill in combination with other already acquired components. Having become nearly automatic the new component is added to or embedded within other components. Thus in motor or sensorimotor skills integration is said to have occurred when the modularized act occurs in the context of other motor acts when performing the skill.

Differentiation and integration occur over time and across contexts. Differentiation proceeds as a skill component is decontextualized. In this process the component becomes generalizable, able to be accurately and easily applied to contexts beyond the familiar ones in which learning was initially activated. Indeed, one could only claim that differentiation had occurred by observing instances of generalization. This generalization is sytematically probed in reading by a structured test of item knowledge, or it is naturalistically observed as a child uses that knowledge in a novel context such as a new word, as Sally did in the example at the beginning of the previous chapter.

The processes discussed for differentiation apply equally to instances of integration. The essence of integration is a connection of modularized components to produce novel combinations. It arises from the same creative learning found in the solutions of perturbations discussed so far. Again the extent of integration would be judged in terms of generalizable or flexible combinations. The degree of integration would be dependent on learning activities expressed in specific strategies.

The same structural concepts can be used to explain the basis for these strategies. It can be argued that the degree of integration which occurs with any one component is a product of interaction between task environment and the child's knowledge base. From that knowledge a plan of action provides guidelines for performances. The probability of an adaptive and independent (that is uncued) act of integration varies with the availability of an appropriate knowledge base and plan of action. It further varies according to the strategy used to achieve generalization.

If degrees of integration partly vary according to the deployment of task-specific strategies one would expect to find inter- and intra-variability in the characteristics of spontaneous generalization. The reading studies we have been examining contain such instances of individual variation in the degree to which learned components are spontaneously combined.

For example Soderbergh describes at least two different strategies for integrating already learned material when trying to read new words. In the sixth month of her learning Soderbergh's child read several new words spontaneously either by putting two separate components together, or by deleting components and substituting others. Again, observations by Francis can be added to these. They show both inter- and intra-individual variation in the children's attempts to produce novel combinations.[2]

Studies of generalization in children can suffer from adult egocentrism. That is in the process of acquisition generalization is seen as inaccurate in comparison with adult-defined boundaries of appropriateness. This implies error or faulty learning. But a child learning to speak or read is reliant on others to find out the conventions, to acquire the rules of the game and the definition of the elements within the game. If there is a fault it exists in the interplay between the learner and the task environment. It is the latter which provides the necessary information, doing so in a clear or difficult manner.

It is important to note that this is the strength of a behavioural explanation of generalization. It locates the sources of generalization within the contingencies. Given failure to generalize, or problems in generalization training, the fault is seen to lie in the interactions engendered by the contingencies. But what this framework does not provide is a useful account of the act of generalization. Just how is a child influenced by the contingencies within which he or she is developing a skill?

The present analysis of strategies involved in differentiation and integration provides the missing analysis. From it there arises a more appropriate conceptualization of generalization in the process of structural change in a symbolic skill. An active learner interacting with a task environment faces a problem. It is one of discovering what the defining and critical characteristics of skill components are, and how these can provide greater expertise in the functional use of the skill. The strategies involved in that learning determine the potential and limits for generalization.

If for example a child often employs a 'try it out and see if it fits' strategy this will result in early attempts at testing modularized components in new contexts. Given components that are critically dependent on information provided by others, then these strategies, seen as local expressions of a general (reality testing) activity, are likely to facilitate progress (see Nelson, 1973; Smith, 1978).

Modularization and practice

The next chapter deals with learning that does not initially arise from performance-directed regulation. Before this, modularization itself needs to be examined. This term refers to changes in the dynamics of a skill component; the speed and fluency which performance takes on with practice. But inspection of the descriptions of modularization and equivalent terms such as 'automatism' suggest that the referent also includes notions of change away from unwieldy and inexact performance (see Chapter 1).

Modularization is usually associated with concepts of practice. Yet it is apparent that some authors use practice to refer to any instance of an independent application of a skill with intent to learn via performance-directed regulation. This would include all the phenomena we have discussed thus far. But there is a special case of self-regulated learning that deserves examination in its own right because of how it refines our understanding of practice and its effects. This is captured in descriptions of the modularization of high-level reach and grasp in infancy. What changes in an infant's performance is its rapidity, smoothness and the probability of immediate accuracy.

These characteristics are also described in A. Newell and Rosenbloom's (1982) recent review of the law of practice. Many of the studies they review describe change, not in terms of the acquisition of new components or novel combinations as has been described in the previous section. Rather, the change is in the performance characteristics of a discrete skill, particularly the rapidity of that skill in concert with the quality of its performance (for example accuracy). The review also demonstrates how ubiquitous practice learning is. Their 'power law of learning' is applicable to changes in performance in a range of tasks including perceptual and problem-solving tasks.

There is, therefore, learning that needs to be accounted for having examined learning from specific problems and after a component is modularized. But it too can be considered another case of overcoming a perturbation. As with differentiation the perturbation is general, being an intent to become more skilled and make performance more exact. Like the other cases of perturbation the essence of the learning comes from performance-directed regulation, captured in this quotation from Bartlett: 'it is not practice but practice the results of which are known that makes perfect'.

The structural analysis of skill suggests that what is learned with practice is a higher order, or more abstract plan for carrying out the performance. This produces the phenomena which lead researchers to talk of freeing-up of attentional capacity. The phenomena do indicate that step-by-step control is eliminated and the learner's knowledge of a particular routine becomes extensive and generalized across contexts.

This automatic responding derives from successive performances in different contexts which are closely monitored. Patterns and cues to performance are extracted from feedback. This creates a general plan of performance. The learning strategy is the task-appropriate version of practising, repetition of an act or learning by rote. When this arises from performance-directed regulation it is more than blind repetition, and with older people practice can be a deliberate act to modularize a component. Performance is engaged in with the express purpose of 'trying out' the skill and becoming better at performing a particular component.

This is illustrated in the following description of practice in the everyday world. Its author attempts to explain how practice results in performance change by using the concept of knowledge of results.

> An ambitious young basketball player can teach himself how to shoot baskets by nailing a rope to the side of the barn and practising by himself. He can see the degree of his error, adjust his behaviour to reduce it, and learn. [He] . . . has internalised the

usual standard for a correct shot, and the comparison of visual feedback with the standard of correctness in his perception of error. The error perception is subjective, and knowledge of it is subjective reinforcement.

(Adams, 1978, p. 237)

Basketballers are not alone in practising. According to Gombrich (1979) painters have engaged in an equivalent form of practice in perfecting their art. Changes in how Rembrandt, for example, represented gold braid across successive paintings are referred to as occurring in a 'rhythm of lumbering advance and subsequent simplification'.

Yet Gombrich's description introduces a further complication into our picture of practice. For an artist the standard which is the equivalent of the proficient shooting of the basket on the barn door is not nearly so fixed. The standard itself may be clarified in the course of practising a component of representing nature. However, the basketball player and artist are alike in that the course of perfecting the particular component is not likely to be a simple conformity or adherence to one route to mastery.

The course of perfecting a skill, even more so with a symbolic skill, is marked by inventiveness in how to use the instrument effectively to obtain the goal. Sequences and routines are varied to test their effectiveness in the course of becoming effective. And it is here that the distinction between practice and play, the freedom to vary routines with minimal threat, blurs.

These are descriptions applicable to quite sophisticated children and adults. With young children the engagement in performance may not rise from a recognizable intention to practise. Indeed, awareness that learning may be a by-product of acting may be completely lacking as young children acquire expertise in symbolic skills (Vygotsky, 1962). But practice, even that described as rote learning, can occur unintentionally. The impetus to performance may be delight in performing the skill, trying to repeat the achievements of growing expertise, wishing to demonstrate that expertise, or simply perceiving frequent occasions for using the skill for its primary purpose. In each case the bases for performance exist *without* the express purpose to practise the skill. But practice is an outcome and modularization of practised acts follows. We shall see in Chapter 7 that such contexts for practice characterize precocious readers, the children who learn to read without formal tuition.

Describing practice for modularization in this way leads to clarification of a thorny pedagogical controversy. Rote learning usually connotes dictatorial classroom practices which are devoid of meaning. One therefore reads with surprise no less a radical educationalist than Ivan Illich (1973) advocating rote learning in 'Deschooling society'. But the important feature to notice in Illich's account is that the repeated performance is under the control of the adults who wish to learn. Their knowledge of the skill to be obtained and what they need to know in order to become proficient suggests rote learning is an efficient procedure. Additionally (and this may be a curious paradox for a 'deschooler') having been to school they also know rote learning can be an efficient way of rapidly acquiring a discrete performance ability.

The situation is very different for young children. Rote learning imposed externally, without a clear plan of action of the task which controls intentions and the need to learn, suffers from the major problems of other-directed learning. These are identified in the next chapter. For young children rote learning, that is practice of skills, is essential. Effective learning is based on generalized proficiency in the modularized component. To guarantee this the conditions of practice must involve performance-directed regulation.

5 Dominance during instruction

The two previous chapters have focused on learning activities which are cued and directed by children from their own performance. It was argued that the bases for learning occur in the relationship between performance-directed regulation and two types of perturbation. These are either a general need to be more effective or a need to overcome a particular problem in performance. Such situations represent one mode of learning. There is another.

Performance-directed regulation and other-directed regulation revisited

Children learn a symbolic skill by encountering task environments which define the skill as functional. They then set about solving these environments thereby acquiring the skill. These task environments are essentially social. Learning to read does not occur in a vacuum; it is rooted in social contexts which provide these task environments.

Social contexts vary along several dimensions. Some of these involve characteristics of the tasks that learners are faced with. Others involve attributes of people's behaviour who influence the learner. In combination they set up the conditions for learning.

Up until this point those episodes of learning have been discussed which have almost exclusively involved performance-directed regulation. Thus the discussion has been restricted to conditions which have supported learning which is self-initiated.

The role of people participating in that learning, who instruct as well as provide other attributes of task environments for self-instruction, has been to aid the overcoming of a problem. For example instruction might occur through the provision of directions about how to solve a perturbation.

Other instructional episodes can occur which are not initiated by the learner. The need is initially identified by someone other than the learner. Acting as an external regulator a tutor then enters into or cues the child's performance and attempts to define a perturbation for the child. In doing so the usual pedagogical intent, at least when interpreted ideally, is twofold. It aims to engage the child in learning about the features of the task and skilful performance that will meet the tutor's criteria for overcoming the problem. The intent also may be to sensitize the child's regulatory activities giving the capability of independently overcoming further examples of the problem. Even though initiated by someone else it is possible for such instruction to enlist some performance-directed regulation within the episode. This might be so for example where there are many other episodes of self-initiated learning which provide a facilitative context. Instruction in these instances enters into and can speed up learning cued by performance-directed regulation.[1]

But in contrast to the sorts of episodes which are dominated by performance-directed regulation learners can also experience settings which are very intrusive. Episodes can occur which usurp both the child's intention to perform and the continued overseeing of that performance. Thus learning episodes which involve another person who constructs the task environment can be placed along a continuum of locus of dominance. At one extreme situations exist where the tasks or the tutor's attempts to define and overcome a need make little sense to the child. They do not make sense in terms of the child's plan of action, the knowledge of the goals and functions of the skill. The other extreme is represented by a child's task-relevant intentions being aroused. The need to learn something becomes understandable although it may be defined initially by someone else.

Under these circumstances a child is independently able to discriminate attributes of performance. Their action plan lets them know success and failure directly. They can evaluate the results of the interactional episode in terms of performance requirements for overcoming the problem. In the latter case, from the point of arousal of intention onwards, the interaction between tutor and child becomes similar to self-initiated learning which simply has an external mediation component.

Dominance during instruction

These two situations represent two extremes of tutor dominance during instructional episodes and the degree to which performance-directed regulation is made possible. The question is what effects do these two extreme situations have on learning. Stated most boldly those episodes dominated by external regulation will always lead to less effective learning. The domination has its effect by restricting the extent to which performance-directed regulation is possible, or by restricting learning activities which can arise from performance-directed regulation.

Interactions which are primarily externally regulated make little sense to the learner. The lack of sense can occur in at least three ways. The tutor's attempts to communicate the need to learn in overcoming a problem may disrupt or depress the child's performance-directed regulation. On such occasions the physical and motivational characteristics of the act of tutoring reduces the child's intention in, and monitoring of, performance.

Other-directed regulation may not make much sense in a second way. Tasks which are presented may so compartmentalize the skill that only limited performance-directed regulation is possible. With tasks that are denuded of significance, connections between the tasks and the function of the skill are made very difficult for the child. When children have a limited knowledge base the meaning of the task resides not in a growing awareness of functions of the skill, but in an approximation to the demands of the tutor. The tutor supplies criteria for performance conveyed in the external regulation.

The third extreme case of external regulation not making sense is where the tutor's definition and information conveyed to the child are ill matched to the child's understanding and skills. If the definition of a problem contains elements which are not presently able to be attended to then the definition is meaningless. The external regulation fails in its intent to engage learning which will provide generalizable knowledge.

The untoward effects of external regulation

Explanations for the untoward effects of other-directed regulation, and their associated learning outcomes, come from the
analyses of regulatory processes and knowledge in earlier chapters. However, recognition of the significance of these phenomena in learning is not limited to skill theorists. For example the
concern for active involvement in learning is central to Konrad
Lorenz's analysis of the development of human knowledge
(Lorenz, 1977).

Lorenz's arguments for its importance are based on an extensive
review of ethological research. He claims that being able to monitor consequences of intended acts is of decisive importance both
ontogenetically and phylogenetically for many species. As
examples he cites classic studies such as those of Maier, or Held
and Hein, where visual consequences of voluntary movement
were shown to be critical in the development of an animal's
knowledge of space.

But Lorenz's analysis goes beyond the acquisition of spatial
knowledge in animals to human insightful learning. He claims
insight depends on the acquisition of knowledge through self-
generated feedback. Such feedback is at a maximum in acts of
self-exploration and curiosity. He claims that the motivation for
this learning is an a priori, a phylogenetic given in humans,
which he terms an innate learning disposition.[2]

Not being able to receive performance-directed feedback is a
major form of disturbance. The second case of disturbance in
performance-directed regulation has received considerable
theoretical attention from the *Gestalt* theorist Kohler (1927) and
from the Russian psychologist Vygotsky (1962). Indeed, it was
Kohler's central criticism of American learning theory that
researchers constructed laboratory environments that did not
allow for insightful learning to occur. American rats showed the
relatively inefficient form of trial and error learning because the
structure of their task environments did not permit a 'scrutineering' of the whole. The animals were not able to analyse the relationship between parts of the problem space.

Kohler's position was that more would be learned and able to
be generalized the more that scrutineering could occur under the
control of the problem-solver. Additionally learning would be

interfered with the more that the problem-solver could not gain an overview:

> The less one takes into consideration all the relevant conditions, the more one will be embarrassed by an apparent failure. By not grasping parts the chimpanzee is influenced just as much by a mistake methodologically unimportant, as by an error in principle, and will then, because subsidiary circumstances spoiled the first attempt, give the whole thing up in despair.
>
> (1927, p. 141)

This quotation from Kohler could be altered to make predictions about the effect of a tutor within an interactional episode.

The third case of external regulation not making sense was discussed in Chapter 3 in the context of Siegler's studies of children's rules with the balance problem. The concept of mismatched instruction was introduced. In terms of the transmission of information, learners at different stages of development are prepared or ready to comprehend different types of information. Other types or too much information reduce the utility of that information. As Siegler's studies showed, learning is interfered with when information is 'mismatched'.

Making reading meaningless

The first two types of meaningless learning and the explanations associated with them are central to our analysis of learning environments in Part 4 of this book. It is therefore necessary to highlight the empirical support that exists for the claim that episodes dominated by other-directed regulation produce less effective learning.

Control by others   Lorenz, as we have already noted, grounded his claims in studies of animal learning, studies in which learners were either actively involved in or passively guided through their learning.

The experimental methods adopted by Held and Hein (1963) provide a striking physical image for the phenomena. One cat could actively investigate a circular environment while another was literally yoked. Held at the other end of a beam which pivoted from the centre of the circle the second cat was passively led through the space by the activities of the first. Their studies graphically demonstrated how limited the learning could be when activities were initiated, monitored, indeed fully regulated, by another.

There are equivalents of these studies in human learning. The most obvious are those which have investigated what has been termed the 'preselection effect'. Not unlike Held and Hein's cats, in these studies blindfolded child and adult subjects have either made a voluntary finger movement traversing a certain distance along a measure or have been moved passively to an experimenter-defined location. When required to reproduce that movement the performance of the active choice group is found to be considerably enhanced compared with the passive groups' accuracy (see Kelso and Wallace, 1978).

This effect is very general in movement research and has been found under a variety of conditions. However, its relationship to the symbolic skill of reading might be questioned. To the researchers who have studied the preselection effect the finger movement is seen as a simple, yet representative motor skill. Given that both are skills, then the effect and the associated explanation are equally applicable to the case of reading.

But the most persuasive empirical demonstration that excessive external regulation can interfere with learning to read comes from studies of reading.

In Chapter 1 a study of oral reading was described in which performance-directed regulation was modified. The readers' self-corrections or errors were modified by the timing of a tutor's feedback. The same effect as the 'preselection' effect was found. Like Held and Hein's cats and like Kelso and Wallace's human subjects excessive external control of performance interfered with accurate performance.

Compartmentalizing tasks   Interactions with tutors are but one expression of a social context. There are other ways in which a reader's performance-directed regulation might be interfered with in an environment constructed by a tutor. The effects on learning are predictable from the studies that have already been reviewed.

The circumstance occurs when tasks are presented in such a

way to limit performance-directed regulation. Performance of the skill is so compartmentalized that tasks have little significance, and learners come to rely on tutors for definitions of success or failure.

Again, studies of animals learning about environments provide the prototypical data. Maze learning as studied by associationist learning theorists showed that when rats learned to run through a maze they did so like unthinking inflexible machines. The automatic nature of their performance was thrown into dramatic relief by studies which involved changes in parts of the maze. Well-trained rats would repeatedly bang into walls erected into the runways which previously led to food, would run past food newly placed in the middle of a runway, or would run into empty space where previously there was an end wall and the goal – food (see reviews by Olton, 1979, and Gallistel, 1980).

However, in contrast to such behavioural stereotyping it is apparent that even the lowly laboratory rat can demonstrate insightful flexible learning, when given the opportunity to do so. Insightful detour behaviour is shown by rats when they spontaneously generate a new but purposeful route to gaining food. From the rats' performance it can be concluded that an overall map of the environment was synthesized from separate experiences with different parts of the environment comprising the detour. In a similar fashion rats can also be shown to learn a general principle about how to move through an environment which provides for immediate solutions when changes in position occur.

Such ability to learn features of an environment and behave flexibly within it, to maximize adaptation to it, is very different from the description of habitual behaviour. The two types of learning are a product of different training conditions. The latter occurs when flexibility is not possible. Limited choice is available but errors are effectively punished and repetitive acts are required by the apparatus. The former occurs where there are opportunities to explore the environment, where there are no negative consequences for exploration and flexibility.

There are similar situations in studies of verbal learning where the conditions of training produce different types of learning. For example Bransford (1979) has reviewed a set of experiments which systematically manipulated the conditions under which

novel concepts were learned, and examined how these conditions influenced the ease of recognizing new instances of the
concepts.

Two training conditions were contrasted. In one the verbal
definition of concepts used uniform examples; in another a
mixed set of examples were used. For example the concept of
'minge' defined as ganging up on a person or thing could be
trained with scenarios involving cowboys, or from a wide range
of different scenarios. Placed in direct contrast the training conditions produced different characteristics of learning. Practice with
same-context examples produced a minimum of initial confusion
in learning but it restricted the learner's ability to transfer the
conceptual knowledge to new examples. Practice with varied
context examples facilitated transfer, particularly to completely
unfamiliar scenarios. But it also resulted in errors and confusion
during the initial stages of learning. Further measures showed
that learners in the former group were unable to evaluate accurately the adequacy of their level of understanding of the experimental concepts until faced with the tests of transfer.

In the series of studies described by Bransford a judicious
balance between same and varied context training produced
most effective early learning coupled with accurate transfer. The
point of these studies for the present argument is this. Conditions of learning can be set up which restrict the learner's overview. Rats running mazes and children acquiring concepts are
similar. Learners can face tasks which are compartmentalized.
Like the effects of an instructor who interferes through their
instruction, the way in which the tasks are presented or structured also can be interfering. Learning within the confines of the
experimenter- or tutor-defined limits can be efficient. But because
of the block to performance-directed regulation and learning
activities derived from those activities additional learning is
limited, and bound to the context of the instruction.

The case of errorless learning   Surprisingly the situations just described are deliberately engineered in some behavioural training
procedures. One is the errorless training paradigm originally
developed by Terrace which has influenced behavioural procedures for teaching reading (Terrace, 1966; Skinner, 1968).

It was originally developed to analyse the motivational bases of
behavioural effects when training animals to discriminate between

two stimuli. But in *The Technology of Teaching* Skinner applied Terrace's work to symbolic skill learning. He said that in learning to discriminate symbols and in learning to form concepts, errors are associated with non-reinforcement. This produces inappropriate side-effects such as avoidance responses which are made to symbols associated with errors. The symbols take on aversive properties.

This disarmingly simple motivational analysis of the effect of errors led to instructional programmes being designed which kept these to a minimum. Appropriate responses to stimuli were made highly probable by the presentation of the material to be learned in very obvious ways. For example in discriminating Q from O a defining feature is exaggerated, perhaps the stick on the Q is enlarged. Thus visual exploration is constrained because the stimuli are exaggerated, in some way made more salient by the experimenter or trainer. Over time the exaggeration is reduced, for example

Q Q Q Q

In these programmes discriminations are acquired without the opportunity to learn which enables the learner to correct responding. This makes this situation an example of externally dominated learning. Thus in learning to discriminate Q from O children are seen as having little opportunity to clarify critical features of a comparison via performance-directed error feedback.

Such programmes are not merely examples of the first case of not making sense. Because presentations of stimuli deliberately constrain what features can be attended to, they can also be seen as compartmentalized tasks which restrict a child from exploring or 'scrutineering'. Both pigeons and children can learn very quickly with errorless training. But they both show some unintended effects of errorless discrimination training. Despite rapid acquisition of a required discrimination the learning may be flawed in two ways which indicate the learning may not be very robust outside of the training environment.

Children may not learn the relational features of stimuli which are critical for a generalized ability to discriminate them. Unless the training procedure is very precise, well defined and carefully controlled children may not attend to the critical dimensions of stimuli (Sidman and Wilson-Morris, 1974). And yet to do this requires a further simplification and compartmentalizing of tasks, to such an extent that further problems are generated such as limited generalization, dependence on instructional support and less effective learning (e.g. Nitsch, 1977). This can be predicted, at least partly, because in order to maintain children's interest and engagement in compartmentalized tasks it becomes necessary to provide powerful external incentives (e.g. tokens exchangeable for food or highly desirable activities). There can be unintended but documented effects associated with 'behavioural overkill' (Wheldall, 1981).

Children learn symbolic skills by solving the task environments they are presented with. This is partly achieved by processes of monitoring and evaluating performance, but the focus of that regulation is critical. With appropriate conditions it is embedded in the performance of the skill as performance-directed regulation. Otherwise it becomes focused somewhere else; performance is evaluated not in terms of a task-relevant action plan but in terms of other criteria.

Externally supplied incentives can produce such a situation by overshadowing the reinforcement inherent in performing the task. This being the case the child's monitoring may shift. A child may become relatively more concerned with the match between performance and the tutor's intentions. These latter are the tutor's criteria for skilful performance as expressed in instructions and the contingencies of positive reinforcement. If this happens attention to attributes of the task environment and performance is restricted to essential information in the interests of maximizing the pay-off by a perfect match.

When powerful extrinsic reinforcers have been used as reinforcements for skilled behaviour an unintended effect has been noted. Relatively competent students do not perform as well, and may not learn as much about aspects of the task, or problem solve as effectively, as they had previously (Lepper, 1981). They may also become less interested in the activity. The effect of 'behavioural overkill' with relatively competent students is to reduce sensitivity to task-related but not immediately functional sources of information, by altering the focus of regulatory activities.

Decades ago Kohler argued for just such a problem occurring as an outcome of shaping procedures used to produce problem-solving. Nearly thirty years ago Bruner, Wallach and Galanter

(1959) described such effects on the pick-up of information during the acquisition of learning sets. And the same effects are found in cases of behavioural 'overkill'.

Learning can be flawed in a second respect. There are negative motivational outcomes of having learned without errors. Children are less able to cope with mistakes. When faced with errors having first learned with an errorless procedure, performance is disrupted and there is reduced persistence (Terrace, 1966; Chapin and Dyck, 1976).

It has been argued for example by Skinner that since the contingencies that exist in the world may not produce the ideal conditions for errorless learning the problem of the paradigm is simply a lamentable case of the world not being perfectly constructed. But the argument offered in this book is that it is a good thing to be able to make mistakes. Not because of some metaphysical belief that being proved wrong is good for one's well-being, but because mistakes are the stuff of active learning.

Active learning enables the learner to go beyond the deliberate instruction and information in the task environment. It is as though children having learned without error became dependent. Certainly the studies indicate that they learned but they were limited to detecting those patterns made readily observable by experimenter definition.

Dominance in language learning   Less effective learning accruing from externally dominated task environments can also be illustrated in the case of language learning. Over more than ten years of research Betty Hart and Todd Risley (1980) have been analysing preschool environments which will facilitate 'disadvantaged' preschoolers' language. The changing structure of their language programmes represents a shift from externally dominated tutoring to tutoring which responds to the child's intention to perform. It also represents for the two researchers their learning via performance-directed regulation.

Initially, specially designed clinical situations were set up within the experimental preschool. Behavioural engineering principles available in the mid-1960s were utilized in their language training. They produced potentially significant gains in the children's use of qualifiers and complex sentences. Unfortunately the children did not transfer their burgeoning expertise to their normal contexts for using language such as the playground, nor were there major instances of untrained learning taking place.

But a serendipitous observation provided the vehicle to overcome this perturbation in the researchers' performance. Their observers' records showed an increase in the complexity of playground language when a particular teacher required a child who made a request for a toy to supply more information about which toy. This led to a different approach which capitalized on the natural ongoing interactions between children and their peers and teachers in normal conversation. Their 'incidental teaching' strategy used the potential reinforcers specified in a child's initiation of an interaction to gain elaborated speech. Learning occurred incidentally from the vehicle provided by the child's instrumental use of language. It proved to be a remarkably generative procedure which produced considerable transfer including significant instances of learning which were not directly trained.

This programme of research illustrates a shift from learning which was dependent on the control of a tutor, to learning which came from a child's self-initiated performance. The interactional conditions were engineered by the preschool staff but the episodes were dominated by the child's intention to use language instrumentally. From that use the tutors were able to define a need to be overcome by the children which was a pressure to communicate more effectively. The resulting increase in more sophisticated language, beyond that contained in the interactions where 'incidental teaching' occurred, is attributable to an increased sensitivity to information and more extensive knowledge being gained of the skill in action.

Identifying basic learning activities

It has been argued that what is learned depends on how the learner is involved. Learning which arises from episodes dominated by performance-directed regulation is superior to learning from episodes which are dominated by someone else's regulation of performance.

Underlying this analysis of the sources of learning has been a view of learning which is essentially behavioural. That is learning is seen to result from activities in which the learner engages. Before a change in focus occurs and the critical features of social settings which influence learning activities are examined, the concept of such activities needs elaborating.

A distinction was made in Chapter 3. Reference was made to general learning activities and their deployment in task-specific strategies which produce learning. The former are a limited set of covert acts while the latter, the strategies used in acquiring symbolic skills, vary across skills and between individuals, and in the developmental progression of an individual from novice to expert. In this section these activities are outlined. Three arguments are offered for making the distinction between general activities and specific strategies in the learning of any skill.

Concepts of basic learning activities

The first argument follows those put forward by Baron (1978) and Langley and Simon (1981). These writers refer to 'central' or 'general' learning activities and distinguish these from acquisition strategies which are domain-specific. For these writers the usefulness of the distinction comes from a concern to identify invariant and general principles of either intelligence (Baron), or learning in cognition (Langley and Simon). They introduce the distinction to deal with the variability found in how different skills are acquired. Baron suggests several candidates for these higher-order mechanisms which are discussed further below. Langley and Simon do not attempt to identify any general activities as such but rather describe principles and conditions of their deployment. However, they add two important points to the discussion. Like Baron they raise the possibility that the emphasis or predominance of a general activity may vary according to task and task environment. But more than this they raise the possibility of development in the general activities. The central activities can develop because they can affect each other. Thus Langley and Simon claim that children possess a limited set of learning activities and they are capable of *acting on each other*. A child starts life with these in rudimentary or weak form. But in application to each other they create activities which become more powerful.

Commonalities in descriptions

The second argument, like Baron's, is a logical one, a semantic version of factor analysis. It is based on perceived commonalities between statements made by different theorists. Irrespective of the skill domain under discussion one often finds similar expressions used to capture the most general level of activity the learner appears to engage in. This does not occur because of extensive cross-referencing; there are sufficient differences between theoretical interests and domains to guarantee some independence and idiosyncratic statements. [3]

There appear to be four relatively distinct categories which different writers have discussed. Using the most general of the descriptive expressions these could be termed *pattern detection*, *reality testing*, *task analysis* and *pattern matching* (or imitation).

The first of these terms, pattern detection, has been described as a core process underlying the learning of more expert performance strategies. It is essentially an inductive activity involving the 'identification of recurrent regularities', as Bruner put it in 1959. It includes those activities referred to by Baron under the heading of relatedness search and is formally equivalent to the Piagetian concept of 'reflective abstraction', a process by which a common element in experiences may be identified and conceptualized (see Donaldson, 1978). In order to make a strong contrast with the next category writers tend to stress the inductive nature of this activity by concentrating on how patterns are recognized and how the retrospective analysis is also involved.

The abstracting processes of pattern detection cannot alone account for the development of complex solving behaviour. Thus the characteristics of the second activity, reality testing, are needed. The essence of reality testing is planning ahead and checking the adequacy of this foresight. It is often discussed in formal logical terms such as hypothesis testing or, in young children, as primitive deductive inference, although the formal model does not necessarily represent a child's own understanding of his or her behaviour.

Different writers tend to emphasize different components in the sequence of anticipation and checking, and the degree to which anticipations are actually tested in performance. The checking component is focused on by writers like Baron. In contrast others focus on the functions of anticipating which provide the roots of inventiveness. Also the component of generating alternatives to gain feedback and engaging in means-end analysis allows for spontaneous variation.

Task analysis, the third category, refers to the analysis of stimuli and events which a child meets in a task environment. When inspecting or exploring a compound stimulus this activity was called stimulus analysis by Baron. But the activity can be seen in wider perspective when multiple features of a problem and its context are systematically examined and related to present expertise. This wider activity is captured in Wood's discussion of a problem-solver representing the problem space and its components and his or her own behaviour in relationship to that space. Kohler's term for this, already encountered, is 'scrutineering'.

Imitation or pattern matching is a learning activity of considerable significance to the development of socially transmitted symbolic skills. Kaye argues that imitation is the most important mode of interacting with the world when the differentiation and integration of skills is considered. This strong claim is based on a suitably general definition of imitation, that of 'any process in which the form of an act is guided by comparison with an observed similar act'. This definition includes learning from verbal models such as verbal instructions; being more social in its exercise it was not included in Baron's list.

A developmental analysis

This cursory review of different concepts suggests that a limited set of basic learning activities might be identifiable. It supplies a second logical argument for the two-level conceptualization of learning acts in complex skills. There is yet a third basis for this conceptualization and the identification of basic activities. It is a developmental argument based on the detection of the activities early in a child's life. This is essentially a search at the roots of all skills, early in development where basic activities might be seen more nakedly than in complex forms of task-specific strategies later on in development.

Contemporary researchers of infants' learning provide impressive evidence for learning capabilities which match the general categories we have outlined here. These categories are not neatly separated as they have been here for discussion purposes. They are seen as occurring in mutually supportive operations as infants adapt to and learn from their environments.[4]

The general characteristics of those activities which were labelled reality testing and pattern detection can be found in infants. They are present in Watson's description of activities he calls 'contingency analysis'. He claims that infants have a strong motivation, and indeed the expertise, to perceive relationships (contingencies) between behaviour and events in their immediate environments. These capabilities to perceive and respond appropriately to the patterning of stimulation provide a means to become socially responsive.

Other research, by Haith and Bornstein, also shows the early availability of simple task analysis activities and pattern detection. And these activities, incorporated with Watson's contingency analysis have been described in a model of infant learning developed by Rovee-Collier and Gekowski. These authors describe infants of 1 month as active problem solvers in an ecological niche. In their account, infants are able to extract actively and test out the contingencies available within their environment.

The final category, that of imitation, is currently receiving much attention. At issue is the reflexive, instrumental or intentional nature of instances of imitation in the first weeks of life. But irrespective of the exact psychological nature of the capability the various studies still provide demonstrations of the early availability of a pattern matching capability.

Learning activities and overcoming perturbations

By way of summary we can now describe how overcoming perturbations, either those supplied at least initially by performance-directed regulation or those defined by a tutor, produce learning. In solving these problems a child uses strategies which are local expressions of basic learning activities.

Examples of learning activities in learning to read

The studies reviewed earlier of word-solving in context, particularly the deliberate problem-solving route, can be used to illustrate this claim. Confronted by an unknown word and having

paused in their fluent reading the readers in those studies systematically analysed various sources of information. Highly
informative graphemes, those occurring at the front and ends of
words, were systematically explored and information picked up
was added to that available from syntactic cues and semantic
cues. The strategies involved in this solving were applied forms
of pattern detection, reality testing and task analysis, appropriate
to the task at hand.

The readers could be said to have been engaged in task analysis
when they surveyed the various elements of the problem's
requirements. This occurred at several levels. One level of task
analysis is represented by their integration of information from
the variety of cues and stimuli available. At a more general level
they made decisions about when to leave words out and when to
use different strategies to gain the ends required.

Pattern detection was involved to the extent that children
matched patterns such as letter combinations and sounds in the
target word with similar combinations in known words. The
detection of a recurrent pattern across successive encounters
with a word is a further way in which pattern detection may have
operated.

Finally, reality testing found expression in attempts to solve a
target word, based on the pattern detection and task analysis activities outlined above. Attempts were tested and evaluated against
the reality of the textual requirements such as graphemic, syntactic and semantic appropriateness. Across several attempts with
varying success the results of checking and evaluation produced
consistent success leading to fluent and accurate responding.

Learning by various means

Two final issues need to be raised about learning activities. The
first is that learning activities which might be deployed during
problem-solving may vary in several ways. One source of variation is the extent to which the activities are utilized. If a solution
which is acceptable to the learner and the task environment can
be achieved using ordinarily available performance strategies
then learning activities need not be involved. Thus the problem
may not demand or receive any more attention than that required
in the available performance strategies. Alternatively, learning

activities can be incorporated into the solution thus forming a solving strategy with learning outcomes. The more extensive the activity around a solution, the more effective the learning.

The data collected in the studies of problem-solving suggest that learning was not an all or nothing affair. The younger or less expert the reader the more instances of a problem and its solution were needed to produce fully transferable expertise. While this may show that learning is dependent on the sophistication of the problem-solving strategy, it may also indicate this point that learning activities can be present to varying degrees.

A second issue concerns the awareness or deliberateness of learning. Most of the preceding discussion of learning has been couched in a form which might imply deliberate conscious acts. But both solving and learning from that solving do not need to involve the learner's complete awareness in the sense of there being a conscious attempt to overcome and learn from overcoming perturbation.

One of the routes which lead to learning words in the problem-solving studies was seemingly non-deliberate. With some words there was no hesitation, and no pause which was followed by an attempt at the word. A response was immediately available within the overall fluent performance strategy used by the readers. Yet over successive fluent encounters with these words some knowledge was gained which enabled them to be identified across different contexts and, finally, out of context. Learning activities, expressed in task-specific strategies, can proceed in a way that is almost automatic.

Part 3
Learning to be skilled

6 The conditions of learning

Skills do not develop in a vacuum. Children learning to read act in particular environments. The analysis of reading in the earlier chapters carries with it a view of learning. Learning involves attempts to solve problems set by children's immediate environments. These dual concepts, of solving and environments which set problems to be solved (or tasks to be achieved), can be shown in the development of a range of skills.

Performing as solving

Although sensorimotor skills such as reaching and grasping have a strong maturational component, even they are sensitive to different environments which may influence the rate or even the sequence of development. Put another way, these most natural of skills are sensitive to different nurturings. They influence strategies of performing at different stages of development (White and Held, 1966; Zelazo, Zelazo and Kolb, 1971).

There is an amusing example of this which comes from personal observation. It involves an infant who, in the course of learning to walk, not only never crawled but also developed a style of movement which could only be described as a cross between a caterpillar and a seal's gait. He used his arms with elbows pointing out either side and extended forwards as anchors to pull his body forward by contraction of the shoulder muscles. As he grew up in a house with smooth polished wooden floors this was a most effective and well-adapted locomotory strategy.

Solving language problems

Children learning language can also be seen as adopting different strategies. They do so at different times or under different conditions in order to solve communication and learning tasks posed by their linguistic environments. Their strategies represent a particular solution to their current environments.

An example is provided by Annette Karmiloff-Smith (1979) who studied a particularly slippery task that children face, learning the many functions that articles have in speech. French children face this task with an extra dimension to solve, that is to use the appropriate form of an article (for example *le* or *la*) to indicate the gender of the noun to which it refers.

The children Karmiloff-Smith observed particularly the youngest of them, used what she describes as a 'phonological' strategy. With this strategy the child chooses the form of an article by considering the endings of nouns and the presence of phonological markers. The children could have adopted other strategies such as using already existing knowledge about gender (for example a cow is female, therefore *la*), or using syntactic rules. Indeed, Karmiloff-Smith found the latter 'semantic' and 'syntactic' rules came to augment the older children's dominant phonological strategy especially where suffix clues were ambiguous.

Faced with the task of indicating gender in the production of articles the French children she studied adopted a particular strategy as judged by its regularity and the types of 'errors' made. The particular strategy adopted and its development with age make sense in terms of the characteristics of their linguistic environments. Karmiloff-Smith argues that the early dominance of the simple phonological strategy occurs because it is through phonology that the most consistent patterns of gender marking are present. The gradual shift to the use of semantic and syntactic cues occurs because the linguistic environment offers frequent exceptions to the phonological rules; there are discernible patterns in the exceptions.

This explanation comes from a formal analysis of language patterns. But having examples of the end product, the linguistic stimuli presented to the children in this example is only one aspect of the 'task' environments that children confront when learning symbolic skills. They also enter into interactions with more skilled people who deliberately or unintentionally organize and modify the tasks through behavioural interactions which are 'instructive'. Another study of oral language strategies illustrates this point and its consequences.

Katherine Nelson examined the structure and acquisition of single words from the time eighteen toddlers first acquired comprehensible words around 12 months to the beginnings of multiple word utterances around 2 years (Nelson, 1972). She describes how the children performed the task of communicating in their social environment, and more generally, how they used language to control their immediate environment.

From an analysis of the first fifty words in each toddler's vocabulary two groups of language users emerged. The first, the 'Referential' strategy children, had a largely object-oriented language. Successive probes of the growing vocabulary and also the total first fifty words showed that more than 50 per cent of their vocabulary fell into a general nominal category. These were words used in labelling, demanding objects, ostensive reference, and so on, such as 'ball', 'he', 'milk'. In contrast to the ten Referential strategy toddlers, a second group of eight developed an 'Expressive' strategy. Less than half of their vocabulary was made up of general nominals. A significant proportion of their vocabulary were personal-social words for expressing affective states, needs and social relationships (for example 'no', 'want', 'please').

The regularity in behaviour was found by successive observations of the children's growing vocabulary when using language in natural settings. For the two groups the strategy rules relate to choosing particular attributes of social situations in which to talk and different objects and events to talk about. These strategies can be described as being used to get from the perceived need to communicate (the immediate problem) to the particular problem solution, the production of a speech act involving a single word.

Consistent with this view Nelson uses the terms selection or processing strategy when referring to the basis for the regularity in the children's behaviour. The strategies adopted were a generalized method for solving immediate problems. But they enabled more linguistic skill to be acquired.

Environments and solutions

Drawing these examples together with the arguments in previous chapters an important conclusion emerges about skilled performance. A child's intention to act on an occasion can be seen as a solution to the task environment. On this view environments present tasks and children are seen as engaged in solving and performing the task more or less adequately. In this way task environments pose the immediate or prior problem. Embedded within this problem are the specific and general perturbations we considered in the last chapters. The immediate problem is to act as skilfully as possible on this occasion.

The term task environment was originally introduced by A. Newell and Simon in 1972. It is apparent from their original discussion that the concept was closely tied to physical attributes of environment and rules of behaving associated with tasks within a particular setting. In the present analysis the concept of task environment needs to be broadened. Attributes of the social environment, as well as materials, are added. Together, these aspects of environments engender and constrain problem-solving activities.

Children learning to read are set multifaceted tasks by their environments. In the environments designed by schools there are a variety of daily tasks derived from the curriculum. They include many separate sorts of discrimination learning, association learning, and concept learning problems as well as the more complex problem set by reading books for meaning.

These are immediate instances from which the specific and general perturbations arise. The perturbations are present in each instance but solving an instance may not advance solutions for the problems of becoming more expert. Each time a text is read it presents an immediate task to be solved, to decode and construct the author's meanings accurately. It also provides opportunities for solving the problem of how to read well. Just how that solving occurs has been the subject of previous chapters.

Learning and active environments

Environments exist which pose problems for children learning to read. A novice confronts those environments. Learning is possible. But our analysis is incomplete. What causes learning to occur?

Answering this question in detail occupies these next four chapters. But in order to make the answers coherent and believable three things are needed. First, we have to establish a view of learning in which both children and environments are seen as determining what takes place. Then a framework for identifying the significant dimensions of task environments is needed. Finally, the adequacy of this framework needs to be tested against the available research.

Different theories of how children acquire skills adopt one of two perspectives on learning. The longstanding distinction is in terms of where the theory locates the source, or the control of learning. Is it within the child as organismic theories would have it, or is it within the environment as behavioural theories would claim?

In the introduction it was suggested that the distinction is misguided. Venerable does not mean viable. A believable account of how a child learns to read requires a theory of learning in which both the child and the environment are potentially active. The child makes a contribution, as do the environments within which that child acts. The developmental outcomes of both these contributions are fashioned by the structural properties of skills.

The present account of how reading skill develops adopts the metaphor of a construction. Development is constructed from interactions into which the novice enters with task environments. The child's contribution to this construction is in terms of learning activities. These activities can arise out of the child's ongoing regulation when performing the skill. Or they can be primarily cued and controlled by someone else who acts in place of the child to regulate performance. Of critical concern in the child's contribution are the extent of performance-directed regulation, the strategies by which perturbations in performance are overcome, and the learning activities which are expressed in those strategies.

This is a model of active learners. How can the ingredients of active environments be identified? Variables are needed which can be related to the development of the skill, that is variables which engineer a child's intention to perform, a child's ongoing regulation of that performance, or a child's overcoming of perturbations and the learning activities they engage in. The needed framework for analysing environmental variables comes from several sources. Together they provide a means of categorizing and generalizing about the nature of the significant variables. One comes from Urie Bronfenbrenner in the form of typology. It identifies two naturally occurring environments or contexts within which development takes place (Bronfenbrenner, 1979).

A second is a product of recent behavioural research on environmental variables. Using that research two sources of events can be looked for which are predicted to influence the effectiveness of those contexts of learning. A distinction is drawn between moment-by-moment interactions and other events in task environments impinging on those interactions (e.g. Glynn, 1982).

The third follows from studies of maternal strategies when teaching problem-solving which provide the concept of scaffolding. With this the system made up of learner, contexts and events which provide the mechanisms for learning, can all be viewed from a developmental perspective (e.g. Wood, Bruner and Ross, 1976).

Contexts for development

Recently Bronfenbrenner carried out an analysis of developmental research in natural settings. From it he derived a significant generalization about two contexts which provide ideal conditions for development. The development of reading skill would be predicted to be facilitated to the extent that these contexts are available for learners.

Bronfenbrenner makes his claim about these contexts in the form of two propositions. He claims there are

> two types of necessary conditions [for development] which are mutually exclusive in time, but they can take place sequentially either within the same setting or from one setting to the next. Proposition 1 is a prerequisite for Proposition 2.

> Proposition 1. A primary developmental context is one in which the child can observe and engage in ongoing patterns of progressively more complex activity jointly with or under the direct guidance of persons who possess knowledge and skill not yet acquired by the child and with whom the child has developed a positive emotional relationship.

Proposition 2. A secondary developmental context is one in which the child is given opportunity, resources, and encouragement to engage in activities he or she has learned in primary developmental context, but now without the active involvement or direct guidance of another person possessing knowledge and skill beyond the levels acquired by the child.

It is clear that Proposition 2 cannot be operative in the absence of the experience stipulated in Proposition 1. But the converse also obtains. If there is no setting in which the child can exercise newly acquired capacities without intervention by more competent others, the developmental process remains incomplete.

(1979, p. 845)

This generalization about contexts is based on studies of general developmental phenomena, notably cognitive, language and social development. As argued in the introduction, learning to read is also a developmental phenomenon. This generalization therefore can apply to the case of learning to read.

Table 4   Observations of a child's reading activity at home: average minutes per day

| Age | Reading activity | |
	Being read to	Looking at books alone
1:8	44	1
2:0	47	0
2:4	80	9
2:8	80	2

Source: Personal records

The existence of situations that have the same general features as Bronfenbrenner's two contexts for children learning to read is obvious. As an example, Table 4 contains the results of systematic behavioural observations of a 2-year-old and her reading activities taken over a week at four-monthly intervals by her parents and grandparents. [1] Within her weekly routine many minutes per day were spent with family members as they read her stories; she also spent time by herself looking at books. The record underestimates time spent in either reading activity. It did not extend to the child's time at a university creche, nor did it include times when one of the adults involved might have been otherwise occupied and unable to observe relatively brief periods of independent reading. But it shows the potential for primary and secondary developmental contexts in a family setting.

Obviously some children are engaged in primary and secondary developmental contexts at home which are focused on literacy skills. Features of the two contexts are also observable at school. At the outset of schooling children continuously interact with an 'expert' with whom they have an ongoing relationship. It might be expected that in most classrooms there are also many opportunities for spending time alone with print. As we shall see this expectation may be naive. More than this, achieving the major features of both contexts may be more difficult at school than at home.

A behavioural analysis of task environments

Primary and secondary developmental contexts, or at least approximations to them, supply the immediate task environments for children learning to read. But apart from very general notions such as 'complex activity', 'jointly', and so on, the specific elements of naturally occurring task environments for beginning readers are not derivable from Bronfenbrenner's generalization. The analysis of environmental variables requires further concepts. To guide the analysis there must be some definition of the major elements within task environments and their relationships with each other, as illustrated in Figure 8.

Tasks, learners and tutors

Many task environments have the three elements shown in the diagram: a task (for example a book), a learner and a tutor.[2] To the extent that the tutor and reader are the same over time, and that they enjoy a positive emotional relationship, this task environment approximates Bronfenbrenner's ideal. As such this identification is stating the obvious. Perhaps not so obvious are the assumptions made about the patterns of influence between these elements: how they interact with each other. Most developmental

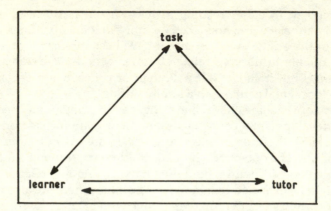

Figure 8   Major patterns of influence within task environments

models of interaction between children and older, more expert persons assume that the processes of influence are reciprocal. That is they assume that behaviours of one both effect, and are affected by, the behaviours of the other. Not only can a parent's behaviour change an infant's, but also the infant can control or modify the parent's.

While developmental theorists have for some time been documenting reciprocal phenomena and examining their theoretical implications, the same is not true of researchers of reading. Much of that research has not progressed beyond a simple unilateral model of where teacher instuction is being seen to affect reader's behaviour. However, the presence of reciprocal influences may be critical to understanding learning in classrooms. Classroom phenomena such as the labelling of children and grouping may increase the potential for teachers' behaviour to be unwittingly influenced by their children's behaviour.

A simple demonstration of the influence of a group of readers on their teacher is shown in Table 5. The data came from a study of six children in a learning disabilities classroom who received extra tutoring from paraprofessionals. Data were collected over several months in a series of experimental phases (lasting up to two weeks) which each child went through. In some phases the children received the extra tutoring on successive passages from their texts in special individual sessions in the morning. Later in the afternoon each child read as usual

Table 5 Teacher behaviour with readers reading with high or low accuracy following extra tutoring

Teacher behaviour	Condition	
	Low accuracy (84.1%)	High accuracy (92.8%)
Error correction		
% Errors attended to	55.8	39.7
% Models	56.3	62.9
Approval rate (per minute)	0.6	0.6

Source: McNaughton (1981b)

with their teacher. In tutoring phases this was the passage on which they had received tutoring. In non-tutoring phases there was no extra tutoring in the morning for the passage they read with the teacher.

The data in Table 5 are averaged across four phases of tutoring (twenty-seven days) and five phases of non-tutoring (thirty-seven days) for six readers. They are measures of the teacher's behaviour in the afternoon reading sessions. Not surprisingly the children were more accurate when they had received extra tutoring. But when they were more accurate the teacher's behaviour, particularly in terms of her corrective feedback, changed considerably. With increased accuracy the *proportion* of errors which were attended to by the teacher decreased. This decrease occurred with each reader. Thus the teacher's behaviour altered systematically according to changes in the readers' behaviour and perhaps her expectations about the readers. She corrected a smaller proportion of their errors as a consequence of how the children acted for the teacher.

Reciprocal influences are a feature of learning. However, even an analysis in terms of reciprocal influences between the reader and the person who acts as tutor is insufficient: a more complex model of influence is needed. In Figure 8 a distinction is made between the reading task which is set and the instructional behaviours of the tutor associated with the task. The distinction is important because the task is an important source of influence.

It is well documented that attributes of reading tasks such as whether or not children are identifying words in context or learning them in isolation will affect the learner. What is less obvious is that these attributes will also affect the tutor's behaviour. Some of the effects will be indirect, arising from changes in the child's behaviour which is a function of the task, and some will directly influence the tutor's behaviour. This effect can be quite unintentional. When a teacher switches from instruction based on words presented in isolation to providing instruction while a child reads a book, the cues for the teacher's behaviour, such as providing feedback, change.

So the analysis of task environments identifies three elements which interact with each other in complex ways. There is a subtle implication here for analyses of interactions involving the learner: to understand the processes of instruction it is necessary to look further than the moment-by-moment interchanges between a tutor and a reader. There are immediate or proximal influences on a child's learning carried by the interactions which the child is engaged in. But also there are more distal or general events which alter the form that these interactions might take over time. This distinction emerges as a fundamental perspective which organizes the discussion of environmental variables within developmental contexts.

Setting events and specific interactions

During the early stages of becoming a skilled reader learning occurs within situations which approximate to greater or lesser degrees the ideal of primary and secondary contexts. In analysing the effects of environmental variables on how learning occurs within these contexts the focus becomes the interactions in which a child engages. It is within these interactions that the immediate effects of variables on child activities are to be located. But Figure 8 also suggests by a double-headed arrow that the relationship between a reading task and a reader is also interactive. It is inappropriate to conceive of a reader simply reacting to the stimuli which make up a task. In comparison with a tutor, a book, and even more so a card with an isolated word on it, is a very static partner in an interaction indeed. Nevertheless, the concept of interaction is still applicable.

It is applicable because of what was earlier described as the structure of reading skill. The reader brings a knowledge base to the task. Stimuli which are confronted are defined in terms of that knowledge. That is the nominal 'stimuli' in the task are made functional, are defined, by what the reader brings to the task. This means the reader in some way determines what the stimuli become. Thus the reader acts on the task.

Furthermore, given that the reader is able to regulate performance there is a stronger sense in which the reader and task interact. With feedforward and feedback processes operating that are rooted in the child's performance, the task itself enters into the performance. The child's performance strategies are modified as a consequence of the effect that information supplied in the task can have on performance-directed feedback.

This sense of interaction is most apposite when a child reads a book for meaning. In reading a book a beginning reader responds to the stimuli supplied by the text. If children perform with an intention to gain the author's meanings rather than, for example, to identify individual words, and conditions enable them to do it, readers' strategies can be seen as 'anticipatory'. That is semantic and syntactic properties of upcoming words are anticipated on the basis of what has been read. Together with their regulatory activities this means readers act as though asking questions of the text, and modifying those actions in the light of what the text offers. The notion of tasks influencing a reader's behaviour contains an important implication. Our analysis would be incomplete if it were restricted to the relationships obtaining between discrete reading responses and the immediate stimuli antecedent to or consequent on that response available from the text and the tutor. A single episode is not self-contained. For a start it is necessary to examine the context which preceding interactions supply, which brings us close to a distinction between 'interactions' and 'setting events' for interactions, but not far enough. Previous interactions are not the sole source of influence on an interaction.

More distal events influence the course of an interaction. The most general of these range from the temperature or lighting of a room through to the physical well-being of the learner. Bijou and Baer had these general events in mind when they defined the concept of setting events: 'a setting event influences an interactional sequence by altering the strengths and characteristics of the particular stimulus and response functions involved in the interaction' (1978, p. 26).

The authors of this definition made the distinction, as they put it, for convenience. The concept of setting events is a generalization about influences on learning. It summarizes findings from different areas of behavioural research. It supplies a guide not so much of where to search but how to widen the searching. It cues researchers to consider multiple sources of influence and relationships between different (potentially functional) events.

Such sources specific to reading will be identified and analysed in the next chapter. They have been chosen partly using the theoretical model of reading skill developed in earlier chapters, partly from established concepts of setting events for human learning and partly as generalizations from the growing data base on setting events from behavioural research.

It should be noted that this analysis of setting events for reading interactions can be taken as support for a relatively new change in the focus of behavioural learning theory. Although the concept of setting events is not foreign to such theories its significance has long been unrecognized. It is not difficult to see conditions which contributed to the lack of recognition.

The early concern for experimental control severely reduced the role or variation in role that environmental events could play. There was a deliberate intention to reduce potential variability in behaviour during conditioning which might be due to attributes of the experimental space. The Skinner box is an example *par excellence* of a carefully designed experimental space. It conveniently reduced potential variation in distal sources of influence such as temperature and light, or other members of the species. The only setting events that were used were chosen because they had a relationship to the reinforcement. The reinforcers or unconditional stimuli that were used in instrumental or classical conditioning studies tended to be the direct object of basic needs. The setting events most pertinent to these needs, such as level of satiation, were therefore of primary concern. As such they were seen as methodological adjuncts, not as variables of interest in their own right.

The impetus for the change in the status accorded to setting events is as easy to document as the reasons for the original disregard. Once behaviour analysts applied themselves to real problems in naturally occurring situations they realized what a limited case of behavioural change the Skinner box really represented. Having to analyse complex behaviour in naturally occurring environments forced a reconceptualization of the significance of setting events.

The development of a primary developmental context

The view of environmental variables which has been outlined has a major shortcoming. It is not developmental; it does not provide a means for conceiving how the interactions change over time as a child becomes more expert. Changes in how children and environments act together to produce reading skill need to be dealt with in a theory of learning to read.

A general concept which has emerged from studies of how mothers teach problem-solving and language skills is useful. The concept is one of 'Scaffolding'. It is consistent with the construction metaphor already adopted in this chapter. The social context, that is the task environment which includes the tutor's activity,

> involves a kind of 'scaffolding' process that enables a child or novice to solve a problem, carry out a task or achieve a goal which would be beyond his unassisted efforts. This scaffolding consists essentially of the adult 'controlling' those elements of the task that are initially beyond the learner's capacity, thus permitting him to concentrate upon and complete only those elements that are within his range of competence. . . . the process can potentially achieve much more for the learner than an assisted completion of the task. It may result, eventually, in development of task competence by the learner at a pace that would far outstrip his unassisted efforts.
> (Wood, Bruner and Ross, 1976, p. 90)

This concept is useful but it too is not primarily developmental. The concept must be expanded to include the notion of progressive removal of scaffolding.

What is suggested here is that the analysis of environmental variables, events and specific interactions, be guided by a third realization of how environments influence learning. Ideally the task environment, determined by both the tutor and the learner, provides scaffolding. The learner's activities are supported by a

task environment that provides conditions for the most competent performance possible, the greatest amount of performance-
directed regulation and the most effective solving and learning
activities available to the child.

This scaffolding is jointly determined by the tutor and child
because the child is able to influence the tutor. This is acknowledged by the authors of the above passages when they claim that
the scaffolding is determined by two theories which a tutor
holds; one is a theory of the task, the other is a theory of the
child's competence. Ideally the scaffolding is systematically
taken down over time. Again it is a product of joint activity as
readers acquire greater expertise in regulating and learning from
their solutions and tutors reduce their support or control in response. Bronfenbrenner calls this a 'gradual shift in the balance
of power'.

The following analysis of setting events and interactional patterns will be guided by this perspective. At issue will be how
variables conspire together to provide the scaffolding and how
they respond with the learner to remove it.

It must be stressed, however, that according to Bronfenbrenner's model of development this is only one context for learning.
A symbolic skill is not necessarily or ordinarily limited to the scaffolding provided in a primary developmental context. It doesn't
develop from dependence to independence in a unitary fashion,
nor is it only an independent skill after it has first been dependent.

At any one time the skill in one form or another is both dependent and independent: able to be used in some form without support as well as developing within supporting structures. A
5-year-old can read a story with a parent or teacher, and also
engage in some solitary reading activities. Both contexts, both
independent and dependent expressions of a burgeoning skill,
can be progressive and produce learning. As Bronfenbrenner
claims, ideally the two contexts are needed for development to be
maximized. [3]

These three frames of reference will guide the analysis of the
conditions of learning in the following chapters. Setting events
and specific interactions occurring in primary and secondary
developmental contexts are identified, and the manner in which
the variables within these contexts can change over time is examined. Many of the research examples are taken from classroom

settings particularly when children are engaged in oral reading. Using experimental data, claims can be made about the ideal conditions for solving and learning from that task. However, as suggested in other examples, the three frames of reference are equally applicable to socialization experiences before school. Ideal conditions also can be plotted for literacy development before school, which maximize performance-directed regulation and learning activities. The application of these concepts to development before school will be a major part of Chapter 10.

7 Making interactions work: Setting events for learning

Demonstrations of the powerful effects that setting events have in natural settings initially came from studies of classroom management. For example, given the task of keeping a group of 5-year-olds listening to a lesson or a story, it can matter a great deal how they are seated in front of the teacher (Krantz and Risley, 1977). Although controlling classroom behaviour and arousing interest in literacy skill may have completely opposite overtones, they are similar in at least one respect. An analysis of the conditions of learning uncovers the presence of significant setting events.

Using the model of primary and secondary developmental contexts two sets of setting events are discussed. Those which influence interactions with the reading task when a tutor is present, and those which increase the probability of independent reading and learning from that reading.

The continued availability of a responsive tutor

One obvious general setting event is suggested by the definition of a primary developmental context. It is the continued availability of responsive 'experts' for one-to-one interactions within a positive relationship. In effect, what is predicted is that the interactions a learner might have with texts and the person functioning as a tutor would be made more productive by the presence of this set of circumstances.

The experimental studies marshalled by Bronfenbrenner to

make the generalization do not include studies of reading as such. However, there is a set of studies by Benjamin Bloom (1984) which do provide experimental data of a more specific sort. Again they are not of reading but they do focus on the learning of school-based skills. In Bloom's research three types of learning environment have been compared for instructing high school students in subjects like Algebra or French. The three conditions involved conventional classroom instruction, 'mastery learning' which involves feedback and corrective instruction based on ongoing tests, and a modified form of mastery learning. The modification was a change from small group instruction to one-to-one tutoring. Groups of students in these studies were randomly assigned to different conditions and were similar on variables such as measured achievement, interests and initial aptitudes. The same teachers taught under each condition.

The performances of students under conventional classroom instruction was used as a baseline against which gains in knowledge by the other groups were compared. On the measures of gains after several weeks the average mastery learning students were shown to have achieved better than 85 per cent of the conventionally instructed students. Under one-to-one instruction this increased further. The average student under this condition learned better than 98 per cent of the students under conventional instruction.

The possible effects of this modification were suggested in a series of observations carried out during instruction. It was found that engagement in the tasks was considerably higher and teacher feedback was systematically different with individual tuition. Bloom's experimental procedures are a weak approximation to Bronfenbrenner's ideal. But the power of the one-to-one setting, complete with reciprocal influence, is suggested strongly in Bloom's data.

At first glance observations of classroom reading interactions do not support Bronfenbrenner's generalization and Bloom's studies. Rosenshine and Berliner have reviewed a considerable body of research on classroom instruction in the first years at school. Out of this review came a puzzling finding. Time spent interacting with only one or two students was negatively related to gains in class achievement, whereas time spent teaching small and large groups was positively related to achievement (Rosenshine and Berliner, 1978).

But the negative correlation arises not because one-to-one interactions are inhibitory, an interpretation that would be contrary to our predictions. It occurs because of the way classrooms operate. The large-scale classroom studies also show that adult presence and supervision was positively correlated with gains in achievement. Those classrooms where group instruction is carried out tend to guarantee that more children are supervised. Students in classrooms tend to be involved more in classroom tasks when a teacher is monitoring. This means classrooms in which interactions with individuals often occur tend to be classrooms in which many children are not supervised for considerable periods of time. The harsh reality is that one-to-one interactions are counter-productive because of how classrooms need to be managed.

So in terms of overall classroom achievement scores individual interactions may not be productive. Yet for individuals, other things being equal, the setting in which the child is most likely to be engaged in learning activities is the one-to-one setting. Classroom observations of early readers show that attention to books or focusing on teacher instructions is guaranteed when a teacher is interacting solely with one reader.

Table 6   Average engagement of forty-six readers during reading lessons under three types of classroom organization

	One-to-one	Group	Individual
Average engagement	97.5%	90.3%	68.0%
Total intervals observed	(56)	(1,829)	(1,931)

Source: McNaughton (1983b)

An example taken from observations in seven classrooms reveals the patterns of engagement by forty-six beginning readers aged between 5:6 and 6:6 years (Table 6). They were observed over three weeks during reading lessons either receiving instruction in a group, working alone, or reading with the teacher. Engagement in the task set by the teacher was scored in ten-second intervals if the child being observed was focused on the task for the majority of the interval. One-to-one instruction did not occur very often but there was only one interval where a child was not attentive and focused on the task at hand. Other researchers have obtained similar data for reading. Together, these results support Bloom's finding.

Unfortunately these observations only indirectly address the specific predictions from Bronfenbrenner's generalization. For example it could be predicted that the effect of the set of circumstances including the continued availability of the tutor would be seen on specific types of interactions. Given otherwise similar tutors one would expect that consistent interactions within an ongoing positive relationship would be associated with different forms of positive and corrective feedback compared with repeated interactions with 'uninvolved' unfamiliar tutors. More precisely, the feedback would be better matched producing more frequent and more effective forms of learning from performance-directed regulation. The tutor's theory of the child would be more extensive and accurate. But such predictions await systematic study.

Text characteristics

Within the relationships set up by someone tutoring a child there is a very obvious source of influence on how a child reads. This is the reading task set by the tutor. There is a considerable history of research into the effects of variations in the major task children face, that of reading books.[1] That research has yielded data about such variables as syntactic and semantic properties of the text and the presence of illustrations.

To the extent that these characteristics can be shown to influence important features of a reader's behaviour when reading with a tutor they can be conceptualized in terms of setting events. This would be so if, for example, the possibility of more effective performance strategies and regulatory activities systematically alters as a function of the syntax of the text.

The linguistic properties of texts which conspire to make a text more or less readable include word difficulty (as assessed, for example, by word frequency norms), sentence length and the syntactic complexity of sentences. The influence of these dimensions on reading performance is easily shown and often dramatic, subject to certain qualifications that research can be used to predict the dimensions of texts that are likely to be setting events for performance-directed regulation and learning activities.

Matching text and reader

From the beginning all aspects of reading skill will be highly dependent on a match between the beginning reader's oral language skill and the language contained in the text. Match in this sense is determined by such dimensions as familiarity, meaningfulness and predictability. With potentially familiar syntax and known vocabulary a novice is capable of picking up and using semantic and syntactic cues to anticipate word classes and even specific words. As was argued in previous chapters this attention to and use of context is a condition of self-regulation that has as a goal the maintenance of meaningful performance. It provides therefore fertile conditions for learning activities.

A simple demonstration is provided by analyses of the performance strategies and self-regulatory activities of children learning in different programmes. Clay has observed development in a programme whose early emphasis is on reading texts designed to approximate children's language structure. Her observations of 100 beginning readers show 90 per cent of them began to self-correct on reading materials written by their teachers from a child's orally supplied text. After six months children were promoted to a graded reading series which continues this emphasis by deliberately approximating the vocabulary and language structures the child might use (so-called 'natural language' texts). On promotion sensitivity to contextual cues was readily apparent. Almost three-quarters of the 5-year-olds' single word and sequence substitutions were judged linguistically equivalent to the text. In addition, high rates of self-correcting errors came to predict progress.

A contrast is provided by observations made of different programmes. Other programmes concentrate on texts in which syntactical complexity and semantic content has been reduced to a minimum in order to manipulate exposure to selected grapheme–phoneme combinations. When reading these texts under these programmes readers tend to make errors which are not words. They opt to produce an accurate phonological equivalent of the graphemes contained in the text words and are less concerned

Table 7 Percentage of errors self-corrected: high progress readers after one year of instruction in different programmes reading two types of texts

Programmes	Texts	
	Code emphasis	Story emphasis
Code emphasis [1]	17%	30%
Natural language [2]	10%	60%

Sources: [1] A.S. Cohen (1975)
[2] Ng (1979)

about producing a meaningful response. Also they self-correct their attempts at words less frequently.

The difference that texts make to self-regulation is shown in Table 7. In it high progress readers from two different programmes are compared after one year of instruction. They are compared reading their instructional texts and non-instructional texts, which are either semantically and syntactically rich (story emphasis) or restricted (code emphasis). Even these high progress readers show the constraints placed on the probability of self-correcting by texts that are not to some extent matched with the children's oral language.

Given what has been claimed about the role of performance-directed regulation in an effective learning, programmes which exclusively concentrate on phonics training in early years make it difficult to go beyond the teaching they receive. That many readers are able to do so in these programmes reflects at least partly the availability of other sources of literacy experienced both in classrooms and in other major socialization settings.

There may be additional difficulties in reducing the richness of the language used in texts as Pearson has found (Pearson, 1974). Too far and children's comprehension diminishes as does their interest in the text. Pearson gave alternative forms of sentences to those which third and fourth grade readers might meet in their reading texts. The alternatives expressed propositions with varying degrees of complexity, for example 'The tall man thanked the young woman', versus, 'The man thanked the woman. He was tall. She was young'. Pearson found that answering questions like 'Who thanked the woman?' was facilitated by more complex sentences; moreover the children stated that they preferred the more complex forms. To the extent that natural language is more likely to be in the former 'more complex' form this study also illustrates the positive effects of a language match.

Obviously syntax and semantics are intertwined dimensions of influence. Thus the concept of meaningfulness or semantic familiarity is needed to augment a purely syntactic analysis of the match between text and reader. This dimension is tapped in measures of word frequency. More generally it is the knowledge readers might have of particular words, and the potential connections between events, objects, actions and characters represented by those words. At a more general level readers also differ in the knowledge they have of how the meanings in books are usually organized and sequenced.

The setting event provided by the degree of match between a child's knowledge of the world and the meanings contained in the words used in texts can be extremely influential. This is clearly demonstrated in a study by Marks, Doctorow and Wittrock (1974). In their study groups of readers differing in reading skill were either given stories matched to their ability or the stories were somewhat more difficult than their current level of ability. For some readers 15 per cent of the words in the story had been changed to more familiar words: words assessed as high frequency words in tables of words used by schoolchildren. For others, 15 per cent of the words were changed to infrequent words, for example by changing 'think' to 'judge'.

The percentage of comprehension questions answered correctly after reading either the appropriate or the difficult stories, when these stories contained high or low frequency substitutions is shown in Table 8. Irrespective of the level of skill, changing only 15 per cent of the words made a considerable difference. Indeed, on these measures a change to more familiar words enabled low-achieving readers to comprehend stories very proficiently. Given that more frequent words coincide with a greater probability of an individual knowing and using these words orally, then the effect of meaning on performances is demonstrated, at least at the level of vocabulary items.

So linguistic properties of texts, in concert with an individual reader's oral language skills, may alter the probability of some

Table 8   Average percentage of comprehension questions correct on stories modified with high or low frequency words

Stories	Achievement group		
	High	Middle	Low
At reading level			
High frequency	73	74	71
Low frequency	48	47	45
Above reading level			
High frequency	61	57	61
Low frequency	47	29	36

Source: Marks, Doctorow and Wittrock (1974)
Reprinted with permission of the Helen Dwight Reid Educational Foundation. Published by Heldref Publications, 4000 Albermarle Street, N.W., Washington, D.C. 20016. Copyright © 1974.

regulatory activities and performance strategies. What might this mean for a primary developmental context? In particular, how might the effects on reading skill alter interactional patterns?

A first way is via the effect that relatively high reader accuracy appears to have on tutoring behaviour, especially the incidence of error correction. If a reader's performance could become more accurate with exposure to better matched texts then it could be predicted that at least the patterning of error correction would change too. A component of this, which is of greater significance, would be the influence on tutor behaviour which might arise from changes in performance-directed regulation and problem-solving. This provides one mechanism for a progressive shift in tutor support which facilitates further independence (see Chapter 6).

When languages differ

There are substantial dangers here for children whose oral language is systematically different from the language represented in the text. Children with non-'standard' language skills might have a built-in source of mismatch between text and reader which affects interactions between tutor and reader. When a linguistic 'match' is expected to mean sophisticated use of the

standard sentence patterns then children may experience interactions of a very different nature. This prediction turns out to be
uncomfortably accurate, at least in the limited American research
available. Semantically appropriate errors reflecting consistent
dialect differences, that could in fact be translations rather than
misreadings as such, are likely to be treated as inappropriate errors
and corrected by teachers. The resulting interactions may take on
the characteristics described in Chapter 12 for low-progress early
readers, becoming disfluent and marked by obtrusive other-
directed regulation (see Cunningham, 1976; Simons, 1979).

Interest and meaning

Although meaning has been stressed here the concept of meaningfulness must itself be augmented. Interest in a book's subject
matter interacts with the knowledge or familiarity a reader has of
a particular text. Interest as such will be discussed further when
self-selection for independent reading (reading in a secondary
development context) is analysed. Here a general finding can be
noted. Comprehension increases with high-interest material
(Asher, 1980).

Given that higher comprehension implies greater facility in
picking up and using semantic information then interest potentially would be an important setting event. It would increase the
probability of performance strategies and regulatory activities
that serve the task of gaining the text's message. What this might
do for the interactions between a reader and a tutor is to increase
the probability of text-related or topic-related questions which
readers might ask (see Chapter 12). Children's interests vary
considerably yet classrooms differ in their use of this setting
event and there are indications in the available surveys that some
children have very limited choices to serve their interests. Again,
there are important implications for children from social and cultural traditions not represented in the topics which early books
contain.

The meanings of illustrations

One further dimension of texts needs consideration, that of text
illustrations. Many early reading books are extensively illustrated,

yet until recently educational psychological opinion held that illustrations had a negative effect on learning to read. The research supplying this opinion is represented in Singer, Samuels and Spiroff's study of word learning by beginning readers. The children were given words to learn by themselves or with a picture, or in a sentence with and without a picture (Singer, Samuels and Spiroff, 1973).

The test of learning was the number of trials taken to be able to identify four previously unidentifiable words in isolation. Training trials, involving presentation cues for where to look plus correction procedures, alternated with test trials during which identification in isolation was tested. The data in Table 9 show the number of trials it took before the readers could identify all four words (cup, cat, bat, bed) on two successive test trials. Also contained in the table is a related measure of the average number of correct responses over test trials.

Table 9   Beginning readers learning to identify words with and without illustrations

	Treatments			
	Word– no picture	Word + picture	Sentence– no picture	Sentence + picture
Mean trials to criterion	8.00	9.69	10.32	11.45
Mean number correct	34.98	28.43	26.23	23.39

Source: Singer, Samuels and Spiroff (1973)
Reprinted with permission of H. Singer and the International Reading Association

The results show that the most effective condition for learning the four target words, in terms of how long it took to identify them in isolation and how many mistakes they made on the way, was training on isolated words with no picture. Next came, in order of effectiveness, word plus picture, and sentence alone. Sentence plus picture was least effective.

The authors suggest a 'focal attention hypothesis' for why training with illustrations is less effective than isolation. They claim pictures or sentence context distract children from concentrating their attention on the graphemic stimuli. However, as compelling as this explanation might be, data on which it is based are limited in a number of important ways. Similar studies, which were discussed in Chapter 4 have been interpreted to show that learning words in context is inferior to learning words in isolation. Like context the negative effects of illustrations are apparent only under some conditions. Further research into the effect of illustrations using similar procedures to Singer, Samuels and Spiroff's has indicated that some children can perform very well with pictures, being able to learn as much as children learning words in isolation. Moreover, there are substantial individual differences in the distractability of pictures. It appears that distractability is most pronounced when the learning that is required and evaluated is a short-term association between word and oral response (see Arlin, Scott and Webster, 1978; Willows, 1978).

There is a further limitation to the data upon which the focal attention hypothesis is based. The effect of illustrations when reading *stories* can be assessed, rather than the effect on learning a small set of target words presented in isolation or in isolated sentences. When this is done a different set of results emerges. For example David Donald (1979) stepped outside the experimental paradigm of paired associate learning and simple measures of trials-to-criterion. He gave average second year readers specially selected meaningful stories to read with or without illustrations. When they read he took various measures of their performance strategies, performance-directed regulation and comprehension.

Table 10   Reader's accuracy and self-correction when reading stories with and without illustrations

	Story type	
Measures of oral learning	*Illustrated*	*Unillustrated*
% Words correct	86.7	82.7
% Errors self-corrected	22.2	10.5

Source: Donald (1979)
Reprinted by permission of Scottish Academic Press

The general measures shown in Table 10 indicate that readers were both more accurate and that they were better able to monitor and correct their errors when reading with illustrations. The measures of strategy were based on ratings of errors in terms of their syntactic, semantic and graphemic acceptability. These showed that the readers' errors were rated substantially more syntactically and semantically acceptable but slightly less acceptable in graphemic terms with the presence of illustrations. The presence of a more effective anticipation strategy relying on context but sampling fewer graphemic cues also is indicated. Finally, the reader's comprehension, rated from recall and inferential questions, was found to be higher.

This study by Donald shows that performance strategies and performance-directed regulation can be enhanced by the presence of illustrations, even in the absence of training. However, consistent with the focal attention hypothesis, the data also show a tendency for readers to identify more exhaustively graphemic stimuli when illustrations are not present. So the issue now becomes what learning is possible when performance strategies and performance-directed regulation are fully activated for gaining meaning and how does this compare with learning about words when training occurs in isolation.

An alternative to the focal attention hypothesis is Frank Smith's claim that children 'learn to read by reading'. In the present context this is a claim that the primary vehicle for learning to read is the act of using the emerging skill for its primary functions. That is not identifying or recognizing words, but reading stories for meaning. The prediction counter to the focal attention hypothesis is that effective learning strategies are made possible when the skill, even in rudimentary form, can operate to gain meaning from meaningful prose. It is possible to learn about words and word components in the act of reading for its primary purpose.

To clarify these two predictions studies are needed which do several things. They need to compare different conditions intensively and analyse different learning outcomes; they also need to take the reader's prior experiences into account. For example, in Singer, Samuels and Spiroff's study, it is not known what the general focus of children's classroom reading programme was. They may not have had any generalizable experience for reading in context and learning from that reading. Moreover, the context afforded by three other words plus an illustration, and training accomplished within less than an hour, hardly allows for a systematic analysis of outcomes.

A more extensive analysis which provides some useful comparison data was carried out by Ehri and Wilce (1979). Readers in their first year of instruction were given lists or sentences to read which contained ten target words. Training consisted of twelve presentations of the target words and supplementary words made into either lists or sentences. If errors occurred correction and some instruction in letter-sound correspondence and pronunciation followed.

Table 11 Learning about words: outcomes from training in a sentence context or in isolation

Measures[1]	Training condition	
	Context	Isolation
Words identified		
Target words	8.2	9.4
Supplementary words	38.3	40.4
Words spelled	2.3	3.2
Sentences produced with words		
Complete	7.6	5.2
Questionable	1.3	2.9
Words detected in sentences	15.5	13.2

Source: Ehri and Wilce (1979)
Note: [1] Numbers of words.
Reprinted with permission of E. Ehri and the International Reading Association

An intensive analysis of types of learning outcomes was made, the results of which are shown in Table 11. The target words and supplementary words were presented on the post-tests in isolation. Readers who received training in isolation could identify more target words and supplementary words. They could also spell more of the target words correctly. But while the isolation training groups learned more about the letter and letter-sound characteristics of words the sentence training groups learned more about other attributes. They could produce well-formed sentences containing the target words and they could more easily detect the target words in long sentences.

The authors of this study suggest that these latter two measures reveal what readers had learned about syntactic and semantic characteristics of words. The study therefore seems to show different aspects of words are learned that reflect the different training conditions. However these data need to be qualified in two ways. First, the differences between groups even on the word identification tasks although statistically significant are very small in terms of numbers of words identified.

This difference of one or two words may be important since it appears that the groups received different amounts of instruction. While the number of times children were exposed to target words was carefully controlled the actual amount of instruction was not. More errors (on average about two per reader) were made under the isolation condition, hence more correction and instruction was received. The sentences had provided contextual support for identification. Such support was not offered by the lists which the isolation group encountered. [2]

The second qualification comes from the researchers' analysis of learning by different types of readers. They divided their children into high and low proficiency readers, essentially those readers with high word identification scores and low word identification scores prior to the study. High proficiency readers in both conditions learned the same things about the orthographic, syntactic or semantic qualities of the target words irrespective of the training condition. For the low proficiency readers the learning was much more restricted to the condition of training.

Again, this study does not desribe the general training the children had received prior to the study and whether this predisposed them to learn better under one condition rather than another. Nor did the carefully controlled sentence condition provide the reader with meaningful stories. Nevertheless, the results and their qualifications suggest one very important conclusion. Children reading words in context can learn about unfamiliar words, including their orthographic characteristics. This learning approaches that achieved by children being trained to identify these words in isolation. Any superiority of the latter group in terms of their orthographic knowledge, and in Ehri and Wilce's study this may be entirely due to the extra training, disappears when high progress readers are compared. Such readers are capable of going beyond the training they receive, the phenomenon introduced in the introduction.

A similar conclusion comes from the research on problem-solving described in previous chapters. High progress 6-year-olds solved words when reading unfamiliar stories by themselves, and learned to identify previously unknown words from their solving in context. These readers were from a reading programme which focused on training in context. The stories they read, although unfamiliar, were taken from a classroom series deliberately written to be like natural language. Again, high progress readers are shown learning about words including their orthographic and graphemic attributes, even while reading in context.

In a further unpublished study in the problem-solving research a direct comparison was made between encountering unfamiliar words in lists or in context. Similar high progress readers were selected. Matched groups were formed using readers from the same classrooms in several schools on the basis of their position in the reading series, and from tests of reading achievement. As in the previous studies the children were given pre-tests from which a set of target words were defined which they could not identify in isolation. The children then encountered these words either in a story context using unfamiliar stories from the classroom series, or in a list. Lists were formed simply by taking the same text passages, mixing up the words and typing them into lists. Because of this matching the groups were exposed to similar new words at a similar frequency over the same period of time. On average there were eighteen new words embedded in passages (or lists) of 700 words, which were read over four sessions.

Nine readers at each of three age levels, 5:6 years, 6:0 years and 6:6 years, read either lists or stories appropriate to their instructional level. The number of previously unidentifiable words which could be identified in isolation after exposure in lists (word study) or stories (context study) is shown in Figure 9. A general increase across age levels is noticeable for both groups. At each age level there were small differences between groups which yielded an overall significant difference in favour of the context group. This group acquired 2.9 words for every 10 new words they encountered, while for the word study children it was 2.1 for every 10 new words.

So like Ehri and Wilce these results show that learning about words can proceed just as effectively in context as in isolation,

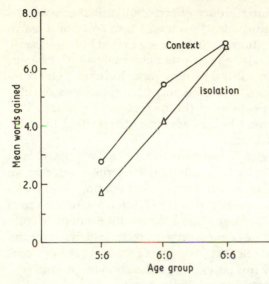

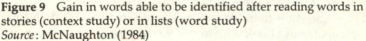

Figure 9 Gain in words able to be identified after reading words in stories (context study) or in lists (word study)
Source: McNaughton (1984)

when the readers involved are those who are effectively learning in their general classroom programme. The 'focal attention' hypothesis at least in its general form is not supportable. During text reading an appropriate context (including illustrations) can function as a setting event which increases oral reading accuracy and performance-directed regulation for meaning. But it can also provide for learning activities which can be focused on orthographic and graphemic attributes of words. These setting events may be particularly significant for heightening an average or low progress reader's performance-directed regulation.

Text difficulty and the sequencing of texts

Variations in the text characteristics already discussed make a text difficult or easy for an individual reader. While the general notion of a match between reader and text has been introduced a question remains unanswered: what counts as the most appropriate level of difficulty for an effective match? Presumably ideal conditions would require fewer errors to be made than would produce substantial interference effects, but sufficient potential errors to provide perturbations from which to solve and learn. Having posed the question it is disquieting to find how imprecise and untested our knowledge is. Systematic analyses of different accuracy conditions in natural reading tasks have not been completed, yet the notion of text difficulty and gradations of difficulty hold a central position in the pedagogy of reading. It is assumed that texts must be systematically controlled in order that learning be supported.

There are pedagogical guidelines which have passed into instructional lore. The criteria adopted by writers refer to an independent reading level, an instructional reading level and a frustration level. It is assumed that for children learning to read there is an optimum accuracy band for reading independently (usually set at 95–100 per cent words correct), and an optimum band for receiving instruction (usually set around 92–5 per cent words correct). Below this latter band frustration reigns and performance strategies break down (Betts, 1946).

The suggestion then for instructional settings is that children should *first* read a book with above 90 per cent words correct, and be promoted to higher difficulty levels when able to read with above 95 per cent accuracy. Going to the sources of these criteria one finds little empirical support for the levels offered. However there are data which give support for the rough guidelines at least for low progress readers. There are remedial tutoring programmes which have adopted and systematically evaluated the general effects of placement levels that have been at the lower end of the instructional level band (e.g. McNaughton, Glynn and Robinson, 1981). These indicate that with careful monitoring and well-designed instructional support remedial readers can make rapid progress under these conditions. However, the same degree of support may not be needed by high progress readers as shown in the studies of independent problem-solving.

Because sustained one-to-one interactions may be impossible in classrooms teachers often rely on readability formulae and publishers' recommendations to group students. This produces many instances of mismatches between readers and texts as shown in several surveys. In New Zealand Wade checked the instructional texts used by a representative sample of urban 7- to 8-year-olds (1200 children in all). A criterion of 90 per cent accuracy as a lower limit (plus comprehension questions answered correctly) was used to assess difficulty levels. Nearly half the children were reading texts in a graded series two levels below where they could still read above 90 per cent accuracy. While these readers were being instructed on very easy books, more than one in ten children were being given material that was too difficult by those criteria (Wade, 1978).

A similar situation was found when Southgate and her colleagues tested nearly 200 8- to 9-year-olds in England. Over half of these children were receiving instruction on books which they read with one or no errors per 100 words. At the other extreme several children were receiving instruction on books that were too difficult using the criteria adopted by Southgate (Southgate, Arnold and Johnson, 1981).

So some classroom conditions might restrict the progress that competent readers might be able to make and a smaller proportion of readers may be trying to learn under very difficult conditions. It must be concluded that there is no substitute for continued monitoring of individual performance. Strict accuracy criteria are not needed so much as conditions which allow monitoring of individual progress.

The verbal context for text reading

Texts are an obvious focus for analysis. But they come to be reading tasks for children because of someone's decision. Organizing and selecting texts which are matched to a reader's expertise are important instructional activities in their own right. A tutor's decision, even in terms of making books available to choose from, sets up those setting events described in the previous sections.

There are other aspects of a tutor's behaviour before reading which affect the subsequent interactions between the reader, text and tutor. A major event is the conversation which might precede oral reading. Earlier a simple yet powerful demonstration of this variable was described. In Wong's study a conversation highlighted the story to be read, its title, likely events and participants in the story, and new vocabulary. It lasted less than five minutes and its effect on a child's performance strategy and self-correction was dramatic (Wong and McNaughton, 1981).

The effect is explained in terms of preparedness. The conversation increased the salience of syntactic and semantic cues which could be better utilized in an anticipation strategy and would provide a stronger basis for monitoring performance. A similar effect with a similar explanation occurs in studies of reading comprehension and recall of text passages. Writers such as Ausubel and more recently Bransford have examined how knowledge and skill can be primed before reading so that comprehension is enhanced (Ausubel, 1968; Bransford, 1979).

The effect is well known. But does this setting event, usually in the form of conversation between reader and tutor, actually feature in primary developmental contexts for reading? Classroom observations have not intentionally focused on this variable. But there is information contained within the categories and definitions used by some researchers.

It is apparent that conversations in classrooms around reading texts are not only present, but also vary tremendously from class to class. Two British studies, one small scale and intensive, the other large scale and less sytematic, show this. In one, observations of oral reading interactions included a category of verbal moves termed 'comprehension questions' some of which were identified as occurring at the start of the interaction. In observations of five teachers this category accounted for 13 per cent of the teacher's verbalizations (see Campbell, 1981). In contrast, the Bullock Report (1975) contains casual observations by more than a thousand teachers of the time target children spend on 'oral English'. This category included but was not limited to conversation deliberately occurring during reading instruction. The classrooms for 6-year-olds and 9-year-olds varied from no oral English times recorded to many minutes per week. On average teachers of younger children reported they received around sixty minutes a week, while the figure for the older children was thirty minutes a week.

Durkin's American study of classroom instruction in comprehension included a category termed 'preparation for reading', which is similar to the phenomenon in question. The data, totalling some 4000 minutes of reading time in twenty-four fourth grade classrooms, are revealing. Instances of the teachers identifying new words, posing questions and referring to children's experiences in conversation preceding reading occurred about 6 per cent of the time the teachers were observed. Translated into individual reader's experience this is a very small amount of time. Indeed, when three individual children were further observed over three weeks no instances of such preparation for comprehension were recorded at all (Durkin, 1978).

Further American research also highlights the presence of variability, this time not between classrooms but between groups within a classroom. On this measure high and low progress readers may interact with the same teacher very differently. A case study of one first grade classroom carried out by Eder observed the two extreme groups which had been organized by the teacher. The high ability group initiated many more topically relevant comments during reading than those in the low ability group. The proportion of these comments that the teacher acknowledged was very similar. But even given the same rate of engaging in a conversation initiated by a reader this meant that the frequency of verbal exchanges relating to reading experienced by the high ability readers was four times more than that experienced by their low ability peers (Eder, 1982).

Eder's study and others like hers suggest that conversation may be both more frequent and more salient for high progress readers. It is partly a function of the child's influence on the teacher, and perhaps attributable to the more extensive knowledge base and interest which more skilled children might have.

Playing reading

Bronfenbrenner's definition of a secondary developmental context was given on p. 108. Applied to the circumstances of learning to read it covers those occasions where novice readers independently try out their burgeoning skills. Bronfenbrenner's concept has some similarity to developmental models of play (e.g. Pepler and Rubin, 1982). Like them it claims that occasions for self-directed independent activity have significance in development. Development is enhanced to the extent that such occasions happen. But it goes further than the general notions of play. It also *explicitly* implicates socialization agents. The independent activity occurs as a consequence of ongoing socialization influences which provide the child with opportunity, resources and encouragement.

In and out of classrooms

In the time-constrained world of the classroom opportunities for independent reading need to be made. Both American and British studies document the considerable variation that exists across classrooms.

It is illustrated in the survey of British schools contained in the Bullock Report. The survey found that in 9 per cent of the classrooms for 6-year-olds no time at all was programmed or used for independent reading. At the other extreme, 2 per cent of the classrooms reported more than one and a half hours per week in both class time and optional time devoted to independent reading. Similarly, Durkin's observations of average American students in early grades show silent reading occurring between 4 and 12 per cent of the total time schedule for reading and social studies. For some readers this represented a total time of five minutes per day.

Assessing the frequency of opportunities for independent reading outside school is a difficult business. The concern for time and scheduling is not nearly so great. Observations need to be extensive and consequently the data are limited. Nevertheless the parental reports and child diaries that are available show that children differ remarkably in their predilections to read by themselves at home as well as at school.

Terman's gifted children, most of whom were very good readers, provide one extreme. After one year at school they read an average of 10.4 books over two months. This estimate was based on a diary in which school-allocated books are mixed with others chosen outside school (Terman, 1925). A similar diary measure was also used in a national survey of 10-year-olds conducted in Britain. The 3000 children reported an average of three books read over a month. But many had not read any: 10 per cent of the children were non-book readers (Whitehead *et. al.*, 1977). A final estimate is provided by a small group of predominantly middle-class parents who kept child records in Chomsky's study of American 8-year-olds. Over a week the record showed children varied from reading 22,000 words to 322,000 words (Chomsky, 1972).

Functions

So the opportunities and the use of those opportunities to read independently at home and at school varies considerably from child to child. Does it matter? There is limited support for an affirmative answer, much of it coming in the form of correlational evidence. Achievement in reading is found to be positively correlated with greater amounts of independent reading. There are also studies which have experimentally manipulated the amount of independent reading by providing opportunities for 'practice'. These too provide evidence for the significance of independent reading (e.g. Heyns, 1978; Leinhardt, Zigmond and Cooley, 1981; Lovitt, 1976).

Setting events for independent reading

Thus it can be concluded that like play generally, independent reading can have developmental significance. Components of the skill may be practised, refined and modified as a consequence of unimpeded playful reading. The reasons for the effects on development can be found in Chapter 3. The effects come from the learning activities which arise from performance-directed regulation. As self-regulation is the only form of performance monitoring available when independently reading, this is not simply the most effective vehicle for learning, but the only one. Thus the critical question to answer now is what setting events increase the likelihood that these activities occur? Conceptualized in terms of Bronfenbrenner's secondary developmental context the question becomes what events function to increase the opportunities, resources and encouragement to engage in independent reading which is marked by performance-directed regulation and learning?

The availability of a primary developmental context

In the general framework supplied by Bronfenbrenner there is a major event which supplies the motivation to engage in independent reading: the primary developmental context within which some transmission of skill is occurring. Within this context both interest in what the skill can accomplish through its functions and interest in becoming proficient in the skill are aroused. The salience of the skill is perceived in social settings and constructed in social interactions.

There is an intriguing developmental issue here. What attributes of a primary developmental context, which in its early stages is characterized by a relationship of dependence, produce the motivation to be independent? Part of the motivation may be a direct outcome of social learning. During interactions the tutor provides a model and positive feedback; subsequently vicarious reinforcement for matching or imitating the model's activity is available. Reinforcement for independent reading may also arise from attempting to recapture the meanings which were constructed by tutor and learner when reading together.

By themselves these variables would be unlikely to produce sustained interest which generalized to unfamiliar books and which provided the conditions for performance-directed regulation. However, from the primary developmental context knowledge is gained about the functions and properties of being skilful. Knowledge of the functions of the skill, ideally to gain meanings, provides an interest in going beyond reconstructing shared meanings. That is interest in utilizing the skill to gain meaning provides the conditions for wanting to be independently competent so as not to be dependent on the availability of someone else.

A final influence can be predicted to arise from what Bandura has termed 'perceived self-efficacy' (Bandura, 1982). This is the child's knowledge and beliefs about how easily the skill might be learned and how competent they might be as a learner. Bandura has demonstrated how this self-knowledge not only affects how much learning occurs when engaged in a task, but also partly determines interest in that activity as measured by free choice. He argues that socially mediated feedback, particularly descriptive positive feedback, provides the basis for early interest and continued learning of a skill because it affects perceived self-efficacy. [3]

Concurrent models for independent reading

There is a different sense in which someone can have an influence on independent reading as a model. It is the model afforded by a valued person who is themself seen to be engaged in reading independently. It can be predicted that if a valued person is observed at least occasionally to be functionally engaged in the activity, then the probability of independent reading is increased. The most obvious candidates for such models are grandparents,

parents and older siblings at home, and peers and teachers at school.

Southgate's interview data suggest that teachers do not perceive personal example to promote independent reading. This self-report appears to translate into behaviour. In Durkin's observations of teachers in twenty-four fourth grade classrooms not one instance was recorded of a teacher engaged in independent silent reading, in 7000 minutes of reading and social studies lessons. Yet even for those children who have been at school for several years the model provided by a teacher also engaged in silent reading can have marked effects. At least the effects can be marked for those children who would not ordinarily read with much concentration. This is demonstrated in a classroom study where the teacher set aside opportunities and required her children to engage in recreational reading (Pluck *et al.*, 1984).

During the fifteen minutes which were set aside on two days a week the children were meant to select library books and read silently. Normally the teacher would occupy herself in classroom organization, marking or preparing work, or tidying the room. In the study the teacher's behaviour was systematically varied across days. On some days she carried on with her normal routines. Other days, however, she sat at the front of the room reading her own book silently, but with obvious enjoyment.

The children were judged to be engaged in silent reading if during ten seconds of observation they had their eyes oriented towards their open book and they were not talking. The percentages of intervals in which children were engaged in silent reading are shown in Figure 10. The data are given for five low achievers and five high achievers selected from standardized achievement test measures.

On days when the teacher carried out her usual routine the low achievers were engaged in reading around one-third of the time they were observed. With the teacher concurrently engaged in reading these low achievers consistently were engaged in reading for a majority of the time, on average 65 per cent of the intervals they were observed. A smaller and less consistent difference was found for the most competent readers who were often engaged in their reading irrespective of what their teacher was doing.

As for recreational reading at home there are similar data which

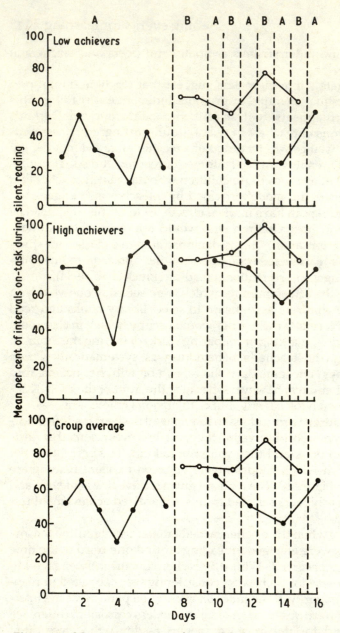

Figure 10 Mean percentages of on-task behaviour by groups of readers during normal teaching days (A) and concurrent reading days (B)
Source: Pluck *et al.* (1984)

show that a valued person who models independent reading can increase the time that a child spends reading by her or himself. The studies discussed in Chapter 11 also show that the homes precocious readers live in are marked by the presence of valued family members who themselves are seen to read and enjoy reading.

Self-selection

The analysis of reading as a skill would predict that choosing to read would make a difference to performance-directed regulation and problem-solving. The simple distinction implied here is between choosing to use an opportunity to read versus being directed to read whether one would choose to do so or not.

There are classroom observations which report high involvement or attention on self-selected tasks versus low concentration on tasks which are required and ordinarily would not be engaged in if given a choice. Similarly there are studies which show no effects on reading achievement from directing or constraining children to use opportunities for recreational reading. The actual amount of reading done is a critical variable in these studies and it varies independently of exhortations and directions to engage in recreational reading (Southgate, Arnold and Johnson, 1981; Heyns, 1978).

But such studies do not provide an analysis of reading activities related to intention or choice. More directly relevant information comes from research which has examined the effects of 'interest' in books that are read independently. Interest is related to choice in that interest is judged by a propensity to engage in an activity. To the extent that interest in the content of a book would translate into choosing to read that book given the opportunity then the predictions about choice on reading skill can be examined.

Downing and Leong, the recent authors of a 'psychology of reading', claim that teachers and parents have often observed that interest affects skilful performance (Downing and Leong, 1982). They should have included film-makers in their list of observant people. There is a remarkably evocative film directed by Ken Loach called *Kes* which captures the effect that interest has on the acquisition of skills which are instrumental in pursuing the interest further. In Loach's film a boy's interest in a kestrel becomes the driving force behind his acquiring skills at school which enable him to learn more about kestrels and share his ideas with others. Necessary empirical support, the pedantic equivalent to Loach's cinematographic insight, has been elusive. Early studies of interest produced inconsistent results which Asher has attributed to serious methodological inadequacies (1980).

Asher's own research overcomes these problems. He has shown that children indicate a strong desire to read passages that correspond to topics that are rated high in interest. Moreover, reading comprehension is shown to be superior on high-interest material. The effect on comprehension comes from two interacting factors. Children are more motivated to read material that interests them and in trying harder pick up more information, but children also have a more elaborate and differentiated knowledge base for things that interest them.

Availability of appropriate material

This dimension of interest and the earlier discussion of the difficulty level of texts suggests a further setting event. Independent reading will be influenced by the availability of appropriate material, that is books of an appropriate difficulty level and interest. Their availability is particularly important for independent reading because a reader is distant from the support provided in a primary developmental context. Therefore that reader is reliant on available cues within familiar texts to reconstruct meanings and carry out whatever level of decoding is presently possible. At very early stages of development, textual cues function as general prompts to recall and respond with segments of text. These segments may be only minimally decoded as such. Therefore such dimensions of 'difficulty' for familiar texts as visual clarity, or the clarity of the relationship between illustrations and text, become important. With clear associations able to be established between segments of remembered speech and segments of a text a child is in a position to carry out learning activities such as pattern detection. Also, it is essential for the transfer of the training received with a tutor to have available relatively unfamiliar books.

In order to acquire generalizable knowledge and skills, particularly of those skills that are supported by the tutor in a primary developmental context, it is necessary that there be unfamiliar books which provide opportunities for practice. It therefore follows that these must be books which make it easy for emergent skills to be deployed.

'Easy' in this context means able to produce near-perfect accuracy for the individual readers in gaining the text's messages with some opportunities to learn from perturbations. Comics may fulfil some of these functions at different stages of development in that meaning can be constructed through picking up information afforded in the illustrations and their sequencing. Books which are similar to those read with tutors, their similarity based on such attributes as common syntactic forms, themes and lexicon, are also early bases for easy books. With development, similarity becomes progressively less significant and skills become less dependent on simple syntax and a reduced lexicon.

Acts of writing and related tasks

The last of the setting events to be discussed does not arise from the social environment, nor is it a product of the interaction between a reader's skill and the type of task being presented. It is a setting event which would affect both independent reading and interactions with a tutor. It concerns the effect of developing expertise in another task involving written symbols.

The act of writing is one of creating meaning constrained by the conventions of spoken and written language. The creation has a particular communicative purpose, including maintaining social interactions, instructing, remembering, planning, elaborating personal experiences, evaluating one's environment and creating imagined environments.

There are differences between reading and writing. Writing involves symbol production rather than symbol decoding, and the recipient of the symbolic communication varies according to the purpose of the writing. Nevertheless writing bears a close relationship to reading. One obvious equivalence is the use of the same conventional symbol system when engaged in both tasks, and meaning is created within these conventions. The equivalence in knowledge exists at many levels, from knowing about the distinctive features of graphemes through to having plans of action for constructing meaning in symbols.

Given this equivalence it is not surprising to find claims that the two skills influence each other during development. What is perhaps surprising is that systematic empirical investigation of this relationship and how the twin developments might be most effectively co-ordinated is limited. There are studies of the development of literacy before schooling which show that the precocious development of reading skills is characterized by accomplishments in both reading and writing. Indeed, the observation of children who have not been deliberately taught at home suggests that developments in writing appear to precede new developments in reading (e.g. Bissex, 1980).

To add to these studies there are formal correlational analyses of progress in reading and the development of writing skills of children at school. Such studies tend to show high positive correlations, even on simple measures such as the number of words able to be written correctly in ten minutes and progress relative to classroom peers (Clay, 1980).

It is interesting to note that observations of writing behaviour in classrooms suggest that interest and the likelihood of engaging independently in writing is strongly correlated with reading ability. The questionnaire data from the Bullock Report indicate that at both 6 years and 9 years above average readers were much more likely to be writing original stories and using writing as a tool in personal investigations than below average readers.

Acts of writing can be conceptualized as setting events which influence the effectiveness of oral reading interactions because they provide further opportunities to acquire reading-related knowledge. Writing affords practice in reading words as well as writing them. In the case of writing, the words read have been self-generated. Furthermore, writing provides occasions for differentiation and integration to occur at the level of word and sentence formation. Given such opportunities learning activities are also likely. Finally, experimenting with rules of written language and the functions of written language become possible.

8 Knowing from a 'no': The case for error feedback

Observe someone tutoring a beginning reader and it is very likely that you will be impressed by the verbal activity which is generated. A prodigious 7000 items were counted by Robin Campbell (1981) after observing 6 classroom teachers hearing 156 readers. These verbal interactions provide a major vehicle for instructional processes. The vehicle is fueled by setting events, such as those which were discussed in the previous chapter. But the instructional force of an environment is expressed in specific interactions (including both verbal and non-verbal behaviour).

Types of interactions

Tutors do not act randomly. Certain classes of child behaviour predictably follow and are predictably followed by tutoring. The significance of this unsurprising conclusion is that it provides one basis for a simple categorization of some interactional sequences: those where the tutor does something as a consequence of faulty or faltering performance, and those where the tutor's behaviour is contingent on some correct performance. These events are not discrete or isolated, but occur in an ongoing interaction stream. Each contingent tutor behaviour also sets up a further relationship from which further classes of child behaviour are a predictable consequence. Nevertheless, the patterning and content of the tutor's behaviour suggest the source of the interactional sequence is some attribute of the child's performance.

Three types of interactions will be discussed in this and the following chapter. One involves interactions cued by perturbations in the reader's performance such as the occurrence of an error. The remaining two typically follow some aspect of appropriate performance. Three terms describe these interactions: error (or negative, or corrective) feedback interactions, positive feedback interactions, and conversational interactions. These terms are relatively neutral descriptive terms. There are possible alternatives, such as reinforcement and punishment which imply particular functions. But these are not used here for one major reason. It will be argued that tutors' behaviours, although contingent on inappropriate and appropriate attributes of performance, rarely specifically function as a reinforcer or a punisher.

Error feedback

The probability that a child's oral reading error will receive some verbal attention from a tutor is generally very high. Various studies of children learning to read at school indicate that on average it is around 0.5, that is one error in two receives attention in some way. But this probability varies according to a child's relative skill within a classroom and across time, the range being somewhat higher for a child who is identified as making low progress to somewhat lower for being or becoming relatively skilled. This range may be different for parents, who appear to be more likely to attend verbally when their child makes an error reading from a book (Glynn and McNaughton, 1985).

The data which Allington (1980) collected from twenty first and

Table 12 Feedback to errors during oral reading: differences between classroom groups in frequency of error feedback (f) and percentage of errors receiving feedback (%)

Reader group	Total errors	Errors resulting in feedback (f)	(%)
Good (N = 66)	5.8	1.8	(31.0)
Poor (N = 78)	9.4	6.9	(73.4)

Source: Allington (1980)

second grade classrooms illustrate the variation between different groups of children. Even given the different numbers of errors made while reading with the teacher the group defined by the teachers as 'Poor' (an instructional grouping based on reading achievement) received significantly more feedback (see Table 12).

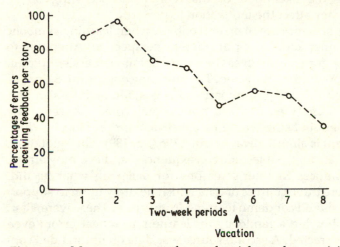

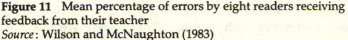

Figure 11   Mean percentage of errors by eight readers receiving feedback from their teacher
Source: Wilson and McNaughton (1983)

Variability across time is illustrated in Figure 11 from a study by Murray Wilson (Wilson and McNaughton, 1983). Here the percentages of errors which received feedback for a group of eight average progress readers are plotted over sixteen weeks (averaged per story over two-week periods). The *between* group differences noted by Allington are paralleled by the changes *within* this group of beginning readers over time. The high percentages occurring early on in their first year of instruction systematically changed to lower percentages, around 40 per cent, towards the end of their first year.

What does error feedback do?

Error feedback interactions are ubiquitous and apparently they are related to the expertise of the reader. How might this feedback operate and what are its demonstrable functions? There are two approaches to this question which have traditionally been taken by learning theorists. Through Skinner and the more radical proponents of the behaviourist tradition has come an analysis of consequent events that emphasizes motivational functions. In the general case events which are contingent on behaviour and influence the likelihood of that behaviour occurring do so because they affect the motivation to perform.

For the specific case of error feedback when learning symbolic skills Skinner adopted a punishment perspective. Attending to errors, he argued, involves the presentation of aversive stimuli. The performance is punished. The following quote from Skinner's *Technology of Teaching* summarizes his position on errors and his solution thus, 'We can avoid troublesome consequences of the punishment in being wrong by constructing programs in which the student is almost always right' (1968, p. 189). This quotation, which refers to 'troublesome consequences' and avoiding errors, also introduces Skinner's reasons for believing what he did. There were three sources of data which he drew upon to support his analysis and condemn learning from errors. These were, first, studies showing a tendency for learners to repeat errors even though corrected. A second source was data on unintended consequences of punishment during discrimination learning which showed interference with learning. Third, there were demonstrations of the superiority of 'errorless' learning in terms of rate of learning and the avoidance of negative consequences.

But each of these sets of phenomena has been shown to apply only under exceptional circumstances. Errors that occur in the early stages of learning certainly do tend to be repeated as von Wright showed in 1957. However, the repetition effect is limited to particular tasks, notably those tasks that require rote associations to be made (Elley, 1966), those tasks that make it difficult to recall either the response or its previous outcome (d'Ydewalle and Buchwald, 1976) and those tasks where the learner has no basis of judging confidence in responses (Kulhavy, 1977). Generally when learners are faced in laboratory studies with more meaningful tasks the difficulty of forming and overcoming inappropriate habits is not found. Errors which receive even simple feedback (e.g. 'wrong') are not as likely to be repeated.

Similar qualifications can be placed on the other demonstrations. Certainly in Terrace's (1966) laboratory studies of discrimination learning by pigeons the stimuli associated with 'errors' can acquire inhibitory and emotional functions. Assuming children behave like pigeons they would be predicted to become anxious faced with reading tasks on which they have made errors and would avoid the tasks where possible.

But this prediction does not hold up in many laboratory analogues of classroom learning tasks. Bransford's (1979) recent review of meaningful verbal learning or concept learning experiments demonstrates this. Again, the untoward consequence may be limited to settings, like those engineered for studying pigeon learning, which involve powerful extrinsic incentives for being right and the absence of these potential reinforcers when wrong or even reprimands and loss of reinforcers. In them the discrimination to be learned is arbitrary, meaningless and presented entirely at the whim of the experimenter.

So too with the third of the sources of data. Although errorless learning may be effective in some senses it is so only under limited conditions. These include the continued absence of errors (or else further learning is disrupted); learning with precisely controlled stimuli and changes in these stimuli (otherwise learners may attend to irrelevant aspects of the task), and simplified compartmentalized, and sequentially presented learning tasks in order to keep errors to a minimum. But this in turn produces problems of transfer and generalization and reliance on powerful external incentives (see studies by Chapin and Dyck, 1976; Holland, 1979; Lepper, 1981; and those discussed in Chapter 3).

It must be stressed that Skinner's analysis is not wrong: rather it is exceptional. The analysis and recommendation for how learning should be engineered obtain more validity the more classroom environments approximate to those exceptional conditions used by Skinner and his colleagues. But the earlier arguments need to be emphasized. Performance-directed regulation and learning activities are reduced when settings are relatively meaningless and compartmentalized. In the long term generalized independent learning may be interfered with.

Ordinary functions

So it would be expected that under all but exceptional circumstances error feedback does not punish. But how does it ordinarily function? When the task to be learned is relatively meaningful, most importantly when conditions support performance-directed regulation, then the answer to this general question is clear. Just as in laboratory studies of meaningful verbal or concept learning, when children are learning to read meaningful texts, error feedback is associated with learning.

This can be demonstrated in a study of remedial tutoring carried out with a class of children experiencing learning difficulties. Some children received tutoring from community helpers in morning sessions before later reading their books to their teacher. The single subject research used each child as their own control 'group'. Thus phases of no tutoring alternated with phases of tutoring. For some children the tutoring consisted solely of error feedback procedures, which operated whenever an error was made which was not self-corrected. Results for two readers are shown in Figure 12. With the addition of error feedback, their accuracy of reading with the teacher was considerably enhanced. In phases of error feedback the percentage of words read initially correctly increased on average by 8–9 per cent words correct. This overall gain, the difference between no tutoring and error feedback, is summarized in the accompanying table in Figure 12: see subject (1) and subject (2) in the first column.

Because of the design of the study some of the gains detected when the readers read in the afternoon might have been due to increased exposure to the books in the morning. Consequently some matched subjects simply got the same ten minutes of extra reading but without any instruction. The two matched subjects for S1 and S2 are termed 'Practice' tutoring readers in the table. On the afternoon measures of reading with the teacher they did not gain as much from practice as did the readers receiving error feedback. Moreover, the tutoring did not immediately raise their accuracy much, as shown by the difference between a test of their accuracy immediately before and immediately after the morning tutoring sessions (the second column in the table). However, a drop in accuracy from immediately after tutoring to reading with the teacher in the afternoon occurred for all readers although it was less of a drop for error feedback readers (the last column in the table).

These results for single subjects have been described in some detail. They illustrate a major conclusion about how error feedback

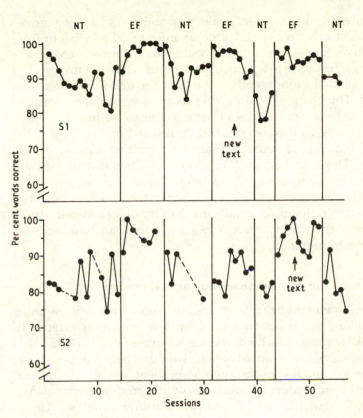

Summary table

Tutoring type		Changes in accuracy (%)	
	No tutoring to tutoring	Before tutoring to after tutoring	Morning session to afternoon session
Error feedback (S1)	8.4	6.7	−2.1
Practice (S5)	3.1	2.3	−3.2
Error feedback (S2)	9.5	12.3	−2.6
Practice (S6)	8.3	7.3	−3.5

Figure 12 Percentage of words read correctly across phases of no tutoring (NT) and error feedback tutoring (EF)
Source: McNaughton and Delquadri (1978)

can often work. Certainly the probability of making errors decreased either measured after ten minutes of tutoring or from one phase to the next. But this could hardly be the avoidance of making a response to a particular stimulus. Rather it involved an alteration in the topography of the performance. Errors were corrected. The probability of making an accurate initial response to words in texts increased as a function of error feedback.

This is the conclusion reached by researchers working in the various models of verbal learning or cognitive learning theory (Hulse, Deese and Egeth, 1975; Borger and Seabourne, 1982). In this tradition negative feedback is found in all but exceptional circumstances to produce learning, often in the absence of positive feedback. The learning usually involves modification in the topography of the original error response. In their analysis feedback provides information.

Dimensions of error feedback during oral reading

Earlier it was argued that feedback from someone else is essential, particularly in the early stages of the development of a symbolic skill like reading. Much knowledge about reading, particularly of the arbitrary codes used in the skill, would be nearly impossible to acquire in a socially insensitive environment. Ideally a task environment should provide conditions which produce performance-directed regulation and associated learning activities. Under such appropriate conditions error feedback can increase the rate at which knowledge can be acquired, relative to some sort of 'discovery' learning in an insensitive environment. It would provide information.

The information that could be provided would be that a perturbation exists and possibly that there are ways in which the specific problem might be solved. A novice may not know in any specific way what needs to be known, or indeed how to go about getting this knowledge about items or performance. For that novice the information is essential. Thus with ideal conditions error feedback is a particularly functional variable substantially increasing the learning possible from perturbations.

Timing and frequency

Despite the part in learning that error feedback may play the most significant dimension determining its effectiveness is how intrusive it is. Intrusive has a particular meaning here. It is interference with, or the usurpation of, learning activities and performance-directed regulation which a reader would otherwise be able to engage in. Error feedback is made intrusive by the timing of its delivery or by the frequency of its occurrence being given too quickly and/or too often.

The timing study, discussed in Chapter 1, showed how immediate error correction can curtail self-correcting and consequently limit accuracy. These results which have been replicated in other studies show that delaying error feedback provides opportunities for readers to regulate their performance (Singh, Winton and Singh, 1984). Supplied only when readers are unable to overcome the perturbation themselves it is then minimally intrusive and maximally functional. In this respect timing could be seen as a setting condition for the effectiveness of yet further dimensions of error feedback.

Given that feedback is delayed does it matter how often it is given? More precisely the question is how many errors that remain unselfcorrected should receive feedback? This question has not received the same degree of experimental attention that timing has. Nevertheless, the data that are available suggest a similar principle of 'intrusiveness' operates in determining the effectiveness of scheduling.

In a series of studies Klein (1976) has examined performance on reading tasks when interrupted by a second task. Readers perform a word boundary task where they are required to draw slashes between words. The words have been printed with a space after every letter but with no additional spaces between words. In some studies performance on coherent passages has been compared with performance with randomly arranged words. Students are able to utilize syntactic and semantic contextual cues in the coherent passages and their rate of identifying words (by slashing word boundaries) is considerably higher.

In one of Klein's studies he also examined the effects of different secondary tasks which college students had to do while completing the word boundary tasks. Again coherent passages facilitated

Table 13   Mean number of words per minute correctly identified on coherent passages

	Secondary motor task	Secondary memory task
With no extra task	43.0	38.2
With additional task	32.7	34.0

Source: Klein (1976)

identification. But the secondary tasks reduced the rate of identification back to the levels that were achieved with random (incoherent) passages. The results are summarized in Table 13. The secondary tasks included a motor task which interrupted reading (to circle as asterisk every fifth word), or a memory task (to remember digits and write them down after a time interval). The secondary tasks signficantly reduced the rate of identifying words relative to performing on coherent passages without any such interference.

Simply stated Klein's data show that when extra demands are made on readers their performance suffers. In these studies the students' expertise in utilizing contextual cues is interfered with. The suggestion, and it is only a suggestion because this laboratory study bears an undetermined relationship to classroom realities, is that error feedback may have the same properties of interference. At least when given frequently, and requiring readers to carry out additional tasks, error feedback during oral reading may reduce performance.

In keeping with Klein's data and his interpretation, a decrement in performance would be expected in the use of contextual cues. Repeatedly giving readers extra tasks to perform such as occurs when a teacher says, 'No, that's not right, sound the first letters out', can interfere with remembering the meaning and syntactic structure of what has been read. A further, as yet untested prediction, would also claim an effect on performance-directed regulation. With many errors and a high probability that errors will receive feedback, the need to self-monitor and check performance may be reduced.

Prompts, models and the support provided by error feedback

Having described an overriding 'intrusiveness' principle which determines the effectiveness of error feedback, informational properties can now be examined. A simple typology is outlined in Figure 13.

TEXT   The cat ran into the house
READER: 'The can ran into the house'

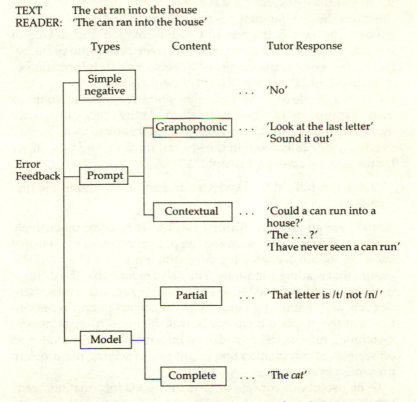

Figure 13 Typology of error feedback during oral reading interactions

Apart from a simple negative, feedback usually takes one of two forms. It is given as a request or instruction to do something, that is the reader is prompted to perform in a particular way to overcome the perturbation. Or feedback is given in the form of a model which specifies an appropriate response to the text.

These three types, an unelaborated negative, prompts and models (and more often combinations of them) appear regularly in observational records of interactions. For example in Allington's (1980) American study, and Campbell's (1981) British one, models represent at least one-quarter of the total feedback given.

Information which supports and is well-matched   In determining the functions these different types might have, two concepts become critical. The first is the amount of information and degree of structuring provided for the reader in overcoming the perturbation. The second is the relationship between that information or structuring and the reader's level of performance.

Carrying the least information are simple negatives. No information is provided on how to proceed. At the other extreme are multiple prompts which provide detailed information on how to overcome difficulty, both in the specific instance and potentially for the general case, for example:

'Look carefully at the last letter and add its sound to the first two /c/ . . . /a/ . . . ?'

Models are ambiguous in this analysis. They comprehensively structure the task of overcoming the perturbation, in the sense of showing the reader what the correct response is. They thereby ensure that reading continues. They also ensure that the difficult word is immediately added to the available syntactic and semantic cues, and that the topography of the correct phonic representation of the graphemic stimuli is available for scrutineering and matching. But a model provides no information on the strategies on sources of information one might use in solving the problem presented by an error.

To be useful this concept of structuring via information needs to be tied to the concept of a developing skill and a match between the reader's expertise and the information provided. As was argued in Chapter 3 problems are commonly engendered by a mismatch between feedback and the level of skill possessed by a child. Error feedback can be mismatched in terms of what information is provided. This sense of mismatch is discussed in the next section. Here the concern is with structuring or amount of information; corrective feedback can provide both too little and too much information.

There are experimental programmes in language and reading, based on behavioural techniques such as shaping and backward chaining, which operate a matching procedure. They specify several levels of information, from a nonspecific cue through increasingly descriptive prompts to general support for the required response usually in the form of a model. Error feedback is first given in the least informative way, and greater support is offered only if that is not effective.

The experimental demonstration of the effectiveness of this simple matching is provided in two studies of remedial intervention by Hansen. She compared a single level of feedback involving graphophonic prompts with a sequence graded from nonspecific ('Try another way') through to providing the correct word. In each study the graded sequence was associated with improved performance including greater accuracy and higher rates of self-correcting errors (see Table 14). Her explanation for the greater effectiveness of this 'matched' feedback focuses on how the single level of prompting restricted the strategies readers could use and learn to use to solve words.

Table 14 Average measures of oral reading under two different forms of prompting

Phase corrections	% words correct	% comprehension questions correct	Frequency of self-correction
Single level prompt	93.3	55.0	10.8
Graduated feedback	94.6	70.5	11.5

Source: Hansen and Eaton (1978)

Nevertheless, in such studies the probability of correcting an error following a nonspecific prompt has been found to be surprisingly high (for example Hansen found ' Try another way ' proved successful 40 per cent of the time in correcting errors). It is apparent that when setting events are appropriate, and this at least includes salient meaningful texts which support performance-directed regulation, then simply highlighting the occurrence of a perturbation is generally effective.

The functions of models In this conceptualization models are seen as providing complete support and hence being the most restrictive feedback condition; this view is generally supported by descriptions of classroom interactions associated with readers making high progress. For such readers, the probability of error feedback being first given in the form of a prompt is high, higher than its being a model. These prompts often successfully cue the reader to overcome the specific problem.

This balance characterizes early readers already making rapid progress and similar readers after three or more years of instruction (see Allington, 1980; Campbell, 1981; Ng, 1979; Southgate, Arnold and Johnson, 1981; Weinstein, 1976). It appears to generalize to other school-related tasks. In a study conducted by Steinert and her colleagues (Steinert, Campbell and Kiely, 1981) teachers and mothers were compared when teaching readers to solve pattern matching tasks. The high progress readers (in contrast with their low progress peers) received few instances of physical help involving comprehensive or complete structuring of the task. Feedback via verbal prompts was much more frequent.

But this picture of models may be too simplistic. While less often employed than prompts, models do occur with noticeable frequency in these studies. In Murray Wilson's (1983) study of beginning readers, the low frequency of models remained relatively stable over four months. In contrast, the support provided by prompts decreased as did the probability of providing any feedback at all. There are also suggestions that high progress readers under some conditions are more often given information directly (either with full or partial models) rather than being questioned, and this is not the case with low progress classmates (McNaughton, 1983b). It may be that models have other uses which dictate their low rate but continued use with high progress readers. Early on a model may provide considerable structure for those words which are unable to be identified using current skills, or solved even given specific prompts. The model provides an instantly modularized response. It could, with successive use, be differentiated with learning activities. Later in development models may still be provided to short circuit prolonged problem-solving cued by prompts, simply because there is little to be gained long term from being prompted to do with some words what can already be done very efficiently.

However, even given this special function associated with a small number of models the general principle of match would still apply. Ideally, over time, a mixture of nonspecific cues and supportive feedback, given in models and detailed informative prompts, yields to minimal support. This occurs as the learner assumes more and more of the activities supported by the earlier structuring.

The information provided by error feedback

Prompts can vary tremendously in terms of both the amount and sort of information they provide. Sources of information that might be used or the activities a reader might engage in to overcome a specific problem are many and prompts can reflect this diversity. At issue is a three-way relationship, between the content of the prompt, the general requirements of the task environment, and the reader's level of expertise. The effectiveness of a prompt is to be gauged by its usefulness to the reader at a particular stage (often judged by the 'type' of error the reader makes) within a particular task environment.

The taxonomy in Figure 13 defines a simple categorization based on what attribute of the text the reader is prompted to use. Allington (1980) has referred to this as the 'direction' of the prompt. The major distinction suggested in Figure 13 is between prompts which direct the reader to use graphophonic cues and those which direct the reader to use syntactic and semantic cues.

In what ways might the information conveyed in a prompt be well-matched? There are two levels of answer to this question. The first concerns the match between the general programme requirements and the prompts. In an exaggerated fashion this is illustrated in the following example of a text from a highly controlled curriculum. It would be unproductive if not absurd to do what is done in the example. That is to prompt the reader of this sentence to use syntactic and semantic cues when they have been deliberately minimized in constructing the text.

TEXT: The cat and the rat had a hat
READER: 'The cat and the rat had a . . . '
TUTOR: 'What might they have had?'

Yet the potential match between the general emphasis of the task environment and error feedback is not an obvious one where, for example, graphophonic cues are needed for children in phonic programmes. Task environments in school programmes are often deliberately constructed to change, and readers also change and exert influences over the tutors who interact with them. The data reviewed below show a complexity which is due to these two reasons.

Before they are introduced it should be noted that they provide a clue to the intriguing phenomenon described in the introduction. The phenomenon, the impressive ability of high progress readers to go beyond the teaching they receive, has already partly been addressed through the discussion of performance-directed regulation and self-initiated learning. However, there are also environmental sources of this inventiveness. One source is the error feedback that high progress readers receive.

Table 15 Percentages of error feedback which directed high progress readers in two studies to use different sources of information

Study	Direction of prompts	
	Graphophonic	Context
Natural language[1]	40	23
Mixed[2]	18	32

Sources: [1] Ng (1979)
      [2] Allington (1980)

The first observations shown in Table 15 come from a 'natural language' programme. Ng (1979) observed highly competent readers in their third year of instruction interacting with twenty-seven teachers. As indicated by a high incidence of contextually appropriate errors and high rates of self-correction these readers were adept at exploiting the general emphasis of the programme. They were, however, the same readers as those described in the introduction. They had acquired detailed information that was not specifically taught in the curriculum.

One source of that information comes from error feedback interactions. They received prompts which cued them to use graphophonic information in their texts. A majority of prompts to these readers did this rather than concentrate their attention on contextual cues. Other studies of first year readers making good progress in similar programmes also indicate that this information in error feedback is available early in instruction (McNaughton, 1983b; Wilson and McNaughton, 1983).

In contrast, Allington's data for twenty teachers, also with high progress readers, show a preponderance of contextual prompts. It is not known what programmes Allington's readers came from. But as he has noted (personal communication) if these New York schools were representative of American schools generally they would be likely to involve programmes which stressed knowledge of grapheme–phoneme association or word classes. In which case the discrepancy between the two sources of data might be solved. These latter readers were also receiving information to help them go beyond the formal requirements of their programmes.

The second level at which the 'direction' of prompts can achieve a match is with the reader's skill on a given task and what the reader needs to do to overcome perturbations due to inadequate performance. This is most easily assessed by looking at the relationship between error patterns and error feedback. At this point Ng's data from twenty-seven teachers become even clearer. The carefully selected high progress readers did not make meaningless, ungrammatical errors, they were already concentrating on semantic and syntactic cues. It would have been redundant to prompt them further; this expertise very likely cued the style of prompting adopted by the teachers.

Setting events which change feedback to punishment

The idealized analysis of error feedback, which has stressed its informative functions, is dependent on particular setting events. Under exceptional circumstances different functions can be observed. The most usual of these is punishment, the function which Skinner originally attributed to all instances of feedback to errors.

A number of setting events can be listed which individually are exceptions to most reading programmes and which would increase the aversive properties of error feedback. They are similar to the ways Frank Smith described in which learning to read can be made difficult. The first of these are events which reduce the meaningfulness of the reading task for the reader. This occurs when the frequency and timing of feedback interferes with performance-directed regulation, where the compartmentalizing of the task reduces that regulation and where the information contained in the feedback is mismatched with the reader's level of skill. There is also a more general sense in which reading tasks have reduced meaning. That occurs in situations where a learner has a restricted knowledge base about the functions of the skill to be acquired or the components of the skill.

There are two further conditions which in themselves would be likely to make it punishing to receive feedback about one's errors. The first of these concerns the positive consequences available for accurate performances, particularly the nature of the consequence and its contingency. Where there is an impressive external pay-off for being right when responding to discrete stimuli such as individual words in the text, then error feedback would take on aversive qualities. 'Impressive' in the context of this discussion would mean consequences that had considerable social or biological significance. Food or high classroom status for a child wanting food or susceptible to peer comparisons would be an impressive pay-off.

A more direct form of punishment occurs when the error feedback actually signals an aversive consequence. The verbal expression of error feedback may convey disapproval, rejection or even disgust. If its occurrence is such a signal then the feedback is likely to operate as a punishment. Similarly if in previous social interactions error feedback has had this form, being associated with unpleasant emotional (including lack of classroom status) or even physical consequences, then current interactions which are conveyed positively are likely to contain residual aversive qualities.

Such a situation is strongly suggested in Heather Pohl's study of high and low progress readers in their eighth year at school (Pohl and McNaughton, 1985). When asked whether they preferred silent or oral reading both groups opted for silent, but for very different reasons. In their answers high progress readers referred to the benefits of silent reading ('I can go at my own speed', 'I can reread', 'I can skim the boring bits'). In contrast, the low progress readers referred to aversive socially mediated consequences of oral reading ('I'm nervous when I read out loud', 'Because people laugh out loud', 'If I don't know a word no-one knows').

Some of these conditions were reviewed earlier. They are re-iterated here for one very important reason. There is reason to suspect that the environments that some low progress readers and their teachers construct take on these exceptional circum-stances. Meaning is reduced and making mistakes becomes aversive. More will be said of the plight of the low progress reader.

Highly trained or highly tuned?

All that has been said, and indeed will also be said in the follow-ing chapter, suggests that the person providing the feedback needs to be a highly trained and theoretically sophisticated tech-nician. There is reason to doubt this conclusion. Highly 'tuned' yes, but not necessarily highly trained. The necessity for con-trolled techniques is increased as soon as children are 'taught' in an artificially organized environment. That is in classrooms where an almost arbitrary decision is made to engineer skill learning, the need for technical expertise becomes stronger. And stronger still when remedial efforts are called for.

However, when a primary developmental context exists in which there are ongoing, mutually influential interactions, and where other appropriate setting conditions obtain, the tutor's behaviour is likely to be closely cued by the learner. While some model of 'teaching' and what needs to be taught (a theory of the curriculum) will be held, even by the most reluctant or uninten-tional tutor, the critical component will be the tutor's sensitivity to the cues and developing expertise provided by the learner.

There is a parallel here with children learning language. Their tutors, primarily their parents with whom they have developed close attachments, are not theoretically sophisticated. They are just relative experts. They can use language, but more importantly they 'read' the cues their novices supply. Without necessarily being aware that they do so these tutors alter their responses during interaction in accordance with response characteristics.

9 Praise, conversation and putting it all together

Teachers do not merely correct errors. Out of the 7000 events which Campbell (1981) studied many were statements of appreciation or affirmation. During reading they also conversed with the children about what they were reading. What are the functions of these two types of interaction?

Being positive

In the previous chapter it was argued that the attention teachers pay to errors typically functions as feedback of information, not as punishment, the function that some behavioural theorists would predict. However, the case for a standard behavioural account of the positive statements that teachers make is considerably more compelling. Among theorists of learning who examine real world situations there has long been an agreement that contingencies of positive reinforcement must account for much learning. Furthermore, it is assumed that at school these contingencies operate through teacher praise. That is it is assumed that much academic skill learning is the result of interactions which are understandable through principles of positive reinforcement.

These are explanations of behavioural change which are couched in terms of positive consequences which alter the probability of behaviour. Among the simple predictions from these principles there are those which have obvious relevance to learning to read. For example they would predict superior behavioural change with human learners when contingent, descriptive praise (perhaps tied with more tangible reinforcers) is scheduled in a way that 'shapes' behaviour (Holland, 1979). At issue then is whether the ordinary function of teacher positive feedback functions to reinforce and shape definable classes of reading behaviour.

The ordinary characteristics of positive feedback

A teacher's positive feedback takes different forms.[1] Teachers can make statements about the correctness of performance, they can express affection or they can merely affirm. It appears that when measures of all these are gathered during interactions with normal readers in classrooms the rate of approval is around one or so per minute per reader. But when only descriptive contingent praise statements are considered, that is expressions of explicit approval or affection which describe the reason for the approval the rate drops to something like once every two hours (Brophy, 1981; Campbell, 1981; Leinhardt, Zigmond and Cooley, 1981; Weinstein, 1976).

Jere Brophy, the reviewer who extracted this summary statistic, apparently suffered a crisis of theory. The observational studies in his review indicated that in normal classrooms which don't have a specially designed and monitored behaviour modification programme, appropriate praise is faint. In the opinion of the reviewer this finding damns the usual, and up until his review his own, interpretation of the function of teachers' positive feedback. It does so because contingent specific praise is used infrequently. Yet children were learning in these classrooms. He therefore reaches the conclusion that praise is seldom used intentionally as a reinforcer, nor does it usually function that way.

There are dangers in uncritically accepting this conclusion. For example, the studies he reviewed were not developmental. They did not investigate how praise rates might change over time as a consequence of interactional histories. Perhaps the approval that is given, although non-descriptive, is clearly contingent on certain classes of reading behaviour and the contingency gradually changes over time shaping towards more and more complex levels of performance.[2]

The first line in Table 16 shows the frequency with which one teacher of normal first year readers made positive comments during reading. The eight readers on average received four such comments per story, and this was the same rate in each month of study. But the frequency did change when one considers the data in terms of a ratio: a ratio of frequency to the number of words read. Stories were getting longer hence the feedback did become less frequent dropping from twelve per hundred words to three per hundred words. In very general terms this looks as though some 'leaning' of the schedule was taking place. That is feedback was becoming more intermittent, as would occur in shaping a rat towards high rates of stable responding; but the impression of shaping is not borne out when one searches for the contingencies. The great bulk of the feedback was nonspecific comprising statements like 'good', 'right' and 'nice'.

Table 16   One teacher's positive feedback with eight normal readers over four months

| | Months | | | |
	1	2	3	4
Frequency per story	4.0	4.1	3.9	3.7
Frequency per 100 words	12.1	5.9	5.4	3.1
% nonspecific	95.0	82.0	99.0	99.0

Source: Wilson and McNaughton (1983)

It does not look as though this teacher had a deliberate intention to pinpoint certain responses for reinforcing. Nevertheless, it is possible that a specific contingency on increasingly expert performance could have operated, without an explicit verbal component. This does not seem to be the case either. Fewer than 16 per cent of the positive comments followed clear instances of expert performance such as successfully solving a word, or self-correcting. Mainly the teacher commented at the end of pages and sentences, and these were being read at the same high level of accuracy over time. Because of the setting events deployed by the teachers the average accuracy for the group remained high and stable.

Thus this study shows a group of children at the early stages of learning to read receiving positive feedback. That feedback became less frequent over time but was basically non-descriptive and non-contingent. There is very little evidence here for a shaping interpretation. This teacher's behaviour adds to evidence that positive feedback normally does not function to reinforce specific attributes of correct responding.

In fact experimental evidence consistent with this view has been obtained by some behavioural researchers who have attempted to change patterns of correct responding on academic tasks by altering the schedule of positive feedback. Many of the studies have been of student comprehension when reading programmed texts. In these studies various ratios or distributions of feedback have been given for answering questions correctly. In sum, the studies illustrate the inadequacy of viewing positive feedback in reinforcement terms. There is a history of failing to replicate the effects of reinforcement schedules. Researchers have been unable to obtain patterns of responding which can be produced in less meaningful highly controlled task environments such as a Skinner box. Reviewing these data Kulhavy concluded that:

> not one study has shown a pattern of results consistent with what might be expected from work done with intermittent reinforcement.

> (1977, p. 214)

Providing information in positive feedback

It would seem that teachers do not ordinarily attempt to use their positive comments to reinforce, and thereby shape up skilled performances. Given this it would be tempting to provide a parallel analysis to error feedback for the case of teacher approval. It would start with a taxonomy going from simple affirmations such as 'yes' and 'good', to very detailed descriptions of what was right in the appropriate response, like 'Good you saw there was an /s/ on the end and you corrected yourself'. From this, notions of structuring equivalent to those provided for error feedback might be developed.

However, the data just reviewed suggest the irrelevance of such an exercise, at least for normal and high progress readers reading texts for meaning. The ideal model of a self-regulated reader actively engaged in learning also suggests that such an analysis would be largely misplaced. That is not to say that positive feedback does not convey information, but the ideal function is not one of shaping or structuring the response for the reader; it is to confirm what readers already do, and it is done largely without detailed specification.

It can be argued then that the level of generality is hardly surprising. In many circumstances the processes by which a child might produce a correct response would be difficult to determine with any degree of specificity. Indeed this may be why some programmes set up task environments in which the processes the reader uses to perform adequately are obvious (for example as would occur in a tightly controlled phonics programme). The need for making such responding overt may in fact say more about the tutor and the programmes than any absolute necessity for a child to perform in this way. Making response processes overt and obvious enables a tutor to know directly if the programme is 'working' and hence has considerable potential for positive feedback for the tutor.

Yet even in programmes which do not deliberately set out to make the subtle obvious there are often instances of overt regulating, checking and solving. But even with these instances the likelihood of clearly specified feedback would seem to be low, judging from the available studies. The difficulty of pinpointing specific activities is not the only impediment to using specific information. There is another because the principle of interference applies here too. Specific detailed information could interfere with learning.

The process of becoming fluid and automatic was earlier described in terms of modularization. Clumsiness or tentativeness is a characteristic of the early stages of skill learning, and may need assurance. Feedback underlines for the learner that important changes in expertise are occurring. However, unlike the learning possible from a perturbation, insinuating detailed descriptions of how the performance is adequate potentially disrupts practice. With a perturbation the conditions exist for a reader gaining specific knowledge or performance capabilities, which are needed at that point. This is not the case with new expertise, however tentative.

The language needed to describe all but the most simple or circumscribed of appropriate performance is considerable. Even a cursory examination of textbooks on reading would convince an adult, let alone a child, that the whole business must be quite complex. Consequently making explicit through a verbal description what is currently tentative can reduce a child's ability to perform that skill.

In the development of a complex, symbolic skill spontaneity often precedes verbalizable awareness. For example there are a number of studies, many stimulated by the Russian psychologist Vygotsky, which argue for language coming to be applied to and directing a skill; after that skill has gained a degree of sureness (e.g. Wertsch, 1985). So for oral reading the lack of specificity and contingency in positive feedback at least partly represents a compromise. It is a compromise, between providing information and interfering with ongoing fluid performance. But there is a more positive ideal function for positive feedback which needs to be identified.

Personal efficacy and becoming interested

The general information provided in many classroom teachers' positive comments gives substance to an important motivation for becoming skilled. In Chapter 7 reference was made to Bandura's concept of self-referent thought. Included in the knowledge one can have of personal characteristics is knowledge of how effectively different situations are dealt with.

Bandura makes a very specific claim. The more that the knowledge you have of your own personal competence leads you to predict you would be very effective in developing and using a skill, the higher the performance capabilities, and the lower the emotional arousal when acting. This prediction, a personal judgement of one's capability, determines how much effort is expended. It also determines how long people will persist when faced with a perturbation. This in turn influences the rate and quality of acquiring a skill.

What are the sources of knowledge about personal efficacy? Information about efficacy in learning a skill is derivable from performance-directed regulation. It is also derived directly from social sources. These include positive feedback. Further support for Bandura's claims can be found in a recent study by Schunk (1982). It demonstrates that positive feedback contingent on performance enhances self-efficacy.

A group of 9-year-olds were given graded maths problems to complete. Before being trained the children were tested for their perceptions of self-efficacy. They briefly saw instances of similar classes of problems and rated their ability to do them. Over the next three days as they attempted problems one group received positive feedback. Every eight minutes a tutor asked them where they were up to, then gave comments such as 'You've been working hard'. In fact the setting events ensured a high rate of success on the problems given perseverance and care. There were other groups who either received instructions to try harder or were control groups for monitoring and testing. As they didn't differ much in their results these latter groups are added together in Table 17, which summarizes the results.

Table 17   Averages for different groups, before, during and after training in maths problems, with and without positive feedback

	Positive feedback group	Control groups
Self-efficacy[1]		
Before	44.3	48.4
After	82.3	54.8
Measures of skill		
Number of problems correct – pre-test	1.9	1.7
post-test	17.3	5.2
Number of pages of problems completed during training	33.9	21.4

Note: [1] Ratings on a scale from 10 to 100.
Source: Schunk (1982)

The group who received positive feedback showed significant changes in their perceptions of self-efficacy. They came to rate themselves as very competent. Correlated with this changed self-perception were changes in their performance of mathematical skill. The number of problems they could complete on twenty-five item tests changed considerably and the rate at which they completed pages of problems during the three forty-minute training sessions was high. On each of these measures, including self-efficacy, the positive feedback group was very different from the other groups. The author of this report, like Bandura, claims that the feedback about performance altered self-efficacy judgements which led to increased perseverance and learning.

Studies like this one are not developmental. They do not examine motivation at the roots of a skill. Bandura claims that many of those activities which people enjoy doing for their own sake originally had little or no interest for them. But given appropriate learning experiences, almost any activity assumes intrinsic significance. He argues that the motivation and interest is influenced by positive feedback which enhances self-efficacy. Under appropriate circumstances a tutor's expressions of interest and general responsiveness to performance convey incentives to learn.

In our ideal model a primary developmental context provides a valued expert, one who is sensitive to a child's interests and expression of skill. The valued person's interest in or responsiveness to burgeoning interest by the learner is a primitive source of motivation. Tasks are attempted because of that person's presence and availability for support.

The argument then is that in situations where performance-directed regulation is possible, positive comments by a tutor serve early on to establish and maintain engagement. Under appropriate conditions the structuring and direction of learning occurs from a learner's activities, promoted by powerful setting events and supported by error feedback during interactions. At the root of the skill praise is an expression of the affective base of the primary developmental context. It provides positive conditions for continuing performance-directed regulation. It comes to provide information about the capabilities of the child for learning the task. In so doing interest is aroused and self-efficacy is enhanced.

Thus there is an explanation for Brophy's disturbing finding (1981). It is not that most teachers are very poor agents of behaviour change. It is understandable that observations of teacher positive comments when children are reading should show them to be often non-contingent, non-descriptive and not explicitly affectionate.[3]

Having conversations

Apart from correcting errors and approving children's effort there is one other major activity which takes place between teachers and readers during oral reading. They talk together. Estimates from observations of beginning classrooms in the USA and Britain suggest the following sorts of exchanges take up more than 10 per cent of the teacher's time (see Wilkinson, 1982; Campbell, 1981).

(1)   TEACHER: 'I wonder why he didn't like riding donkey?'
       READER: 'Because he thinks he'll fall off.'

(2)   READER: (reading the text) 'It is red roof.'
       TEACHER   'mmh'
       READER: 'We've got a brown one haven't we?'
       TEACHER: 'What's on your house?'

The conversations are about the stories. They may be relatively mundane but their most compelling characteristic is the semantic relationship. Aspects of the text's meanings are being referred to.

Earlier it was argued that those conversations occurring before oral reading takes place serve as a special kind of setting event. The questioning and discussion increase the salience of semantic and syntactic cues in the text to be read. Following this analysis conversations that occur *during* reading could be seen as a continuation of the setting event. They occur before particular sections of the text and as such might have a similar function to those that are antecedent to the whole text.

Conversations as reinforcement

But there are additional functions for the reader. In one of the examples given above the conversation was initiated by the reader. From the available descriptions it seems those initiations may be only intermittently responded to. This situation is shown in Table 18 which comes from an intensive classroom study by Donna Eder (1982). The percentage of all initiations responded to by the teacher was between 20 and 40 per cent depending on membership in a low or high progress group.

When a teacher does reply it is usually a response to the reader's comprehension of the story. This was the case in Eder's

Table 18   Average initations of conversation during instruction in reading groups and teacher responsiveness, in one classroom

	High groups	Low groups
Reader initiations		
Total	35.5	12.5
% topical	60.0	40.0
Teacher response to initiations		
Total responded to	12.0	3.0

Source: Eder (1982)

study. The teacher was far more likely to respond to a topical comment, one that was relevant to the current focus of the reading group (44 per cent were responded to) than to an irrelevant comment. Non-topical remarks were ignored or, if acknowledged, were reprimanded (only 12 per cent were acknowledged).

Both reader-initiated and tutor-initiated conversations occur *after* a section of the text has been decoded relatively successfully. Thus the contingency apparently involves some association with competent reading and more particularly a strong relationship with the meanings of the text or personalized associations with those meanings.

The conversation between tutor and reader establishes shared meaning. This process involves a joint contribution by both the reader and tutor to the construction of these shared meanings. There are three likely consequences of this construction process. The first is motivation. Contingent conversations reinforce continued attention to and use of contextual cues. This is especially so following interactions that are contingent on a topic-relevant initiation by the child.

One feature of this claim is critical. The act and the reinforcement share the same form and relation. Proficient use of the skill is acknowledged by a contribution to the very act of employing the skill. Meaning is added to meaning. Such isomorphism gives a pleasing symmetry to the interaction, but why should it increase the probability of gaining meaning by influencing the child's motivation to do so?

The point can be argued in several ways. One way is to claim that gaining meaning, and this would include the additional meaning contributed by the tutor, is reinforcing. The notion that identification or construction of meaning is reinforcing is present in many different branches of psychological research including studies of infant perception (Bower, 1977) and infant responsiveness to contingencies (Finkelstein and Ramey, 1977).

Reinforcement and modelling

Conversation is also a demonstration of the uses of reading. Thus, the construction of shared meanings also provides a model to the reader of what can be done when reading effectively. Both the reinforcement and the modelling interpretations predict the same outcome. Increased skill in picking up and using the meanings in texts would develop.

Descriptions of patterns of teacher behaviour with high and low progress readers at school provide some limited support for this view. The support is in the form of positive correlations between progress and conversations that are focused on shared meanings. For example in the study which contributed the data in Table 18 high progress readers initiated interactions at a rate which was three times that of low progress readers, and as shown in Table 18 their initiations were more likely to be topically relevant. This means that the overall amount of meaning likely to be contributed by the tutor was considerably more for the high progress readers. There is evidence that even after eight years at school low progress readers are still more likely to produce irrelevant comments and questions when they are asked to comment on what they are reading silently (Pohl and McNaughton, 1985).

Finally, there is a persuasive analogy to be drawn with the case of learning language. In the late 1960s psycholinguists, heady with the excesses of Chomsky's criticism of Skinner, were quick to attempt critical tests of 'reinforcement theory'. For example Roger Brown (Brown and Hanlon, 1970) tested the adequacy of a reinforcement explanation for syntactic development by extracting from his records instances of mother praise or positive feedback to child utterances. He found exceedingly low rates of positive feedback clearly relating to the structure of utterances, and there was no indication that this was contingent on more sophisticated syntax. This of course is not surprising to anyone who talks with children or listens to other people talking with children. It would be exceptional and somewhat disturbing to find adults saying 'I liked the use of the copula in that utterance', or 'You really formed that sentence well'.

What Brown found was that positive feedback was clearly contingent on the truth value of the child's utterance (for example, 'Yes, daddy is coming home'). Like the case of learning to read this shows a source of reinforcement, or motivation to use more sophisticated language (to convey meanings) which also contains models for how that language might be more sophisticated. Contingently responding to what children mean in their conversations by continuing the conversation produces learning. It is associated with language development (Snow, 1979). It can be shown to act both as a reinforcement and as an instructional device (Hart and Risley, 1980).

Putting it all together

Three models of environmental influences on children's learning were outlined in Chapter 6. In succeeding chapters details of two of these have been explicitly described. Data have been discussed in terms of Bronfenbrenner's twin concepts of primary and secondary developmental contexts. Similarly the distinction between setting events and specific interactional processes has provided a framework for identifying how environments facilitate learning activities.

A third model was outlined in Chapter 6. It was identified by the term 'scaffolding', a construction metaphor, in which the tutor is seen as providing the supports and structures necessary for learning. To complete the metaphor teaching or tutoring is seen as a process of both erecting and removing scaffolding. Unlike a building site, in human learning the scaffolding is designed and detached under the joint control of both tutor and learner. If you like, both are builders who together build and remove the supports. The metaphor is an ideal one. But it serves as a neat summary which enables the variables discussed in the previous chapters to be seen in developmental terms. Ideally the setting events, the interactional processes and the primary and secondary developmental contexts they occur within, provide the scaffolding. Tasks are made easy, within the range of the learner's skill so that some form of performance-directed regulation is possible in which learning activities occur. As a consequence of the interchanges with tutor and tasks the reader gains more expertise. The tasks become more difficult. The supports for performing on those tasks are progressively removed. Independent performance which was limited to a restricted range of tasks becomes increasingly possible across a range of tasks.

A dramatic demonstration of scaffolding can be seen in an intensive study of seven beginning readers and their teachers over four months (Wilson and McNaughton, 1983). Data from this study have been introduced piecemeal in previous sections. By putting them together the mutual process of removing instructional support can be illustrated.

The setting events organized by the classroom teacher ensured highly accurate performances. The readers started on fifty-word stories containing repetitive sentence frames with a limited range of different vocabulary items. They progressed through to longer 200-word stories with complex syntax and many new words. The books were designed to approximate their 'natural language' and the daily lesson format capitalized on this. Discussion and

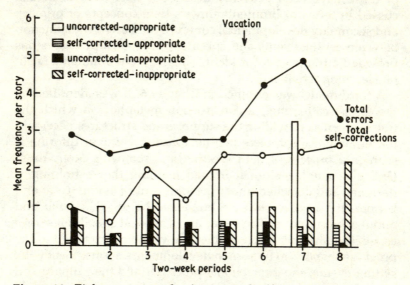

Figure 14 Eight average readers' errors and self-corrections during oral reading, over two months of classroom instruction

conversation with the group introduced each new book which was then reread in one-to-one interactions with the teacher.

With such setting events performance was not only highly accurate as shown in Figure 14 but also engendered very effective performance-directed regulation. Figure 14 shows both the number of self-corrections and what was self-corrected. Errors which were contextually inappropriate (they did not make sense or were the wrong part of speech for the sentence up to the error) became increasingly likely to be self-corrected. Appropriate errors became more likely to be ignored. Thus the readers were becoming more and more expert regulators, increasingly sensitive to text meanings and the meaningfulness of their attempts to decode words.

The readers also were developing other strategies for overcoming perturbations. They were increasing activities such as sounding out difficult words, reading on and rereading from difficult words and pausing before difficult words. In other studies of similar readers pausing has been shown to be associated with word-solving. So too for these readers. The two graphs comprising Figure 15 show both an increasing frequency of these activities and an increasing likelihood that pauses would be followed by a correct response to a difficult word. Self-regulation and independent problem-solving were developing within the setting events provided by the teacher. But just as these setting events can be viewed as scaffolding so can specific characteristics of the interactions. This can be seen in the relationship between the teacher's behaviour and independent problem-solving over time.

It will be recalled that readers' performance strategies became more tuned to the task as seen in the low incidence of contextually inappropriate errors. As this occurred, they also became more expert in monitoring and overcoming perturbations, often through pauses. Over time the teacher waited longer before interrupting, as shown in Figure 16. In the early stages the teacher anticipated errors occurring. The time taken for a reader to produce a correct word once a pause developed was around two seconds. After five seconds an error was likely to occur and the teacher usually intervened at this point. But with the readers' increasing expertise the teacher held back. In the last month of observations teacher interruptions were likely to occur only after six seconds had elapsed. By this time any errors that were not

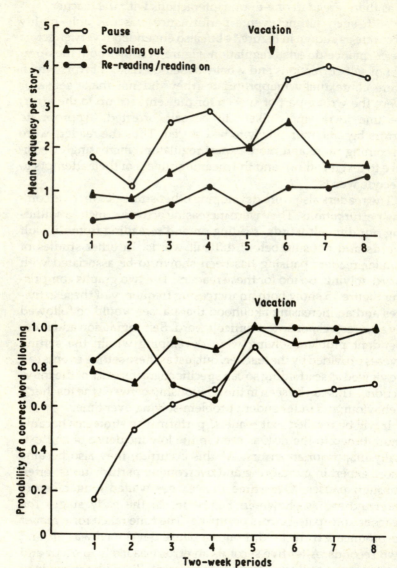

Figure 15 Eight average readers' problem-solving behaviour during oral reading over two months of classroom instruction – upper graph: frequency; lower graph: outcomes

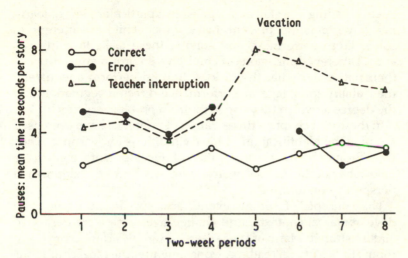

Figure 16   Eight average readers' pause time before errors, correct words and teacher intervention during oral reading over two months of classroom instruction

then self-corrected were acceptable approximations to the text anyway.

More generally, the teacher became less likely to interrupt with all types of errors or potential errors. This aspect of the tutoring was discussed earlier. From the data in Figure 12 it can be seen that over time fewer errors received feedback. Even at the beginning of the observation period the timing of that error feedback was more often delayed giving readers opportunities to detect and correct problems, but immediate interruptions became even less likely over time. Looking at the content of the error feedback it seems that less information was being given as readers became more expert. When the teacher did provide error feedback it was either to provide information about graphemes and phonemes or to model the word for the readers.

So setting events and interactions summed together to provide a supporting structure for performance strategies, performance-directed regulation and learning activities of novice readers. And out of a growing expertise the scaffolding was progressively removed.

The conditions of learning revisited

Seeing reading as a skill has suggested a particular view of learning. Environments present tasks which children attempt to solve. From performing and solving these tasks learning can arise. Different dimensions of children's environments influence their notions of what the task is, how to perform adequately, their ability to engage in performance-directed regulation and the degree to which they can learn from problem-solving.

In these four chapters three frames of reference have been used to guide the identification of ideal conditions for learning. They were Bronfenbrenner's description of developmental contexts, a new behavioural analysis of environments, and a developmental perspective on tutoring.

The concepts of setting events and specific interactions in developmental contexts, and change over time were described and illustrated. Many of the research examples came from classroom studies of oral reading. Consequently, the ideal conditions and functions of various classroom events which have been identified are those which influence performance-directed regulation and learning during oral reading for meaning.

However, some examples were drawn from socialization experience before school. The three frames of reference are equally applicable to and provide productive guides into preschool environments. Ideal conditions can also be plotted for literacy development before school which maximize performance-directed regulation and learning activities. A more systematic analysis of these conditions is the subject of the next chapter. Armed with these frameworks the next chapters examine the realities of home and classroom settings.

Part 4
Socializations

10 The early socializations of learning to read

Faced with idealized descriptions and arguments based largely on experimental evidence the reader's response now might legitimately be 'So, how do children actually learn to read?'. The query is entirely justified. The question remains as to what realities children face when learning to read, and how these realities relate to the processes which have been identified in previous chapters.

The next three chapters examine how different groups of children are socialized into literacy skills. Descriptions of different learning expeiences operating in schools and out of schools are provided, which will enable the effectiveness which different socialization routes have for becoming skilled in reading to be evaluated.

This will then enable the claims about learning conditions and the significance of performance-directed regulation to be examined. The intent is to show how the concepts which have been discussed in previous chapters can provide a coherent integrated account of learning as experienced in the real worlds within which children live. It is argued that 'effective' socialization routes can be identified which arouse a strong intention to perform the skill early in development. These routes are those that repeatedly provide conditions for performances which are dominated by performance-directed regulation and the effective deployment of learning strategies.

Effectiveness is a slippery quality to measure: how can it be gauged? This book concentrates on early reading skills. The question of effectiveness therefore becomes one of the transfer of learning, or generalization. Effectiveness will be gauged by examining generalization across settings, over time, and from one level of skill to another.

The unschooled reader: socialization at home

The major developments of reading skill usually appear under the joint influence of two developmental contexts, the home and the school. This is not so for a small but important group of children who get to school already able to read. The size of the group is difficult to determine with any precision. Only one study has systematically sampled representative groups of children as they entered schools in the USA.

Dolores Durkin (1966) selected her samples first on the basis of a simple word identification screening test which was then followed by a standardized achievement test. Children also able to score on these latter tests were selected. Their median grade level score was 2, meaning they were able to read at second grade level. Between 1 and 4 per cent of the groups sampled on the east and west coasts met her criteria and were judged already able to read. That study was completed by 1966. There has been no further systematic survey in the USA or elsewhere. However, with some reworking of the data reported in two British studies a decade later, one by Margaret Clark (1976) and the other by Cox (1977), similar percentages emerge.

What characterizes the developmental histories of these children who might make up nearly 5 per cent of children entering school? The simplest categorization of the available data shows two groups of early readers. The parents of one group did not deliberately plan to teach reading. Parents of the other group did. Learning apparently was initiated and, at least initially, programmed or controlled by these latter parents who followed a deliberate plan. These are not equal groups, a finding foreshadowed by Terman in 1925. In his survey fewer than 3 per cent of the 197 parents who reported early reading used formal tutoring. The children Terman studied were specially selected as having high intelligence so they might not have represented the 'normal' early reader. However, in both Durkin's and Clark's research more than three quarters of their parents claimed reading skills were learned without deliberate or planned help.

Unfortunately it is not known if there are historical trends operating here. Perhaps since the mid-1970s direct teaching has become more frequent. Some of the many how-to-do-it books bought by parents, 25 million in the USA between 1973 and 1975 (Clarke-Stewart, 1978), contain suggestions about teaching reading. This explosion of advice may have affected some parental practices shifting them towards more deliberate tutoring. It certainly did for Soderbergh who conducted the case study reported in Chapter 4. However, in the absence of more contemporary group studies it must be assumed that early readers are not often associated with deliberate tutoring.

But there is a problem with the data: it is not known what the gradations of learning might be. The research procedures produce a binary categorization: children who did or did not learn before they got to school. Moreover, all the studies commence by identifying children on entry to school or at school who are the 'successes', the unschooled readers. If there are few instances of deliberate tutoring among this group does this represent a true (namely low) rate of intentionally trying to teach young children to read, or does it represent the fruits of a larger number of ineffective attempts? Even in Durkin's questions to a control group of non-early readers there is very little information that would indicate attempts at tutoring that proved to be ineffective. There is no substitute for longitudinal developmental observations which would indicate the characteristics of development in different home contexts.

A further word of caution is needed before the characteristics of the groups are examined. The studies have the logic of correlational analyses. That is they are descriptions of characteristics which are found to be consistently associated with early readers. In Durkin's study these associations are strengthened by the presence of a 'control group' matched for intelligence, sex and first grade teacher. However, the usual cautions still apply; correlations do not show cause.

Informal socialization at home

It is clear that learning to read without deliberate instruction is achieved without it being necessary for the child to come from a high social class, or from a family of a particular size or composition. Nor is it necessary to have parents of a certain age or level of education, or for the child to have high intelligence. Certainly some familial characteristics are disproportionately represented in the early reading groups but they are not requirements for early reading (see Table 19).

Table 19   Family and child characteristics of precocious readers

Study	Total number of families	Number of families upper-middle class or 'professional'[1]	Child IQ[2]	
			Average	Range
Clark (1976)	32	10	122.5	98–146
Durkin (1966)				
(a)	49	7	121	91–170
(b)	30	12	133	82–170

Notes: [1] Clark provides data on number of families where at least one parent was 'professional'.
Durkin provides data based on Warner's 'Index of Social Class Scale'.
[2] Clark: Wechsler Pre-School and Primary Scale of Intelligence.
Durkin: Stanford-Binet Intelligence Scale.

The distribution of intelligence represented in the studies is positively skewed, with group averages of 111 to 133 being reported. But there are many average or below average intelligence children represented in the groups. For example Durkin's groups had IQs which ranged from 82 to 170 and Torrey (1979) even reports a remarkable case of the lowest tested IQ being 34. Given that measures of intelligence are indirect assessments of acquisition in different skill areas it is interesting to find that a child does not need to show exceptional learning across a broad range of skills. The conditions favouring early exceptional development can be relatively specific to literacy skills.

More specific characteristics of family setting than 'letter box' indicators such as class appear to provide the conditions for precocity. The information about these conditions can be loosely categorized in terms of family environments, interactions and

Family environments

1. Reading and written communication as salient activities within the family.
2. Reading as a meaningful activity
3. Availability and use of materials
4. Continued availability of valued family member(s)

Interactions

1. Responsiveness of family member(s)
2. Provision of requested information
3. Initiation and control by learner

The child as learner

1. Generalized curiosity related to written language
2. Interest in text meaning
3. Variety of strategies for acquiring information from available help
4. Generalized use of reading as a tool

Figure 17   Characteristics of early readers and their socialization settings revealed in the group and case studies
Sources: Based on information in studies reported by Bissex (1980); Clark
(1976); Durkin (1966); Terman (1925); Torrey (1978).

expressions of learning by the precocious children. This categorization is show in Figure 17.

Family environments for literacy   Several features of family life reported in studies of precocious readers made reading and written communication very obvious and potentially desirable skills. First, reading was an obvious activity and literacy a demonstrably used skill in their homes; the majority of parents in the studies could be seen as motivated readers. Given a standard to judge themselves by, they reported reading more than the average adult.

If reading was not a salient parental activity the data suggest it was for an older sibling who was already at school. Reading was also a personal and meaningful activity in that children were often read to. Related to both of these was the availability as well as use of reading and writing materials: presence of papers and pencils, blackboards and books (often library books) is consistently referred to in the interview responses.

These characteristics of family environments, in different combinations and in varying degrees of intensity had one profound effect. They aroused interest. Parents were asked to report on what aroused their child's motivation to learn to read. Among the most frequently cited perceived sources were being read to, and the availability and use of materials. Another source is perhaps best described as obvious acts of written communication, ranging from television advertisements and outdoor signs to printing, in which the children became interested. Finally, sibling comparisons were also frequently mentioned.

A further source of support for these features of environments comes from autobiographical and biographical accounts of people with precocious literacy skills. Each family characteristic can be found. For example Marie Curie played school with her older literate sister during school holidays. Her sister, the teacher and biographer, reports she was very effective as a teacher (Curie, 1937). Thomas Edison, being uncomfortable at school, stayed away. He was inspired to learn to read by his mother who read world history and the classics to him (Vanderbilt, 1971).

Interactions: 'to the verge of exhaustion' The children became interested; what then? Given the burgeoning interest all the studies indicate that the children began to ask questions. Now the group of children under discussion had been described as having parents who did not deliberately initiate and control their learning. This negative characterization could be misleading. It is apparent that the children had access to valued persons, often their mothers, who were very responsive to the interest. Their mothers' replies to the questionnaires indicate they responded to any early interest in reading, with positive informative feedback suited to their child's request or comment. They were not a little worried about the effects of their responsiveness, particularly on later schooling, and they may have been tentative, but they responded.[1]

There is a telling description provided by Terman in 1925 which captures this responsiveness. The parents responded 'fully' and 'patiently' and answered children's questions 'to the verge of exhaustion'. So did the parents in the other studies. In Durkin's comparisons all the early readers' parents said they supplied help when the child first expressed an interest. Fewer than three-quarters of a matched group of non-early readers were seen by their mothers to have expressed an interest in reading, and a third of these were, by parental report, *not* given any help even when they expressed an interest.

What sort of information did the mothers supply? The 'facts' of reading and writing supplied to the children were diverse, partly reflecting the way researchers have asked questions (for example 'Did you give – the following kinds of help').[2] Most if not all the mothers said they gave help with identification of letters, numbers, written words and the sounds of letters, and gave help with printing, spelling and the meaning of words. The more open-ended questions have yielded similar categories of talking about the sounds of letters, identifying words, and helping with printing, spelling and word meanings.

These summaries, while remaining close to the data provided in the available studies, are consistent with the idealized analysis of setting events and interactions provided in the previous three chapters. Although not achieving the same level of specificity they nevertheless show the presence of broad classes of setting events, some of which have been experimentally verified as functional events, in the family settings of precocious readers. In important ways then the settings and interactions of precocious readers approach an ideal combination of variables. But in order to argue in terms of the model of self-initiated learning the characteristics of the learners themselves need to be carefully examined. Among other things our prediction would be that these environmental setting events and interactional patterns would arouse and heighten an intention to learn.

Curiouser and curiouser: the child as learner   The children in all the studies have been described as actively curious. The resulting curiosity showed persistence and concentration, as reported by their mothers, and extended to many sorts of written material, from words on street signs to those in newspapers. Indeed after her interviews Durkin 'experienced a conscious and keen awareness of the abundance of words surrounding a child' (p. 57). The children in Clark's study read a variety of print: non-fiction and fiction, newspapers and books, taking considerable enjoyment in using the tool to gain meanings. Their curiosity also extended to the act of writing.

From this curiosity children were learning the skill and they arrived at school with some degree of skill. It was argued earlier that evaluating the effectiveness of learning requires assessing the degree to which the skill generalizes across different settings and over time. This criterion can be applied to the data on precocious readers at school. It would appear that the learning precocious readers engage in is not limited. These children do not read only when they have a pliant domestic tutor, nor do they stop learning when their day is taken over by school.

Again, an early basis for this claim comes from Terman's parents' answers about how much reading had taken place during the preschool years. The average for his sample of gifted children, based on both early and non-early readers, was four to five hours spent reading per week, which means that the average for the precocious readers was at least this. Unfortunately Terman did not examine the continuing reading habits of those gifted children who were early readers. But at 6 to 7 years the whole group (one-quarter of whom probably learned to read before going to school) read on average six hours per week. In a special diary of a small sample Terman found this meant about ten books over a two-month period.

Durkin's data provide more direct evidence. She followed the children who on entry to school were labeled early readers for three to five years at school, and found that the relative achievement of the early readers continued. They remained significantly higher in their achievement in reading even after five years compared with equally bright classmates who were not early readers. At three years it was a difference in reading age of about one year. An interesting relationship with IQ was found which suggested that the early acquisition of skills favoured less bright children. They were at a considerable advantage. High IQ children who did not read early did well at school anyway. [3]

There is a second way to assess the effectiveness of this unschooled learning. Individual attainments supplied by Durkin can be checked for any evidence of reduced progress and underachievement. Rates for unschooled learners might then be compared against general rates of underachievement by same age peers with similar intellectual abilities.

By careful analysis of the data and test information in Durkin's studies it can be deduced that the likelihood of those children not deliberately tutored dropping below grade level was very slight. No instances in one of her samples, and less than 5 per cent in the other. Clark's report does not distinguish between those twenty-five children who were not deliberately instructed and the remaining seven. But the reading attainments after the first year or two at school for the whole group was 'high' or 'very high' in comparison with their classmates. Only one child was less than 'high' in reading comprehension. Clark not only reports on achievement, but also comments on the results of a diary readers kept for a month when they were 7. The results show they were still reading often and widely.

Not an inoculation Care should be exercised when interpreting these results. Continued progress in acquiring any complex skill is not solely dependent on the conditions of initial learning. More is needed to support generalization. The conditions which support generalization over time are those which define the skill as still functional for the individual. If the conditions remain stable or, more realistically, develop in a way that maintains an intention to learn and use the skill, then generalization is supported. Many domestic and school variables might potentially reduce the perceived utility and interest in using the skill.

Thus it is a mistake to fit reading, and more generally the development of symbolic skills, into an inoculation model of learning. Continued progress in reading is a joint function of prior interactional history and current conditions (see Chapter 11). This means that any analysis of continued learning must take into account the developing characteristics of the settings within which the acquisition it still taking place.

Despite this caution it still remains an important question the extent to which any socialization route might guarantee independence from tutor support. To what extent does the route produce sustained interest in acquiring a general level of proficiency, perhaps irrespective of the vagaries of instruction? To what extent is interest in using the skill independently of others guaranteed? On these grounds the unschooled non-deliberate learning route can be seen as producing a high rate of success. Apparently the learning does generalize. The skill continues to be used independently across settings and over time.

Deliberate tutoring at home

In the group studies and in some case studies (e.g. Soderbergh, 1971) parents have deliberately set out to teach their preschoolers to read. Unfortunately the characteristics of this deliberate tutoring and its effectiveness at home are difficult to gauge. The distinction between the two groups is blurred because there is not enough information available from the parent reports in the group studies to know how deliberate and planned the parental teaching was. It is clear that some parents in both Durkin's and Clark's studies reported deliberately setting out to teach their children as a response to persistent interest. They deliberately decided, as it were, not to stop the children from learning. This decision was not taken lightly. Both studies report a curious intention, voiced by many parents, to forestall learning, apparently under the misapprehension of there being a right way to tutor reading. The right way was seen to be the prerogative of a professional élite; teachers.

Thus some parents defined as deliberate tutors didn't so much decide on a curriculum and then engage their child in it, as decide that they would enter into a child-controlled incidental curriculum. The plans which the remaining deliberate tutors had are not spelled out in either Durkin's or Clark's studies. Because some of the mothers were ex-teachers or had read books about teaching children to read it could be reasonably assumed that the methods they adopted reflected the variety of plans that are available in schools.

In one case study Durkin describes a deliberate teaching mother who bought a phonics workbook. But even in this instance the programme of teaching occurred in a context not unlike the other less deliberate parents. The book was bought because the girl insisted that someone show her how to read. They worked only when the child wanted to, and the workbook augmented books and reading activities already in operation.

Given these ambiguities it is not at all clear from the group studies how effective deliberate teaching programmes are. The group studies cannot indicate whether deliberately taught children are or are not different from other children in terms of the generalization of their skills over settings and across time. The only indication comes from one of Durkin's samples where eleven parents claimed to set out deliberately to teach reading. As has been pointed out not all of these parents represent a group who initiated and systematically adhered to a curriculum of teaching. Nevertheless, the data show that one of the eleven so-called deliberately taught children had dropped below grade level after five years of schooling.

As the programmes which parents adopt probably resemble the available school practices the comments in the next chapter are equally relevant here. Those programmes which arouse an intention to perform and construct conditions for performance-directed regulation will provide most effective socialization routes, but there is one major difference in tutoring at home compared with school-based learning. It is the likely availability of a major setting event for self-regulated learning *irrespective of the initial programme adopted*.

Tutoring at home sets up the conditions for a primary developmental context. Primary dyads, which remain intact over long periods of time, have considerable potential for learning. Such a situation, where each member exerts considerable influence in a dialectic of growing independence, is a fundamental characteristic of family life. Much of a child's early development, including the learning of emotional behaviours and language skills, are rooted in this context. Experiences within these contexts make the child's contribution to development more easily exercised because of the history of mutual influence. Given that a plan for teaching in the early stages arouses the child's intention to perform the skill, then one major outcome is likely. The ensuing interactions are likely to take on the characteristics of a jointly established curriculum which follows the child's initiation and regulation of performance.

This situation is clearly illustrated in the case study reported by Soderbergh. She set out to teach her daughter to read with an already established programme. There is no mention of an initial interest by her daughter in literacy skills prior to Soderbergh deciding to institute a 'look and say' programme, but it was initiated as a game, drawing on the child's own conceptual knowledge and using vocabulary which had immediate significance for the child.

Two things are apparent from Soderbergh's descriptions of the developing interactions between mother and daughter. First, the child's intention to perform the skill was strongly aroused by the game. Second, the rate, content and sequence of instruction provided by the mother came to be jointly determined. It was determined by the mother's instructional theory and her responsivity to the child's performance-directed regulation. It was not solely the content of the game, the expression of the mother's intention, which was the vehicle for arousing the child's interest. Rather it was the content introduced as play within the context of a primary developmental context.

If this claim is correct we should find in other successful accounts the elements of meaningful content, play and close relationship, even though other specifics of content and methodology might vary. This claim is difficult to test. But from some autobiographical and biographical accounts of deliberate teaching before or outside school these elements appear to be present while the specific games and methods vary.

Varieties of experience

It would seem that only a small proportion of parents deliberately set out to teach their children to read. Out of the remaining group researchers have identified a group of children who show some initiative in a very supportive environment, but that research creates a misleading picture. By categorizing children as able or not able to read on entry to school it implies that environments, setting events and interactions are either available or not available. But both children and the multifaceted environments we have described vary.

For convenience the research has adopted cut-off points. These demarcations were made on what in reality is a gradient of skill development. The range on entry to school in countries like the USA and Britain is likely to be represented at one extreme by a child with a minimal knowledge base and without any capabilities to perform or regulate that performance. At the other extreme children could be found who are very competent readers. So too with the environmental features we have discussed. They would range from those where all the elements listed in Figure 17 are functionally present, to environments where few of the setting events and interactional patterns were available to a child and only available in weak forms. This range of experiences available in homes and their developmental sequelae become more obvious from data reviewed in the next two chapters.

This continuum is reflected in research studies which have identified home variables before school which are correlated with school progress. This list generated by Hess and Holloway (1984) in their recent review identifies availability of reading and writing materials, reading with children, value placed on literacy (for example parental reading), press for achievement (for example responsiveness to children's interest in literacy) and opportunities for contingent verbal interactions particularly those which are related to written language. Each of these has been shown to exist to varying degrees in families and to correlate with early achievement at school. Their list is close to the one offered by way of summary here, although it does not include all the developmental features. The explanations offered here for the significance of these variables stresses their specific power as setting events and interactional exchanges which socialize literacy skill in different developmental contexts.

11 The transition: From home to school

This chapter aims to describe the characteristics of different socialization experiences and their effectiveness but, unlike the previous chapter, deals with two settings. On entering school children come under the influence of a second socialization setting, arriving with different degrees of reading skill. Understanding development at this point requires a consideration of joint socialization experiences. In this chapter the focus will be in home contributions to development at school. The school's contribution is added in the next chapter.

Joint socialization: a model for two settings

An extension to the three frameworks for viewing conditions of learning is needed which incorporates such an extension. The transition to school and the presence of two major socialization settings is shown in Figure 18. The model for two settings has extra features: the child on entry to school now participates in two sets of interactions in two settings which have events which are particular or idiosyncratic to each setting.

It is assumed that the child enters into interaction at school equipped already with a certain expertise in reading skill and with other characteristics associated with that child's membership in a specific socialization setting. These characteristics influence the interactions with a second tutor, the teacher. The teacher in interactions responds to these and in turn influences the child. The child's interactions at home are also modified.

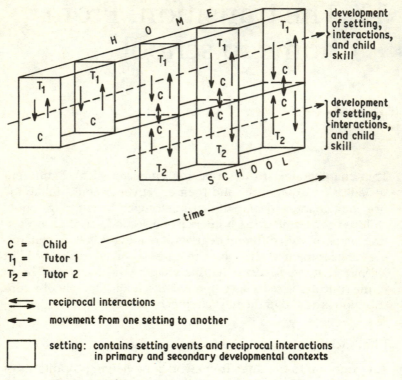

C = Child
T_1 = Tutor 1
T_2 = Tutor 2

⇌ reciprocal interactions

↔ movement from one setting to another

☐ setting: contains setting events and reciprocal interactions
              in primary and secondary developmental contexts

--→ change over time

Figure 18 Patterns of interaction between tutors and a child over the
transition from one socialization setting (home) to two (home and
school)

Whatever learning occurs at school it potentially transcends the
physical separation between home and school. To a greater or
lesser extent it generalizes to home. The child's contribution in
interactions changes accordingly, influencing his or her first
tutors.

These of course are not the only ways tutors in either setting
may influence each other. Direct communication between teachers

or other representatives of the school setting and parent is likely. The content and form of that communication can have profound effects on the behaviour of each socialization agent and the setting events which might contribute to interactions. This is why in Figure 18 the border between home and school settings is represented as semi-continuous.[1] This model draws on other models of human development in social settings. Like those models this one carries several implications for research into the socializations of skills. For example it is inappropriate to conceptualize the effects of early experience as an 'inoculation'. It is increasingly apparent that the development of a skill cannot be isolated from its social context. The ongoing dynamic interrelationships between learners and their tutors functioning in social contexts is what research should focus on. Skill development is not fixed by a short-term experience: it fluctuates as a consequence of how the interactions are developing (see Bronfenbrenner, 1979; Kagan *et al.*, 1978).

There is another implication. The twin settings can fit together well or poorly. They can be complementary or mismatched in how mutually helpful the dual interactions are for acquiring the skill. Bronfenbrenner has incorporated this model of multiple socialization settings into his description of the ecology of human development. The social system within which children develop is much more complex and wide-ranging than researchers have tended to see it. His term for the system which incorporates distinct socialization settings is a 'mesosystem'.

Predictions about development

Bronfenbrenner offers the following predictions about the potential for match or mismatch between socialization settings.

> The developmental potential of a child rearing setting is increased as a function of the number of supportive links between that setting and other contexts involving the child or persons responsible for his or her care. Such interconnections may take the form of shared activities, two-way communication, and information provided in each setting about the others.
>
> (1979, p. 848)

These are general predictions about how settings might function to complement each other. But there are more specific predictions to be made. They come from applications of previous chapters, notably the concepts of skill learning and the frameworks for analysing conditions of learning.

It will be recalled that the perspectives on skills and conditions of learning adopted in the book argue against a simple view of children as arriving at school skilled or not skilled. Through specific setting events and interactions socialization experiences have set the limits for the development before school. Thus children arrive at school differing in how much knowledge they have of the skill, how they perform on various reading 'tasks' and their expertise in regulating performance.

Their development in these areas can be predicted to influence the ease with which children acquire more skill at school. That is the greater the knowledge base and experience in performance-directed regulation of performances the higher the rate of progress will tend to be, and this will be more so if appropriate socialization experiences at home continue to develop.

This is in part an explanation for the phenomena of children's learning introduced at the beginning of this book. Higher rates of progress can be generally predicted because of where children start from. But, more importantly, the more a child has the characteristics noted above the more that a child can both solve task environments and go beyond the teaching received. This prediction is relative. It is made in terms of the degree of learning and support available from socialization experiences before school and accompanying the transition to school.

When children get to school they enter into a set of idiosyncratic interactions with their teachers. Many variables conspire to produce the unique developmental sequences that result. The child brings to school behaviours associated with having lived five or more years in particular settings. So too, teachers enter into interactions with well-developed behaviours and perceptions of their pupils' behaviour. From such things as patterns of oral language and attitudes to authority, through to their clothes and personal hygiene, children's backgrounds cue and maintain special responses from their teachers.

However, one would not expect to find a simple relationship between literacy skills learned before skill and progress at school. Any effect of home learning is followed by successive teachers' reactions to the characteristics of a child's socialization. In gross terms a child's membership of a particular cultural, ethnic or social group is an influence on teacher behaviour, producing in some subtle ways some very unsubtle changes in aspects of inter-actions, such as patterns of error feedback (e.g. Cunningham, 1976; Simons 1979).

Nevertheless, even given these complexities a strong relation-ship would still be expected between the degree of early achieve-ment and characteristics of the child's skill on entry to school. The more experience of performance-directed regulation in liter-acy skills, and the greater the knowledge base the better able the child would be to detect patterns and analyse the stimuli which a task environment provides, relating that information to the developing skill. In so doing the child would be better able to weather the idiosyncracies of classroom environments

Unlocking the realities

To test these expectations studies are reviewed in the following ways. Statistical or experimental manipulations which show the effects of preschool experience or learning on the transition to school learning, independently of the general indices of social class and ethnicity, will be particularly pertinent. The data most relevant to these expectations will come from descriptions of dif-ferent degrees of socialization experience which are related to children's knowledge and behaviour prior to school and upon entering school. Ideally longitudinal studies containing repeated measures of socialization and child behaviour before school and on entry to school would be most able to meet our needs.

Social class and socialization experiences

In general, large surveys and longitudinal studies show a signifi-cant social class effect. Early progress in reading is positively related to the standard indices of social class such as paternal and maternal income, level of education and type of job (Davie, But-ler and Goldstein, 1972; NAEP, 1985). The correlations are partic-ularly strong with material expressions of that reality such as conditions of crowding, poor amenities and lack of personal, social and material resources.

The relationships discovered between family background and early progress in learning are illustrated in several British studies carried out by Chazan and his colleagues (1971; 1977) for the School Research and Development Project in Compensatory Education. But the studies also yield an important qualification. Material disadvantage with its consequent social and political ramifications can exist, yet in some of these household specific conditions for developing literacy skills are present and the impact on school achievement is high.

In an early study nearly one-third of a sample of children from deprived areas of Wales and London were found to have parents interested in reading, who frequently involved their child in reading activities. (Conversely, one-third of a sample of 'advantaged' parents showed little interest or involved their children.) Rating of the interest in reading shown by the 5-year-olds in the sample showed a similar proportion. One-third of the deprived 5-year-olds had high interest in reading. They owned and enjoyed books and tried to read them.

The relationship between child curiosity in reading and these setting events is suggested more strongly in a further study where parents of 122 'deprived' 5-year-olds were given a questionnaire prior to their child entering school. A high proportion of those parents (85 per cent) who reported they owned six or more books also reported their children asking to be read to. In those homes with no adult books only half the parents reported their children had asked to be read to.

These data are consistent with the data introduced in the previous chapter on precocious readers. They show the effects of specific setting events on interest in reading, particularly the availability and use of reading material. To the extent that ownership of books by parents indicates an interest in reading by parents, these data suggest that parental models increase the likelihood of expressions of interest by their children. These setting events existed independently of their membership in social class.

A larger-scale study reported by the project in 1977 suggests the effect on school learning of repeated experiences. Children were identified as both materially disadvantaged and coming from 'culturally disadvantaged homes' where, prior to school, interest in literacy, responsiveness to children's interest and provision of reading and school-related experiences were low. When these children were compared with children from deprived areas which were rated higher on these factors substantial differences in reading attainment and adjustment in school were found.

What can be concluded from those studies? On a group basis social class membership is related to reading attainments. After two years at school in Britain a yawning eighteen-month gap in tested reading age has opened up between upper and lower classes (Davie, Butler and Goldstein, 1972). All the studies which have been concerned with social class show considerable variability in literacy-related socialization within groupings; progress on entering school also shows variability.

Unfortunately in those studies we have reviewed so far the analysis of variability in socialization experiences and development from preschool to school has occurred retrospectively as a secondary question. Consequently subgroups are not well matched on variables such as tested intelligence. No attempt is made to examine the independent effects of the variations in socialization which we have predicted are related to literacy learning.

Table 20   Relationships between home environment, social class and reading achievement

Environment measures at 2:6	Correlation with social class	Independent correlation with reading test 7:0
Toys, books and experiences	0.61	0.54
Language: modelling and encouragement	0.74	0.41
Social-emotional: positive and responsive	0.54	0.44

Source: Moore (1968)
Reprinted by permission of S. Karger AG. Basel.

But there are studies which have done this. An early study by Moore (1968) reported on seventy-six London children followed from infancy to two years after entry to school. At 2:6 years observations and ratings of home life were carried out. From these observations three major measures of home experiences were derived. The first was the availability and value placed on toys, books and experiences. The other two assessed parental involvement with and responsiveness to children in terms of language interactions and in terms of positive responses to their childrens' social and emotional development.

As shown in Table 20 each of these ratings was positively (and all significantly) correlated with social class. Given this, the correlations between the environment ratings and tested reading achievement at 7 years were calculated with social class 'partialled out'. This is a statistical technique whereby the joint relationship of both environmental ratings and reading achievement with social class is removed. A measure is then gained which is not inflated by relationships that might have been due primarily to social class.

The resulting correlations between home environment variables and reading achievement, independent of social class, are shown in Table 20. They were still positive and highly significant. As independent predictors of reading achievement these ratings were superior to other measures of environment such as ordinal position, family spacing, level of maternal education and even sophistication of maternal language. Importantly, they were also superior predictors to tested intelligence at three years.

Moore's study answers the question about the significance of different socialization experiences *within* social groupings. There are distinct socialization variables which can be independent of social class membership which predict the development of reading skill at school. The measures Moore used are more general than the setting events and interactional patterns predicted from previous chapters, but they are consistent with those measures. For example one measure taps the availability and use of materials including books. Although not directly in the area of reading skill the other two measures sample positive and responsive interactional patterns. In the area of oral language they are patterns which provide models for responding and stimulate further responding. Given the first measure responsiveness to language learning might have tapped responsiveness to literacy learning.

Apart from the gross nature of the environmental measures there is another difficulty in Moore's study. It adopts or at least implies an inoculation model of development. The manner in which the correlations were computed implies that early experiences programmed the later achievements. The studies which are now reviewed provide more specific data on the attributes of early socialization experiences related to achievement.

Socialization at home and the transition to school

There is a study that approaches the ideal longitudinal study needed to answer the questions which are central to this chapter. It involved twenty children systematically observed in normal interactions within their family settings over the two years before school. They were followed over the first two years at school. Interviews when the children were 5:0 and 7:0 were used to supplement the observational data.

Three points immediately can be made of the resulting patterns of correlations shown in Table 21. First, certain preschool socialization patterns were associated with the development of reading skill. Two measures of setting events and parent interactions,

Table 21 Correlations between various socialization measures and reading skill over the preschool and early school years

Socialization measures and skills	Knowledge of literacy on entry to school	Reading achievement after two years at school
From 3 to 5[1]		
Parent language (richness)	0.51[3]	0.62
Parent interest in literacy	0.70	0.53
Child interest in literacy	0.43	0.40
From 5 to 7[2]		
Child knowledge on entry to school	–	0.79
Parent provisions for literacy	–	0.59
Parent teaching of literacy	–	0.29
Parent attitude to education	–	0.58

Source: Moon and Wells (1979)

Notes: [1] The preschool measures were based on observations at home.
[2] The parent measures for the first two years of school were based on interviews.
[3] Correlations greater than 0.43 were statistically significant ($p < 0.05$).

namely parental interest in literacy and the richness of parent language, were significantly correlated with children's knowledge of literacy on entry to school. The measure of knowledge was an assessment of concepts about print and letter identification. Parental interest was derived from instances in the observational records of such things as asking questions about words and looking at print. Richness of language was a measure of the extent to which the parent responded to child initiations in ways that were relevant to the meaning and intention of the initiation and produced further interaction. Like Moore's study this measure tapped responsiveness to children.

Second, the children's reading achievements after two years at school was related to the continuation of specific socialization experiences in reading. The extent to which parents provided reading and writing materials (parental provision for literacy) correlated significantly with standardized tests of reading achievement (0.59 in Table 21). This interview measure, taken when the children were 7:0, was in turn significantly correlated with interview measures of parental interest in literacy before the children got to school (r = 0.69).

A third question which is critical to our concerns relates to the measures of the children's skill. The assessment of knowledge of literacy at 5:0 years correlated 0.79 with achievement after two years. This supports the prediction that the development of skill within supportive socialization experience enables the child to enter into and learn effectively from classroom interactions. Children arrived at school with differences in skill, judged in terms of knowledge, and progress at school was predicted very strongly by this knowledge. Significantly progress was not related to the programme the children entered when they got to school. The eighteen classrooms they entered were assessed using behavioural observations of types of reading activities and time spent on different activities. Differential achievement was not associated with different scores on these measures (see Wells, 1979).

Thus the study provides correlational support for the model of ongoing socialization. As far as the issue of social class is concerned it is unfortunate that Moon and Wells did not present their data on socialization variables independently of membership in a social class. However, in another report Wells has claimed that the outcome measures in language development for the children in the project were substantially related to interactional variables, but not to social class (Wells, 1979). Observation of spontaneous language showed greater differences between individuals within class groupings than there were between the averages for groups. Having made this point it was also noted that there was a tendency for extreme scores to be related to class groupings. Standardized tests under controlled conditions exaggerated this trend.

Joint socialization: setting events and interactions

The Moon and Wells study provides general support for the model described on p. 200. It also adds to the claim that socialization experiences can be independent of social class. But there are specific results from this study which need further analysis. They involve socialization experiences tapped by the measures of child interest in literacy, the provision of resources, parent attitude to schooling and parent teaching of literacy.

Child interest in literacy   One of the findings is anomalous, at least in terms of the concepts of skill learning presented in this book. It involves their measure of the child's preschool interest in literacy. This was defined in the same way as parental interest in literacy. Surprisingly Table 21 shows a relatively weak (barely significant) correlation between child interest at 3:0 to 5:0 years and knowledge of literacy at 5:0 years. Furthermore, the correlation with achievement after two years at school was not significant ($r = 0.40$). From the earlier arguments and data it might be expected that knowledgeable children in a supportive environment would be likely to be more interested than less knowledgeable children from other socialization settings.

The measures of child interest are, however, suspect. There is a methodological problem in the Moon and Wells study which suggests they were not able to get reliable data on child interest. The researchers didn't observe at a time when much child reading is likely to take place, namely in the hour or two before going to bed. As the authors note, 'frequencies of reading and writing activities may have been significantly underestimated as a result of the fact that the observations finished at 6p.m.' (1979, p. 60). Related to this problem are others which arise from the ninety-second tape recordings made from transmitter microphones which were the basis of the home observations. Instances of looking at print and interest in books which were not accompanied by recordable language would have been difficult to record.

Child interest on entry to school also has been examined by J. Cohen (1979). Unlike Moon and Wells, she found that preschool interest strongly predicted early progress. Fifty children were studied immediately before and after entering school. From interviews with parents before school and after one month at school parents were placed into several categories. These categories were judged to be reliable in that three independent observers who classified the interview data were in substantial agreement. One group had children who were perceived as taking control of learning and who initiated interactions around literacy skills. For example these children were said to ask questions about words and letters, comment on books, ask to be read to, and attempt to read, without first being prompted to do so. This group was distinguished from others, where parents reported degrees of prompting through to coercion or disinterest. These latter parents said they had children who were not very interested so they (the parents) took the initiative.

Two things are important about Cohen's results. First, parental groupings were not significantly related to social class, nor other variables such as position of child in family, sex or whether or not the children had full experience of preschooling.[2] Second, teachers' assessments of reading attainment after two terms at school were significantly related to child curiosity and intention to read at preschool. For example all of the 'child led' group (twenty-two children) were average or above average in attainment, while all of the below average children (ten children) belonged to one or other of the 'parental push' or disinterested groups.

Unlike the previous study Cohen's suggests that child interest is a significant variable for skill development during the transition from home to school. This is not its only significance: an important corollary to her data should not be overlooked. Her data indicate that there were particular socialization experiences associated with child interest. 'Child led' implies 'parent follow'. Presumably child interest existed in a setting which supported child initiation and control over learning. Such interactional patterns would be consistent with those found for precocious readers, associated with similar outcomes for progress at school.

Cohen does not provide information on the relationship between interest and knowledge. That predicted association, not found by Moon and Wells, needs to be systematically studied in further research. Nor does she provide specific information on socialization experiences before school and while a child is at school. Because Moon and Wells did we now return to their study.

Resources for literacy learning Two measures which they gained from their parents were significantly correlated with continued achievement at school. The first of these was a measure of the provision of materials for reading and writing. It is a setting event identified in the research on precocious readers and has in one form or another been found in large-scale surveys investigating the relationships between home variables and reading achievement.

There is a very powerful demonstration of the significance of having books available and having some encouragement to read books. It comes from an ingenious study by Heyns (1978) of 3000 13-year-olds in the Atlanta school system. The primary focus of the study was to re-examine assumptions about the effects of schooling relative to family background on school achievement. To do this, the author capitalized on a natural experiment that schools unwittingly set up. If one assumes that the influence of home background is relatively constant throughout the school year, then schools can be seen as repeatedly adding on and subtracting a second socialization setting from this background. Thus the rate with which the child acquires a skill can be compared when one versus two socialization settings are in operation.

Heyns compared the rate at which sixth and seventh graders gained in word knowledge over the summer vacation and over the school term. Her results show that overall the rate of learning during summer was substantially less than the rate of learning at school. In terms of grade level gains the Atlanta children progressed about two-thirds of a grade while at school but made minimal progress during summer.

But there were substantial differences between social class groupings (based primarily on income). In the highest income bracket there was no difference in rate of gain over the two time periods while in the lowest bracket children actually lost some of the word knowledge they had acquired at school when not at school. When these two income levels were compared it was clear that between one-half and two-thirds of the annual learning gap between children in the two groups happened during the summer (vacation) months. Summer was a potent contributor to differential achievement. Conversely schools seemed to have an equal effect on children, producing similar rates of gain while at school.

The critical question is what happened during summer? Parents were interviewed about child activities in questions designed to yield frequency of occurrence-type measures. They provided information on incidence of structured activities (such as camps, summer school, organized sport), trips, time spent on hobbies and playing, and reading activities. The one summer activity which was strongly related to summer learning was reading, whether it was measured by number of books read, time spent reading or regularity of library use.

The other activities were associated with minimal gains in word knowledge. By comparison reading activity produced substantial gains, largely independently of income level or race. When children who read six books or more were compared with those who read fewer than six, the former group stood to gain between one and two months in word knowledge achievement compared with the latter group, irrespective of affluence or race. In different terms Heyns calculates this effect as showing that with each additional hour spent reading, or every four books completed during the summer, a further vocabulary word on the standardized test was gained.

Heyns did examine some of the child correlates of book reading, but unfortunately the questions asked did not tap parental activities or their interaction with their children. The variables most highly correlated with reading and household size were not very strong predictors. Again Heyn's provides a delightfully real translation of the statistics showing that living within seven blocks of a public library added about one book to the summer's accomplishment. The importance of library facilities suggests parental encouragement but we don't know the specifics of parental behaviour associated with book reading.

Parent attitude to or interest in schooling   In the study by Moon and

Wells two parent variables were significantly correlated with children's progress once at school. The first has been considered; the second was parental attitude to education.

This variable has assumed considerable importance in both Britain and the USA as a result of several national surveys and longitudinal studies. In Britain data on family backgrounds and schools have been collected on more than 20,000 children ranging from 7 to 12 or more years. The data provide an extensive empirical basis for the significance of this variable (see Davie, Butler and Goldstein, 1972; Douglas, 1964; Fraser, 1959; Plowden, 1967). The burden of these studies has been the effects of social class membership on reading achievement. The variable which has emerged as the strongest expression of the effect of class has been parental interest in children's progress at school, and encouragement of that progress. It was found to be very closely associated with social class; the 'lower' the class membership, the less interest and encouragement.

In most of the studies this measure of interest is an assessment of the relationship between home and school as perceived by teachers. From other data it can be reasonably assumed that such a measure says more about teachers and how their behaviours are affected by social cues than parental interest in the child's competence independently of school.[3] Indeed when the parent interview data that are available are examined clearly a different picture emerges. For example in the Plowden Report there were minimal differences between social class groupings in expressions by parents of interest and desire to help their children in what they can do at home. What differences did exist were attitudes to approaching, communicating and using information from schools. These are variables which may reflect differential class experiences of contact. They may also reflect different perceptions of schools and teachers.

The Plowden Report and one researcher's reanalysis (Acland, 1980) contain other significant qualifications. In the first instance the Plowden Report analysed the degree of relationship between each of three summary measures and achievement in reading comprehension at 7, 8 and 11 years (for 3000 children). One of the summary measures, parental attitudes, was correlated more strongly with reading achievement than either of the other two, which were home circumstances (physical amenities, income and size of family) and the state of the school (class size, length of teacher training).

The data which led the authors of the Plowden Report to conclude that parents' attitudes were associated with most variation in skill learning have been critically examined by Acland (1980). It turns out that this summary variable had in turn been based on several component measures. The components measured aspirations for their child's career at school, visits to school, asking for homework and literacy at home. This latter component measured the availability and use of books at home by parents and children, separately and together.

Out of all the contributing measures literacy at home was the component that consistently yielded the highest correlations. The next most significant variable, parental aspirations, figured prominently at the higher age level, 11 years, when children were first faced with a national exam. Thus Acland notes that the summary in the Plowden Report does not convey an accurate description of the specific variables which are related to achievement.

Home backgrounds loom large in progress at school, possibly larger than the effects of the school in the equivalent large-scale American studies (e.g. Coleman *et al.*, 1966; Jencks *et al.*, 1972). The resources relating to literacy at home, that is the presence of reading materials, is one specific variable consistently related to school achievement. However, unlike their British counterparts, the summary measures are not interpreted by American researchers in terms of 'encouragement' or 'interest'. The summary variable is usually taken to be an indication of status, a feature of cultural environment.

Irrespective of which general interpretation is stressed the basis of the measure is unambiguous. It is a measure of specific socialization experiences. Notably these are the presence of materials for the skill and the active use of the skill as part of the home reality. They are associated with early progress before and on entry to school, and with progress after entry to school.

These are both variables which have been found associated with precocious readers. When identified in Chapter 10 they were analysed in terms of setting events. That is they were seen as influencing interactions for literacy learning. The probability and characteristics of those interactions is affected by having books and writing materials available, which are used as part of domestic life. They are also implied in the experimental research on setting events reviewed in Chapter 7, particularly that research which has examined primary developmental contexts and the effect of different types of reading tasks.

Coaching or help?   One of Moon and Wells's parent measures was not significantly correlated with achievement at school from 5 to 7 years. It is the measure of parent teaching of literacy. Moreover, this lack of relationship is echoed in the Plowden Report. Measures of the level of help for doing schoolwork at home were not strongly related to achievement.

From such findings as those of Moon and Wells, it seems that at least some sorts of interactions with parents may not help children learning to read. Questionable consequences of help were also found by Newson and Newson (1977) in a longitudinal study of 700 children. Their general index of literacy in the home, gained from interview ratings of setting events like number of books owned, extent to which books were used to gain information and amount of parental reading to children, was clearly associated with achievement at 7 years. Children who were good readers were found in 'literate' homes, but parental reports of giving 'help' were not associated with good readers.

Yet at least one series of carefully designed studies indicates the reverse. In these studies help or, as Hewison and Tizard (1980) have called it 'coaching', by the parents of working-class children was examined. Coaching was defined as regularly hearing a child read and not simply reading to the child. This parental help was found to be a highly significant variable in achievement over the first two years at school. In three studies involving almost 300 children, all of whom were from a working-class population, this variable strongly predicted attainment at 7 and 8 years. The correlations between coaching and attainment were higher than any other home variable and coached children were on average almost one standard deviation above their non-coached peers in reading achievement.

Results from two of their studies are shown in Tables 22 and 23. Data from the first study demonstrate that when the tested intelligence of the children was held constant the relationship still remained strong (statistically significant). In each IQ band achievement was strongly related to the significance of parental coaching.

Table 22   Relationships between hearing a child read ('coaching') and reading achievements in third year of school within different levels of intelligence

IQ band	Achievement level[1]	
	Poor readers (N = 55)	Good readers (N = 45)
87 or less		
Not coached	10	0
Coached	1	1
88–102		
Not coached	21	5
Coached	6	10
103–117		
Not coached	9	3
Coached	2	14
118–above		
Not coached	4	1
Coached	2	11

Source: Hewison and Tizard (1980) (second study)
Reprinted by permission of Scottish Academic Press
Note: [1] Children's scores on a standardized reading test were used to categorize this as 'Poor' or as 'Good' defined as above or below the sample average.

Table 23   Relationships between frequency of hearing a child read and reading achievement in third year of school

Frequency of hearing child read	Average reading score
Regularly to third year (N = 39)	104.9
Occasionally to third year (N = 23)	98.3
Regularly to second year (N = 19)	91.2
Occasionally to second year (N = 11)	86.7
Never in three years (N = 12)	81.1

Source: Hewison and Tizard (1980) (third study)
Reprinted by permission of Scottish Academic Press

Hewison and Tizard systematically examined the significance of related variables such as the sophistication of mother's language (measured from the interview transcripts) and the type of school. But in each case coaching emerged as the major variable.

The second set of data shows how level of attainment was sensitive to continued coaching. Regularly hearing a child read over the first three years at school was strongly associated with achievement. Gradations of less than this, ranging from occasional but continual help to no help, were systematically related to less and less achievement, measured on a standardized reading test.

These data are very important. They show the positive effects of an as yet to be clarified style of interaction (coaching) operating within a social class. [4] But their results are contrary to others such as those obtained by the Newsons. The differences may be entirely due to the way questions have been asked in various studies. In the studies by Moon and Wells and the Newsons the questions were asked about 'help' or 'teaching'. Those questions seem to have been interpreted by the parents in terms of deliberate help, initiated by the parents when they perceived their child was in difficulty. This would include help over an error as well as help because the child was making low progress or finding learning difficult.

It is therefore not surprising that 76 per cent of the children judged unable to read in the Newsons's study were receiving parental help at 7:0 years; the same percentage of children judged able to read at 7:0 years were also receiving help. Given the single measure at one age, 'help' tapped responses to difficulties as well as continued positive interactions which may have been developing over some time.

Hewison and Tizard asked about hearing a child read. In their research this is conceptualized as 'coaching' but the actual questions concerned hearing a child read. Responses to that question in two of three studies had to indicate a long-standing involvement of regular coaching – not simply a response to difficulty. In the third study continued interactions (regular interactions or those which had become occasional) in which the child actively participated from entry to school were associated with the greatest achievement as shown in Table 23.

Thus given the model on p. 200, it is possible that these interactions were developments from even earlier interactions before school. They might then represent a continued experience which shifted from a preschool style of interaction in which the parent did most of the reading to one in which the child did most of the reading. It is unfortunate that the question of the initiation of these interactions and their developmental histories are not provided in this study.

Being responsive There is a different connection to be made between the interactions tapped by Hewison and Tizard's category of 'coaching' and Moon and Wells's measures. The connection is with their measure of language richness. This was a measure of parental responsiveness to child conversational initiations. Parents who scored highly responded in ways that were relevant to the meaning and intention of the initiation. An earlier study reviewed by Moore (1968) had similar categories of parental behaviour. In each study the language measure was significantly related to reading skill. Logically this measure would include parental responsiveness to a child's verbally expressed interest in literacy. In time, as a child becomes more competent and especially after entry to school, this would most often be operationalized in hearing a child read. Thus the coaching measure of Hewison and Tizard could be seen as a more specific index of the resonsiveness measures of Moon and Wells and of Moore.

Further research is needed to determine the specific attributes of 'coaching'. But the thread that links the studies by Moore, Moon and Wells, Cohen, and Hewison and Tizard is a sense of interactions which have the primary characteristic of being responsive to a child's developing expertise. This was clearly also a characteristic of interactions with precocious readers.

Not helping From Table 23 it can be seen that parents who had stopped hearing a child read after two years were found with children making slower progress. Why would parents who might start to hear a child read, stop? It has been repeatedly demonstrated in several countries that most parents are interested in their children's burgeoning skill and yet many do not know very much about what is appropriate pedagogical thought and practice (e.g. Plowden Report, 1967; McNaughton, Glynn and Robinson, 1981). They don't know how to help. This state of frustrated ignorance is exacerbated when low progress is detected, as attested to by data supplied in research projects where parents have been directly involved in a remedial effort. The desire to help increases yet the ignorance becomes more painfully obvious.

The plight of these parents, at least until recently, tends not to be alleviated by their contact with schools. Some parental reports indicate that they feel the schools resort to excuses which lay the blame for continued low progress on obscure neurophysiological problems, or on the children's home background. In either case, parents have reported not receiving information and appropriate books on which they could act.

Given this lack of knowledge and materials, when they have tried to help their low progress children there are difficulties. Not surprisingly they tend to do things that at best are ineffective and at worst interfering, in terms of the child's needs to learn (see Glynn and McNaughton, 1985). There is thus the possibility of becoming disheartened and ceasing personal efforts; the interest remains but the personal expression has been extinguished.

The transition revisited   On entry to school children come under the influence of a second socialization setting, but they influence that setting too. By bringing specific attributes of reading skill and general characteristics of their membership in a particular community they influence classroom events; this is why success over this transition and the first years at school is found to be related both to previous experiences at home and continuing experiences in that primary socialization setting.

In a recent review Hess and Holloway (1984) gave their breakdown of family experiences which have been found to correlate with early progress in learning to read. The dimensions were the availability of reading and writing material, reading with children, the value placed on literacy, responsiveness to children's interest, and generative language interactions which have characteristics related to written language.

Their list fits well with the summary provided in Figure 17 for precocious readers. Their dimensions are incorporated in the models of socialization and skill learning that have been developed here. But the present analysis stresses that when such setting events and interactions are strongly present children are provided with a firm basis for taking and making sense out of classroom requirements. With that socialization developing apace at home children have the wherewithal to adapt to and go beyond the teaching they receive.

Thus this review of studies looking at the home effects on the transition to school is consistent with earlier predictions about how setting events and interactions can influence acts of learning. But the specific claims within the model of socialization, particularly about influences on classroom interactions, need to be examined in detail. Moreover, a further question needs to be addressed. In what respects do classroom environments aid or interfere with children adapting to and going beyond the teaching they receive? We now turn to these related questions.

12 Being schooled

The previous chapter focused on one side of the joint socialization. This follows one assumption made by the model described on p. 200 that learning at school is at least partially determined by the previous and continuing socialization experiences at home and how these create and modify classroom experiences for individuals. But the model also assumes that the child's development is influenced by, just as it influences, the ongoing environment of the classroom.

The reality at school

Some of the realities of life in classrooms have been referred to piecemeal in previous chapters. These can be brought together and summarized to make one point: to learn in classrooms is to learn in a group under a teacher who is required to manage time, tasks and tutoring. Under this regimen setting events and interactions must take on particular characteristics. For example the systematic availability of one-to-one interactions, consistent with the concept of a primary developmental context, is jeopardized. It is not possible, indeed it is counterproductive to engineer such circumstances exhaustively for all the individual learners in a classroom, because time doesn't permit it. From this general situation, that is the weakening of the potential for primary developmental contexts, several other circumstances follow.

Significant threats can be found to the availability of an appropriate match between texts and learners. Group management, the vagaries of teacher training and the lack of continued close individual contact can result in a reliance on single text series and misjudgements of difficulty levels. There are also considerable variations between classrooms in the amount of verbal context provided for children learning. Again, a noticeable proportion of classrooms appear to be very restricted in this setting event, and the same can be said for opportunities for independent reading. Considerable variation between classrooms and the presence of classrooms which restrict independent reading are noticeable.

Therefore in some respects children are faced with less than ideal conditions for learning to read, with competition for use of available resources and access to the available setting events. The competition may not be intentional, nor the results deliberate. It may arise through the differences between learners in how they have learned to learn and particularly what they know about reading and classrooms. They influence the teacher. Due to the contrasts between groups and the characteristics of the group members as learners different environments are constructed. The reality of this claim is nowhere as stark as in the case of the low progress reader. In what follows the realities for low progress readers are examined. This represents a very different perspective from that of earlier chapters which have focused on normal and high progress readers. The shift in focus is deliberate. This focus yields the most dramatic demonstrations of how socialization experiences at school develop from earlier experiences, yet also how these experiences place an idiosyncratic stamp on learning.

The case of the low progress reader

It is apparent from studies reviewed in earlier chapters that the experiences of low progress readers are different from their more competent peers. The differences begin very early in school life; perhaps a majority of the otherwise healthy and competent children who begin to fail do so partly because of systematic differences in classrooms experiences. Using the framework of setting events and interactions and recent reviews by Allington (1983) and Cazden (1983) the nature of these differences can be documented.[1]

The differences in primary developmental contexts   There is little evidence to show that children who make low progress come to have less exposure to adult interactions. In fact it is likely that more time is spent in one-to-one interactions with a tutor. This is because when low progress is extreme children become candidates for special remedial attention. Even if not promoted to remedial status children who begin to make low progress may attract more attention from teachers.

But while there is no good reason to expect that less time is spent interacting with teachers there are good grounds for claiming that the interactions and the activities involved in those interactions can be considerably different.

Indications of these differences can be found in observations of readers during reading lessons. In terms of allocated time, that is the amount of time planned by teachers for reading lessons, low progress children are not necessarily at a disadvantage. They are allocated similar amounts of time for instruction.[2] However, when observations of what happens during that time are made a different reality emerges. There is a difference between low progress and high progress readers in the amount of time spent 'on task' during instruction. Here time 'on task' means involvement in the reading tasks set. It is operationalized in terms of attention to task or performance of the task. Virtually without exception, researchers have observed good readers to be more often 'on task' in reading than low progress classmates.

Table 24   Average percentages of engagement in classroom tasks during reading lessons

Achievement group	Total	Teacher monitoring	Teacher not monitoring
High (N = 25)	83.7	89.8	80.2
Low (N = 25)	73.9	80.3	65.6

Source: Flower (1983)

Results from one such study of older readers (10-year-olds) are shown in Table 24. Observations were made in five classrooms during reading lessons over a week. In each classroom observations focused on five good readers and five poor readers selected from teacher rankings. The average percentage of time on task in the lesson was significantly different for each group: the good readers spent 10 per cent more time on task. Interestingly it made a difference as to whether the teacher was watching the child at the time of observing or not. In those intervals where the teacher was watching children were more often observed to be on task. This was true for both groups but the difference was greater for poor readers.

Stated in terms of potential learning time such results show low progress readers to be at a disadvantage, in spite of the similar amounts of curriculum time for instruction. Why are low progress readers less attentive to instructional events and more dependent on teacher control? Two major types of explanation can be found. The first sees the problem as the child's. Deficiencies in processing of information are said to make for low attention and greater distractability. But distractability and attention can be shown to be situationally specific. On some tasks under some conditions, otherwise distractable low progress readers can become more attentive. For example Gambrell, Wilson and Gantt (1981) identified seventy good and poor readers from teacher ratings and then observed their time on task during reading instruction. The researchers also examined the difficulty of the tasks which had been set during the lesson for these fourth graders by taking further observations of words read correctly.

The two groups differed significantly in the accuracy with which they could read their tasks. These data are shown in Table

Table 25   Average percentages of engagement in classroom tasks and difficulty of tasks during reading lessons

Achievement group	Difficulty of task	Engagement
Good (N = 35)	99.3	92
Poor (N = 35)	89.4	81
	easy (95+)	83
	hard (95−)	74

Source: Gambrell, Wilson and Gantt (1981)
Note: Difficulty of task was assessed from individual children's oral word accuracy, expressed as per cent words correct.

25. Associated with the difference in difficulty was a significant difference in engagement (92 per cent compared with 81 per cent on task). Finally, two subgroups of poor readers were identified: those with tasks they could accomplish with above 95 per cent accuracy and those with tasks that could not. Again there tended to be a difference in engagement associated with the two levels of difficulty.

Descriptive data on the tasks which low progress readers face add a further dimension to Gambrell's finding of modifiability. In several studies these children have been found to get fewer opportunities to read appropriate, meaningful, interesting prose compared with their more expert peers. They spend more time on compartmentalized, low meaning tasks such as letter-sound association training. It can be predicted that this dimension of reading task is a setting event for engagement. Like different toys for infants, classroom tasks differ in the degree to which they hold attention. On this view reading stories is likely to have more holding power as an instrumental event than discrimination learning tasks (Allington, 1973).

Even when books are the instructional event they may have different characteristics for low progress readers. In Chapter 7 texts were conceptualized as containing setting events for skilled performance and learning. Difficulty level is one such event. In discussing difficulty levels studies were reviewed which suggested significant numbers of children are given texts to read that are very difficult. Slow reading, high error rates and low incidence of self-correction eventuate.

There are strong indications that low progress readers are particularly susceptible to being misplaced in this way. Both in general surveys of poor readers and in observations of low progress readers prior to application of specially designed remedial procedures readers have been found reading books that are considerably too difficult for them. Presumably this arises partly through the needs for grouping and the difficulties of individualizing instruction.

The modifiability of engagement and the identification of setting events which control this suggest that the source for lower engagement during reading instruction is not simply the child. Alternative explanations focus on the relationships between performance, task environments and socialization experiences. The immediate cause of the differences can be conceptualized in terms of setting events and interactions. But these are the expressions of task environments which are constructed by the participants.

Thus for children who quickly settle in and learn at an acceptable rate for their classroom, the task environment is more generative. On entry to school the learner's knowledge base and existing performance strategies allow some performance-directed regulation within the initial tasks. In an important sense the tasks are relatively more meaningful. Earlier and additional access to stories (addition to what exists already at home) guarantees greater engagement and greater learning. Because of their knowledge such children are better able to cope with the vagaries of classroom life.

Of interactions Differences between progress groups which are found in setting events are also apparent in the interactions which readers have with their tutors. Looking first at error feedback, differences have appeared in four areas. First, overall percentages of errors receiving feedback have been found to be different. Data showing this in one study were presented earlier in Table 12 on p. 150. It appears there is a high probability that the errors a low progress reader makes will receive feedback.

Allington's study (1980) which provided the data in Table 12 needs to be more closely examined. This general finding may have come about because low progress readers perform in such a way that they need constant support. Perhaps their errors simply cannot be overlooked. To clarify this point the likelihood of tutors correcting different types of errors can be checked in Allington's study. One dimension of how problematic an error might be is given by its semantic appropriateness. Semantically inappropriate errors in Allington's study were those that did not make sense given the sentence context. Such errors substantially interfere with ongoing attention to semantic and syntactic cues. Semantically appropriate errors do not and hence are less problematic.

Were the teachers simply more likely to correct problematic errors for both groups and because the low progress readers produced more they were corrected more often? Table 26 shows that significantly higher percentages of both inappropriate and appropriate errors made by low progress readers received feedback. Thus the teachers were systematically more sensitive to their errors, irrespective of the 'quality' of the error.[3]

Table 26 Mean percentage of different types of errors receiving feedback and mean percentage of different types of feedback given to first and second grade readers

	Progress groups	
	High (N = 66)	Low (N = 78)
Error types receiving feedback		
semantically appropriate	11	55
semantically inappropriate	45	79
Feedback type		
graphophonic	18	28
semantic-syntactic	32	8
model	38	50
other	12	14

Source: Allington (1980)

Allington's data suggest that the content of error feedback might be different too. When prompts were given they were more likely to require the low progress readers to use graphophonic information in the text rather than contextual information (that is syntactic-semantic information). The reverse was true for the high progress readers. Allington has interpreted this observation as once again indicating that the low progress readers task is often focused on components rather than meaning. [4] It should be noted that low progress readers often received a model, perhaps reflecting the lack of effectiveness of the prompts used.

Overall Allington's data show low progress readers receiving considerable support from error feedback. This support functions to overcome repeated perturbations in the performance, but it comes from someone else – the tutor – and often it is complete support, in the form of a model. Moreover, and this is to add a further dimension from the comparative research, it is usually given in a way that severely undermines self-regulatory activity. It is often given immediately rather than being delayed to give opportunities for self-regulation and solving.

The data which suggest this latter finding come from several types of research. For some time there have been comments from classroom researchers that immediate correction was more likely for low progress readers. Support for this claim has come from systematic observations which are available in the baseline observations of tutoring studies. They show that while there are some individual differences most teachers of very low progress readers are very unlikely to delay their corrections (see Glynn and McNaughton, 1985).

In contrast, the available data for normal or high progress readers suggest that error feedback for them would be at least as likely to be delayed as it was immediate. For these readers the task environment supports and probably facilitates greater independence in learning. Teachers are cued to 'remove the scaffolding' knowing that these readers can engage in performance-directed regulation and learning activities (e.g. Wilson and McNaughton, 1983).

Information on positive feedback and praise rates is inconsistent. Some studies show an overall lower praise rate with low progress readers, others a higher praise rate. Still others have found wide individual teacher variation. One interpretation of the inconsistency is that several different general patterns of setting events and associated interactions are possible (see Brophy, 1981).

In one, the interactions are distinctly positive. Readers make errors, teachers support readers to correct the errors and are effusive in their praise following those assisted corrections. The general pattern can be seen as one of learned mutual dependence. The child is dependent on considerable teacher support (through setting events and interactions), such support being conveyed positively. Given that attributes of the reader's performance such as assisted corrections and word recognition are reinforcing for the teacher then the teacher is in turn reinforced for maintaining the support characteristics (McNaughton, 1981b).

The final dimension of interactions can be seen in studies which were reviewed in Chapter 9. They indicated that the focus and function of conversations during reading may be different for low groups and high groups (see Table 18, p. 177). These and other comparisons of conversations suggested that interactions are relatively less meaningful for low progress readers. Conversely high progress readers are those children who know what to talk about, how to keep themselves on task, and how to get the most useful information out of their teachers.

The reality for low progress readers   These general differences may of course be entirely appropriate. Maybe low progress readers are receiving instruction which is attuned to their needs. It does not resemble the environment of their more expert classroom peers but perhaps it resembles developmentally similar peers. Moreover, perhaps it changes over time as they become more expert.

There is very little information to answer either of these questions. Nevertheless, the author of one review, Courtney Cazden (1983), predicts that the differences are relatively stable and enduring. Certainly the differences appear early in the first year of instruction. In at least one study she reviews they did not change once the low progress readers had progressed to the point in the texts where their more expert peers had been earlier in the year. She relates this assumed difference to another general finding, that ability grouping increases the range of achievement, enhancing the gains of the higher achievers and decreasing the gains of the lower achievers. The implication is obvious. The differences in task environments increases the developmental differences between students.

The differences in task environments are not malicious. Cazden argues they come about because of 'preactive' and 'interactive' influences. Preactive influences include how teachers plan instruction for different groups of readers and their beliefs and expectations, intentional and unintentional, about the needs of their students. Interactive influences are the processes of reciprocal influence where the teacher's behaviour is determined at least partially by the reader's. Because topics of conversation are different between different groups, because of the haltingly problematic performance, the teacher's behaviour develops certain characteristics which function in turn as setting events and contribute to ongoing interactions.

Cazden's interpretation parallels ours. It would seem that the construction of the different task environments is jointly determined by teachers and readers. The roots are to be found in the transition from the earlier socialization setting to the dual settings of home and school. Children arrive at school with different degrees of reading skill. The differences in knowledge, performance strategies and potential to self-regulate performance immediately interact with the dynamics of classrooms. Out of teacher plans and expectations on the one hand, and setting events and interactions on the other, task environments are constructed. The consequent task environment may severely curtail learning for some children reducing their rate of development even further. However, as Cazden points out, there are programmes which attempt to guarantee increased engagement in meaningful tasks for low progress readers. Even within the ordinary range of classrooms some can be found where more conducive environments are engineered.

The schooled reader: socializations at school

Classrooms, like homes, have the potential to vary in the environments they provide for learning. Although deliberately setting out to teach, teachers, just as parents, can vary in the setting events and interactions they construct with the variously skilled children who enter their charge.

This concern for the way teachers respond to children has been the focus of the previous section. But overlying this source of difference for task environments is another. The second source comes from the reading curriculum classrooms adopt. There is a lengthy history of comparative evaluation research whose deliberate aim has been to show the superiority of one versus another programme. There is also a second source of information, although it has a shorter history. Compensatory programmes, that is special programmes with special curricula for children who are predicted to be educationally 'at risk', have been evaluated and compared, on a scale unprecedented and perhaps unrepeatable in educational research. Both of these sources can be examined for data on the effectiveness of types of conditions supplied at this more general level of the curriculum.

The 'great debate'

Jeanne Chall (1967) called the arguments surrounding how one should teach reading part of a 'great debate'. The debate has not produced a clear winner. Even with independent adjudicators the evidence usd in the debate fails to convince. Why should this be when such disparate psychological and pedagogical arguments are pitted against each other?

It is partly because the debators and their evaluations are

confused about what the question entails, and the form that a useful answer would take. The debate has most often centred around general claims about curricula, which specify in different ways what is to be learned and how the tasks are to be presented and sequenced. For example they might state that grapheme-phoneme knowledge must precede contextual performance strategies, or that early learning should be based on acquiring a repertoire of specific words.

Perhaps it is not surprising that large-scale comparisons of children's acheivements under such curricula have shown no clear superiority for any particular programme (Resnick, 1979; Williams, 1970). There are a number of reasons why this is not surprising. The first is that until recently comparisons have seldom examined how teachers' behaviours express an espoused curriculum in a set of dynamic interactions with their children. Ostensibly the same curriculum can be expressed by different teachers in quite different ways (see Calfee and Pointkowski, 1981; Cazden, 1979).

It is generally accepted that studies are needed of teaching behaviours within and across different curricula. Yet this behavioural level of analysis would still yield an incomplete picture if it did not examine how different curricula construct types of experiences, and what sort of setting events and interactions for performance-directed regulation they contained. Such data are needed to explain how readers might be able to solve and go beyond the formal requirements of the curriculum. To do this analysis justice more is needed than standardized tests of achievements over short time periods. Earlier it was argued that the effectiveness of environments should be judged in terms of generalizations. Generalization can be measured in several ways. One way is to examine continued interest in acquiring and using the skill independently of the programme.

Academic engaged time in programmes

The ideal data requested in the last paragraphs are not available. Nevertheless, some limited conclusions about programme environments are possible. One such conclusion, in the form of a generalization about classroom environments, is called by Rosenshine and Berliner (1978) 'academic engaged time'. This term refers to the amount of time a learner spends actively engaged on a task which is directly related to the academic skill being taught, at an appropriate level of difficulty for his or her current level of skill. The claim is that the higher the academic engaged time for the class, the higher the achievement in the skill. There are numbers of large-scale studies which provide the data for this generalization. And there are some reading programmes, so the authors claim, which do this better than others.

Direct Instruction   The example *par excellence* of a 'better' programme is the Direct Instruction compensatory programme for disadvantaged children. The designers can guarantee in a well-running implementation high amounts of instructional time for reading (about forty-five minutes per day), which engage children in more than 90 per cent of the observed time.[5] Success rates in sequenced tasks and participation in instructional exchanges with teachers are similarly high. The programme therefore is closely tuned to the students' current knowledge at least in terms of accuracy levels on letter-sound and word learning tasks.

This programme has been found to be associated with greater gains in measures of reading achievement over three years compared with other compensatory programmes. It is consistently superior to non-behavioural programmes which do not focus instructional time in knowledge components. Because of its publicly acclaimed success, and because of what its success might say about socialization experiences and skill learning in classrooms, it deserves careful consideration.

Massive funding was provided for the evaluation of compensatory programmes, specifically the 'Follow Through' programmes for disadvantaged children in the USA. Like its progenitor, 'Head Start', Follow Through was an attempt to break into the 'poverty cycle' facing children of parents with little economic, social and political power. The aim was to change children's social and economic future by increasing the effectiveness of educational programmes. Variation in the type of programme which was offered (and therefore able to be evaluated) was deliberately achieved through contracts with a variety of sponsors of educational programmes and school districts.

Each programme intended to influence academic achievement at school, which meant they each contained provisions for teaching reading. The usual range of pedagogical theory was represented in these programmes from those based on concepts attributed to Piaget and Dewey, to those based on behavioural learning theory. The effects of a number of programmes have been systematically assessed both by sponsors who analysed their own programmes and by independent research organizations in national studies.

Understandably these assessments are controversial. For example there are considerable methodological and conceptual issues involved in the national assessments.[6] Despite the controversies there is consensus on at least three data-based conclusions. The first is that the influence that any programme exerted in achievement scores varied tremendously across different communities where it was applied. The variation in means of gains from setting to setting within each programme type was greater than the variation of the means among the programmes. All parties to the national assessment agree that this confirms other findings that the local circumstances, and in particular classroom behaviours, are more significant determinants of learning. As one group of national assessors put it, more so than 'the intentions, theories and rhetoric of outside interveners' (R.B. Anderson *et al.*, 1978, p. 162).

Implicit in this finding is the further conclusion that no one programme could be argued on statistical grounds to be better or worse than another. However, in terms of overall levels of achievement there is consensus that one type of programme can be ranked first among the various models. At first glance the ranking appears to be in direct contradiction to the claims made in other chapters about maximally effective conditions for learning symbolic skills. The most 'effective' programmes could not be more different, for example, from the conditions which children who have learned to read before they got to school have experienced.

The programme consistently ranking higher than the others is noteworthy also because of the data which are available from the designers on the processes of implementation and their outcomes. As noted earlier, the Direct Instruction model, much of it designed by Wesley Becker and Siegfried Englemann, is highly structured, with considerable control exerted by the teacher. It couples a behavioural learning theory analysis of the processes of instruction with a logical analysis of reading tasks. The result is a carefully sequenced programme in which graphophonological components are conceptualized as basic and therefore taught first to produce decoding skills. Sentences are not introduced for reading until later in the instructional sequence, and even then contain highly controlled words which match the blending skills already taught. Daily instruction occurs, often in small group settings using carefully analysed techniques of controlling children's attention, providing positive contingencies for correct answers, keeping errors to a minimum and correcting those that do occur immediately using standard correction procedures.

In content the programme is directly contrasted by the designers with 'wholeword' or 'reading for meaning' approaches. These were among the programmes offered in other Follow Through projects. There were also programmes which operated for similar but non-Follow Through children who were members of control groups of 'disadvantaged' students.

In process the model involves a controlled incremental acquisition from basic concepts. Generalization from one stage to another is explicitly trained by the teaching of general cases. Teachers and their aides received careful training and the format of reading lessons is based on systematic analyses of teaching components.

This programme ranked first, but in what senses could it be said to provide effective task environments? Its 'success' has been interpreted in several places as showing the superiority of those programmes which emphasize basic skills, with learning being precisely structured through teacher control achieved through the compartmentalizing of reading tasks. Such attributes maximize academic engaged time.

Evaluating outcomes   The evaluation of about 2000 Directly Instructed students' achievement in reading conducted by both the designers and the national longitudinal evaluators show several outcomes. The data are based on two reading tests. The first, the Wide Range Achievement Test, is a measure of decoding skills or word recognition. The evaluation data for this measure contained in Table 27 are in terms of percentiles and grade equivalents. A percentile of 18 represents a score which is equal to or better than 18 per cent of the equivalent children based on the normative data for the test. Percentiles can be translated into

Table 27   Achievements in decoding for children receiving 'Follow Through' Direct Instruction programmes from kindergarten to third grade

Measure	Pre-kindergarten	Post-third grade
Percentiles (WRAT)[1]		
Direct Instruction	18.0	82.0
National median	50.0	50.0
Grade equivalent	0.2	5.3

Source: Becker and Carnine (1980)
Note: [1] Average scores in percentiles for the Wide Range Achievement Test outcomes.
Reproduced with the permission of Wesley C. Becker.

grade equivalents, meaning the grade level an equivalent child could be expected to be working at.

The data show remarkable gains after receiving Direct Instruction from kindergarten to third grade. After three or four years Direct Instruction students were on average almost one standard deviation above the national median percentile of 50 and working at a fifth grade level. But Direct Instruction concentrated on decoding strategies and knowledge of words, outcomes which are exclusively tested by WRAT. By contrast, learning to comprehend prose passages was not emphasized. So what effect did the programme have on comprehension? At first glance it seems a strong one given the results on a second test which was used by the National evaluators. The second test was the Metropolitan Achievement Test and it included a measure of comprehension on prose. As shown by the results in Table 28 Direct Instruction ranked first on this measure too. Even so the average achievement by students was only the fortieth percentile, below the national norm of the fiftieth percentile (which has a grade equivalent of 3.5).

The average achievements in eight other Follow Through programmes were even less and ranged from the eighteenth to the thirty-fourth percentile. However, the expected typical performance level of similar ('at risk') children in regular grade classrooms is the twentieth percentile, and the authors argue that this represents the best benchmark to compare results against. The

Table 28 Achievements in MAT reading for children receiving Direct Instruction, and other Follow Through programmes plus control groups

Measures	Direct Instruction	Other programmes
Percentiles (MAT)[1]	41.0	18–34
Grade equivalents	3.2	2.5–3.0

Source: Becker and Carnine (1980)
Note: [1] Average scores in percentiles for the Metropolitan Achievement Test outcome.
Reproduced with the permission of Wesley C. Becker

control groups that were established at selected locations for all the programmes do not provide a good basis for comparison. After looking at their characteristics they turned out to be more 'advantaged' than the programme children. Thus their achievement after third grade was at the thirty-fourth percentile on a variety of programmes. But even given this, when adjustments are made for initial differences between control groups and programme groups, Direct Instruction is found to have more instances of significant gains on reading measures compared with control groups than the other programmes.

After the programme Added to these findings are the reports of progress two to three years after leaving Direct Instruction classrooms and being taught in regular classrooms. Compared with similar but non-Follow Through programme children in the same schools, the Direct Instruction children continued to show superior achievement if slightly attenuated in their decoding and word identification skills. Progress in these skills, which had been deliberately trained to generalize, continued. But the relatively small gains in comprehension did not generalize. The achievement at third grade, where on average children were comprehending better than up to 40 per cent of the national sample of third grade children, was reduced over the following three years. At sixth grade the children were now showing achievement in comprehension only as good as 25 per cent of a national sample of sixth grade readers. This means they did not make the same progress in relationship to a national sample as they had done while in the programme. Their average achievement was now close to one grade below the national average.

This lack of generalization across time and settings to new skills is interpreted by the designers of the programme in the following way. They argue that knowing the meaning of one word can not have any inherent transfer effect. Vocabulary concepts are learned in a much more linear additive fashion than learning to identify words from generalizable rules for decoding. Thus word knowledge from one's oral language repertoire is a prerequisite and needs to be learned item by item. Typically much of what is required in the first few grades is learned at home, the designers claim, but 'often the learning environments of many low-income homes do not support and encourage language development (knowledge of basic words) among children' (Becker et al., 1981, p. 121). Therefore they argue that for these children comprehension items and skills must also require highly structured learning conditions. It follows, so the designers argue, that Direct Instruction programmes for such should be implemented in grades higher than third grade.

In its simple form much of this interpretation is questionable. All word concepts do not have to be directly socially transmitted. They can be learned via performance-directed regulation as a child analyses the linguistic contexts for individual words, for example available when reading books or watching television. Indeed, another obvious learning strategy to overcome a problem of comprehension is to ask someone what the word means. That low-income homes do not provide conditions for learning word-concepts is an empirical question which needs to identify what vocabulary items are learned and their relationship with standardized tests, as well as how they are learned.

An alternative interpretation of the patterns in these results stresses the accelerated but dependent nature of the children's learning. The characteristics of Direct Instruction classrooms guarantee the rapid acquisition and mastery of decoding or word analysis skills. Much of what can be learned is learned within the three or four years spent under the programme. Moreover, it is learned under conditions which guarantee considerable time spent engaged in acquiring these skills. Teacher training coupled with a standardized specification of instructional behaviour has created a programme which is exceptional in terms of 'academic engaged time'.

But the classroom task environment also reduces early performance-directed regulation and acts of learning which take the reader beyond the requirements of the curriculum. Because of the structure of the curriculum the readers are dependent on being given words and their meanings by the teachers, at a predetermined time in sequence within the curriculum.Without a strong intention to perform the skill, which we have argued is dependent on early domination of interactions with performance-directed regulation, little exercise of the skill is likely to occur outside the demands of the externally dominated task environments.

The reality of the terms 'exercise' and 'demand' are that the skill tends not to be used other than for the functions defined by the tutor. These are to analyse words, and to put the skill to use when required by teachers for other tasks. If this analysis is correct, one should expect to find little reading for interest or pleasure being carried out independently by these children. Unfortunately this is not a measure that any evaluator includes in their analysis of effectiveness.

More than this, the model of home–school relationships outlined in Chapter 11 suggests further limitations. If home settings do not match the socialization experiences offered by the school, developmental processes are not maximized. Part of the reason why special programmes for 'disadvantaged' children might be needed is because their socialization experiences at home are systematically different from school. While promoting some skills home socializations may not promote others which schools value, such as literacy skills (see Laosa, 1982; Ogbu, 1981). The nature of the close classroom (stimulus) control over learning in Direct Instruction classrooms almost guarantees that little generalization from school to home, which might influence those socialization practices, is likely.

Survival in classrooms

As stated originally Rosenshine and Berliner's (1978) generalization about academic engaged time appeared to be consistent with certain setting events introduced in Chapter 7. These are the setting events of text difficulty and repeated opportunitis to learn.

But the analysis of Direct Instruction cautions against adopting the unwarranted assumption that classrooms with increased academic engaged time will necessarily produce more skilled readers.

The earlier analysis of setting events and interactions stressed functional relationships between particular expressions of these variables and attributes of reading skill. In particular reading (for meaning) as a skill and learning arising from performance-directed regulation were the attributes of most concern. Thus not task *per se* but text appropriateness was discussed. Not opportunities to be exposed to training but opportunities to learn were discussed.

A bleak picture has been painted. Children whose socialization experiences do not prepare them for the realities of classrooms may encounter considerable difficulties. On entering school they construct environments with their tutors which can increasingly limit their progress compared with their 'advantaged' peers. Even if they get the best available compensatory programmes their initial success may be limited.

Shifting the focus back to more normal readers it could be argued that *their* task is made unnecessarily difficult by the way schools operate. The feature of primary developmental contexts cannot be achieved easily. Consequently the most effective arrangements of setting events and interactions are often not achieved. It is in some ways astonishing that many children can be so good at learning under these conditions. It is one of the primary theses of this book that they can be because they can use what the school offers to build on experiences which have been and continue to be offered by their socialization settings out of school.

Our argument to this point then is that it is very difficult to establish the superiority of one classroom programme over another. Such a finding has eluded researchers who have compared regular classrooms. Even when differences have been found for special classrooms they may be of a very restricted sort. Nevertheless, as our model predicts, classrooms do make a difference. In the first instance it was established in the introduction that different programmes stamp an idiosyncratic seal on development. Children solve the environments they confront, adapting to what the environment offers. The result is that in some respects sequences of skill development differ from programme to programme.

Classrooms have a second influence. Whatever environment is present it can offer opportunities, or provide functional setting events and interactions. If they can make sense of their environments learners capitalize on what is offered in the way of primary and secondary contexts. Because the environments make sense, they are manageable. As adjuncts, complementing already existing settings out of school, classroom experiences can speed up the rate at which learning has hitherto proceeded. So they may be less than perfect as environments but they can be instructional.

However, their instructional effectiveness is limited. It is limited by what socializations have occurred prior to school and how they continue to operate when schooling commences. This is not to say that under some extraordinary conditions classrooms cannot 'arouse an intention' to learn as we earlier argued homes can do. But it is considerably harder to do this (in the absence of matched socializations at home) under the general conditions which are set up by schools.

Over and above these influences classroom programmes can make it relatively easier or more difficult to learn what they require. More significantly, they make it easier or more difficult to go beyond the requirements of the programme. Those environments which provide in strong measure for setting events and interactions, which facilitate acts of learning from performance-directed regulation for meaning, will best achieve the latter sort of influence.

The ease with which a child can solve and go beyond formal requirements is very closely determined by socialization out of school. Herein lies a central dilemma of schooling. There are children whose socializations do not provide a level of preparedness which matches many other children. For these children schools provide institutional forms of socialization. Yet by their nature as institutions schools make it very difficult for just these different children to learn. The more prepared a child is the more that this second deliberate socialization can facilitate their development of literacy skills. For the most prepared children the type of classroom environment probably doesn't matter that much. Unless it is so rigid and poorly matched as to frustrate them, their development will continue to accelerate.

13 Becoming a skilled reader

This final chapter reviews the elements of a socialization theory for learning to read, and implications are drawn for both schooling practices and remedial endeavours with children having difficulties learning to read. But first there is a question that remains unanswered in the analysis of socialization, concerning the development of different types of socializations at home. How do different socializations arise?

Something left to explain

The question is important. It is unsatisfactory to leave an analysis incomplete, particularly if implications for developing children's literacy are dependent on our understanding of the missing components. Knowledge of the processes which influence family patterns is needed if deliberate attempts to influence literacy are to be maximally effective. Three related sources of influence can be found. The first is general societal practices which involve the transmission of patterns of family environments from one generation to the next. The second arises from membership of different social or cultural groups within a society. Third, there are differences in parenting practices within these groups which are affected by particular experiences, including schooling.

Societal practices

In 1973 the International Association for the Evaluation of Educational Achievement published their findings on reading. A variety of measures of reading achievement were gathered from between ten and fifteen developed and developing countries. There is an intriguing pattern in the outcomes which was detected by John Guthrie (1982). One country is ranked first on three measures which reflect ability to comprehend and interpret prose passages. Yet on other measures of word knowledge and reading speed this country was not out of the ordinary: students were found to achieve at an average level.

The country at issue was New Zealand. In measures of reading comprehension and interpretation of literature, representative samples of 14-year-olds and 18-year-olds were ranked first and scored between half and one standard deviation above the median country. The results, especially for the 14-year-olds, are not attributable to selection problems in the participating countries nor are they substantially biased by the measuring instruments.

Table 29   Literacy rate in three countries

	New Zealand		United States	Iran
Newspapers				
Daily	27.8			
Weekly	3.6			
Combined		31.4	20.4	4.6
Magazines		6.6	13.7	0.5
Books				
Purchase	1.6			
Borrow from library	1.4			
Exchange/gifts	1.7			
Combined		4.7	1.1	No data
Other	No data		No data	No data
Total		42.7	35.2	5.1

Source: Guthrie (1982)
Reprinted with permission of J. Guthrie and the International Reading Association
Note: Figures are copies/person/month.

The relatively high reading achievement of New Zealand students raises interesting questions. Guthrie's own analysis of the data leads to the following answer. New Zealand is apparently more of a 'print-oriented society' than other developed and developing countries included in the survey. The data in Table 29 illustrate this conclusion. Guthrie reviewed representative surveys of the amount of reading engaged in by adult populations in New Zealand, the USA and Iran (representing a developing country). From the surveys he constructed a measure of copies of books or magazines read per person per month. This measure of reading volume was found to be different in the three countries he compared. When all types of reading materials are considered, the rate for New Zealand was 42.7 copies per person per month, compared with 35.2 copies and 5.1 copies for the USA and Iran respectively.

There are differences in what these copies are. For example in the USA comparatively more magazines are read. But overall, Guthrie claims the data support the concept of New Zealand being a print-oriented society. The relatively high volume of reading in the adult population matches the relatively high achievement in reading comprehension by New Zealand students.

Guthrie's claim for a causal relationship essentially is that this constitutes a societal practice which makes reading a salient and expected activity. The effect is achieved through variables which he refers to as the availability of materials, language use in the community and child-rearing practices; variables which might be seen as particular setting events and interactional patterns. It would be consistent with the predictions already made that the strong presence of these variables would be associated with an intention to learn and generalized use of the tool.

Thus a general level of influence on socialization of literacy can be found. Societies differ in terms of their practice of literacy. The levels of that practice, and the setting events and interactions associated with those levels, are presumably transmitted from one generation to another. One generation's practice affects their children's achievement which becomes another generation's practice. But this is a very gross level of analysis. Within societies there are substantial differences between families. Some of these differences tend to be found in families that share cultural, political and economic realities.

Child-rearing: beliefs, values and goals

Inequal achievement patterns in reading are found associated with the familiar groupings of socio-economic status and cultural group. In general the lower the status, the lower the school achievement. A similar correlation exists for membership in some cultural groups disempowered in their recent past, through experiences such as colonization, enslavement or immigrant labour. The conclusion in Chapter 12 was that the setting events and interactions which increase the development of those literacy skills having effects on school achievement are similarly unequally distributed within societies.

Two qualifications to this generalization are necessary. The first has been made. There is considerable variability in achievement between families that have been so grouped. From this a conclusion was drawn that it is the presence of particular setting events and interactional patterns, not membership in a group as such, which determines the development of literacy. The second qualification has not been made until this point. A.B. Anderson and Stokes (1984) supply the basis for it in their extensive observational study of low income groups in the USA. The preschoolers in these families were found to participate directly in or observe an astounding 7.5 minutes of literacy events per hour. Their environments teemed with events encountered mostly in daily living (for example as print seen during shopping), and as entertainment (for example print encountered on television). They too found considerable variation between low income families and have claimed that group membership *per se* does not dictate what is learned.

But what studies such as that of A.B. Anderson and Stokes suggest (see also Heath, 1982b) is that literacy events are present in different forms in many environments. Our argument here is that the comined presence of *particular* setting events and interaction patterns in primary and secondary developmental contexts influences the development of particular literacy skills. The concept of skill is central. The focus is on socialization processes which influence the skill components of knowledge, performance strategies and performance-directed regulation in reading for meaning.

What is it about membership in some social class or cultural groupings that is associated with these particular literacy experiences being strongly present or not in family settings? There is a longstanding approach to this question. For many years differences between groups in child-rearing experiences related to academic skill have been seen in terms of a deficiency model, that is general differences in the way different groups socialize their children have been systematically compared with an ideal. The ideal has been the dominant social and cultural group's general practices.

In major western countries these have been defined by white middle-class families, so the trend towards providing the types of literacy-related experiences in these families is idealized. They are adopted as definitive; they represent the 'best' way to rear children. It follows that other social or cultural groups who do not show the same general trends are deficient or inadequate in their child-rearing skills. Certainly there may be a best-fit model for success at school, and in general middle-class white families may define that. How could it be otherwise with an institution which in many ways is designed to serve the majority groups needs? But there is more than a logical point to be made here. Contemporary researchers have argued very strongly against such an 'ethnic' or 'cultural centric' view of child-rearing which judges other groups as deficient in child-rearing techniques. There exist differences rather than deficiencies and these differences require an explanation.

John Ogbu (1981) argues that all parents socialize their children in terms of beliefs, expectations and values which they have about what children need to learn to be competent. Child-rearing becomes an exercise in teaching competence and survival in the cultural tasks adults face.

This argument is repeated by Luis Laosa:

> the values placed on given modes of behaviour . . . vary among social and cultural groups, depending on each group's patterns of coping with and adapting to the surrounding environment . . . each socioculture contains a formula for customary parental behavior which has evolved over time and is largely successful under relatively stable conditions.
>
> (1982, p. 162)

Both writers have considered the case of minority groups. Laosa points out that where patterns of behaviour which are adaptive within one community but are maladaptive within another setting exist (for example school), then change occurs; but change can take several forms. One is the development of dual patterns of adaption. Ogbu describes another: some minority groups, and in particular he refers to the experiences of ghetto Blacks in the USA, may evolve culturally organized competencies which become alternatives to those of the dominant culture.

The implications for our analysis of family environments are that environments in which particular literacy experiences are underrepresented are not necessarily deficient; the child-rearing is not pathological.[1] Whether or not they want their children to do well at school, the setting events and interactions relating to literacy are systematically different. To some extent they reflect the family and group's adaptation to social, political and cultural realities, which include how much economic power is achievable or desirable and what competencies are needed. They relate to beliefs, expectations and values which the group holds, for example about the accessibility and benevolence of schools and the value of school-related tasks.

An extreme example of one group's values about, and needs for literacy, is found in a study of children raised in the scientific community of Los Alamos, New Mexico (John-Steiner and Roth, 1984). In their households one or both parents work outside the home and effective communications are needed to co-ordinate family life. Similarly, because of frequent shifts, effective communication over time and distance needs to be developed to maintain contact with the extended family. In short, adults and children need to write and read in order to manage their lives. But, in addition, their membership of a scientific community makes written communication a valued activity and achievement at school is also likely to be valued.

A sample of writing at home was collected from twelve children over four months. The amount of writing was prodigious: 280 separate items were analysed and they ranged from messages and notes which functioned to maintain family activities, through to poems and cartoons which served creative functions.

Different experiences

So different groups within a society may have different priorities for skills that are needed in order to cope well with their realities. Their different patterns of socialization reflect an adaptation to different conditions of living. Thus socializations for literacy are related to these conditions, included in which are economic and social power and cultural patterns preserved in ethnic member-ship. It is worth emphasizing here the conclusion that Ogbu arrives at with his analysis:

> It follows that the most effective way to improve ghetto or minority school success is to increase and improve their con-ventional economic resources (e.g. provide more and better conventional jobs for youths and adults) to the point where ... significant changes occur in perceptions of opportunity structures in the conventional economy.
>
> (1981, p. 426)

But we have already noted that there is considerable variation within the traditional groupings, particularly that of social class, in socialization patterns. If this is so then the usual groupings must not exclusively or accurately summarize the sources of influence on socializations for literacy.

This has been very clearly shown in a series of studies carried out by Luis Laosa (1982). In these studies the strategies which dif-ferent groups of mothers have used to help their preschoolers in problem-solving tasks have been observed. Previous research has tended to show that the teaching style adopted varies accord-ing to social class and ethnic group. Social class has been judged in terms of maternal or paternal education and occupation, either interchangeably or added together to yield a composite score.

Laosa's own studies separated out particular experiential vari-ables, namely occupational status and formal schooling, and examined their influence within an ethnic group. He compared maternal teaching style of Chicano mothers with Anglo-American mothers. The problems that their 5-year-olds faced were manipu-lation tasks where a disassembled toy model had to be made like one already assembled. The two groups of mothers were selected to be as representative as possible of Chicano and Anglo-American families in the USA with regard to educational levels and occupa-tional status of parents. As a group the Chicanos had completed fewer years of schooling and were employed in lower status occupations.

The general comparison is shown in Figure 19. The frequency of various maternal behaviours is expressed in terms of rate over two five-minute sessions. As a group the Chicano mothers used model-ling (showing how to assemble parts), visual cues (highlighting

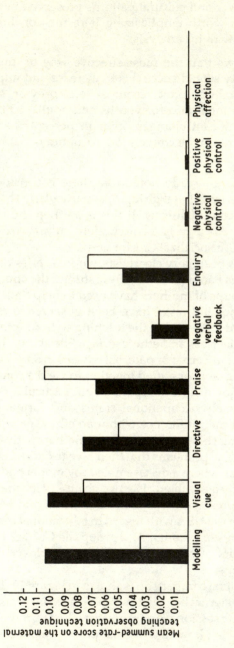

Figure 19 Maternal teaching strategies in Chicano and Anglo-American families before controlling for ethnic group differences in formal education level and occupational status

Source: Laosa (1982)

Note: Solid bars refer to Chicanos; open bars refer to Anglo-Americans.

how parts go together), directives (verbally commanding the child) and negative verbal feedback (disapproval) more than the Anglo-Americans. The latter group, however, used enquiry (questioning the child) and praise more frequently than the Chicano mothers. But these differences, which are similar to previously reported social class differences, disappeared entirely when level of maternal education was held constant.[2] In Figure 20 the results for Chicano mothers with different years of formal education are shown. The higher the mother's level of formal education the more enquiry and praise were used; the lower the level, the more modelling. Thus two different patterns of teaching were used depending on levels of education. Mothers with less than eleventh grade mainly taught through modelling, visual cues and directives. With at least eleventh grade education mothers taught mainly through a combination of praise, visual cues and enquiry.

With level of maternal education controlled, differences between groups in teaching style disappeared. They also disappeared when paternal level of education was held constant, but the differences were still apparent when maternal occupation and paternal occupation were each controlled for. Thus the differences between the ethnic groups were tied to differences in the average level of formal education of the parents, but not tied to occupation, a variable which is often used in ascribing social class.

These results suggest two things. First, that schooling has an effect on child-rearing practices. Indeed, there is a striking similarity between the teaching pattern used by more highly educated mothers and the academic style which includes verbal feedback. Laosa argues that the pattern adopted by more highly educated parents may be better preparation for the educational system. Not necessarily because it is in fact a better style of teaching but because it matches the style at school. This is essentially an argument about what makes for a smooth transition from one socialization setting to another.

This variable, and its suggested effects, are likely to be the case for literacy-related experiences too (as was discussed in previous chapters). Laosa did find that the more highly schooled of the Chicano mothers 'spent significantly more time reading to their children, and a greater proportion of them indeed had children who had acquired at least some reading and writing skills prior to

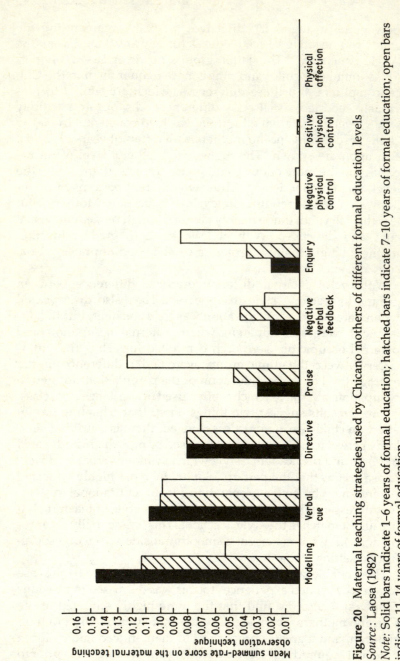

Figure 20 Maternal teaching strategies used by Chicano mothers of different formal education levels

Source: Laosa (1982)

Note: Solid bars indicate 1–6 years of formal education; hatched bars indicate 7–10 years of formal education; open bars indicate 11–14 years of formal education.

kindergarten' (p. 159). What this finding adds to our analysis is an example of one source of influence in the particular adaptation that a family makes to their environment. Within groupings based on occupation or ethnicity years of parental schooling can significantly affect child-rearing patterns. Included in these patterns are those socialization experiences which relate to literacy.

Such a difference within a group reflects a different adaptation to that which characterizes the group overall. It reflects beliefs, values and expectations about the need for and value of literacy. Thus there are a variety of sources of experiences which influence socialization patterns. They range from gross societal ones through to specific experiences such as years of formal schooling.

Testing the theory

A theory of learning to read has been developed in this book which focuses on naturally occurring phenomena. A cornerstone of that theory is the analysis of reading as a skill; to this can be added a second base. As a skill, and even more so as a symbolic skill, becoming an expert represents an idiosyncratic response to particular environments. Being skilled is a social process. Learning takes place in environments as a joint construction of the child and a matrix of active influences.

Before school, setting events and specific interactions which relate to literacy exist in socialization experiences. Together with the child, these experiences construct the routes that development takes. Different socializations at home represent different adaptations to cultural, social, economic and political realities. Thus being literate permeates the environments of some families. For other families, such literacy skills are not an immediate concern of daily life.

In becoming skilled, in being socialized at home, a child learns several things. Knowledge is gained of what being literate means. Accompanying this, some performance strategies for limited tasks develop, and capabilities of self-regulation increase. Out of this regulation learning activities are increasingly able to be deployed on literacy tasks.

From home to school, children arrive with different kinds of expertise. With the transition to school two socialization contexts come to operate. They can be well or poorly co-ordinated. For some children opportunities for learning can be considerably enhanced even given the limited nature of setting events and interactions which a child can engage in at school. There is another extreme: what the second context requires of other children in terms of learning can be literally meaningless.

These then are the elements of the theory: a developing skill, active learners and multifaceted socializations. How are the three phenomena, which introduced this book as tests of an adequate theory of learning to read, to be explained from these elements? The answers have been provided in various sections of the book and they can be easily summarized.

The quotation from Shakespeare's *As You Like It* – 'Learned yet never schooled' – was used to capture the phenomenon of precocious readers. For these readers it can be argued that the particular constellation of setting events and interaction patterns they encounter make it worth their while to learn and keep learning to gain and make meaning using written language. An intention to learn is aroused and maintained.

Their skill is a product of socialization. Yet, in a very important sense, these children generally are active learners, having substantial control of their learning. Given a responsive environment they are able to engage in learning activities arising out of performance-directed regulation. Their knowledge and performance strategies are developed early. Inventive conformity to the requirements of classroom programmes is a characteristic of children who make satisfactory progress at school. Their adaptation to or exploitation of what programmes have to offer can be explained with the concepts used for precocious readers.

Classroom programmes may be more restricted learning environments; they may be more controlling than family environments and they may set up an initially unfamiliar task environment. But children who have some literacy skill on entry to school enter the new environment able to problem solve. What their initial skill level entails in terms of knowledge, performance strategies, regulation and learning activities enables them to learn both efficiently and expediently. This learning is considerably enhanced by continued socialization experiences at home which adjust to and capitalize on the socialization at school. The reverberating socialization experiences accelerate learning.

Inventive conformity is possible as children make sense of

their classroom environment. In so doing classroom experiences are constructed by the child, who not only exploits what the programme has to offer but also exploits the setting events and interactions which are also available.

Independent active learning is also implicated in the final phenomenon. Going beyond the teaching received is possible because independent learning activities add power to the child's ability to solve the problems of becoming skilled. These activities arise out of performance-directed regulation which is possible where sense can be made out of a task environment. This is dependent on some existing knowledge and intention to learn, which is also an outcome of being skilled in a socialization setting that exists prior to school and harmonizes with school.

Thus the claim of this book is that when children find it relatively easy to learn to read, and this can be found in different classrooms which espouse different reading programmes, it is because socializations allow personal meaning and performance-directed regulation in their learning. The phenomena are explicable only with a theory having both socialization and skills perspectives: both a functional and a structural view.

The argument is not absolute. That is it is not argued that people will learn to read easily only if their twin socialization settings harmonize to promote active learning. Children without these, who find learning difficult at school, who may not experience relatively harmonious settings, can still become proficient. Adult 'illiterates' can learn again, given a need to, and conducive environments. What has been explained in this book is how the early stages of learning to read are made easy.

The argument is not absolute in a second sense. The socialization processes identified in this book are not the only variables influencing achievement in reading and writing at school. Homes and schools can be well or poorly matched on a number of dimensions. One dimension of profound importance is oral language. The role of different language interactions at home has only been touched on in the present analysis. Yet it is obvious that language skills developed at home can have a marked effect on achievement at school.

There is a longstanding tradition for attributing differences in achievement to differences in language between home and school. Earlier versions were based on incomplete analyses and are insufficient if not inadequate as explanations (e.g. Wells, 1981).

In general the contemporary claims stress two things. The first encompasses the learning of different discourse rules. It is a claim that the ways different sociocultural groups converse with their children, the ways children have been socialized and hence have developed expertise before school, can be quite distinct. This can be seen in the role of questions. Heath (1982a) has described how the same middle-class white adults, as teachers in a classroom and as parents, attempt to train children to be experts in answering questions about the world, particularly in identifying attributes of objects out of context. Middle-class children coming to school are relative experts at this. Black working-class children, however, find school questions to be 'unfamiliar in their frequency, purposes and types and in the domains of content knowledge and skills they assumed on the part of students' (1982a, p. 123). But these children have their own strengths with the interrogative form. They are able to answer expertly questions asking of analogical comparisons, relating to the whole of incidents and composites of characteristics of persons, objects and events.

The second focus extends this last comment. It concerns a dimension of language which Snow (1983) in particular raises to a position of central importance in differences between home and school. She refers to the comprehension and production of 'decontextualized' information. Both oral and written modes of language use can be required where there is little by way of a familiar context or concrete referents to support the skill. Presenting monologues, engaging in abstract verbal reasoning, and giving metalinguistic jdugements are extreme examples of what she calls decontextualized language use in the oral mode. Reading and writing as normally used after several years at school are given by her as examples in the written mode. Thus she argues

By about fourth grade, many school literacy activities are highly decontextualized. Children are no longer asked just to fill in worksheets or read from books with pictures but are expected to read from textbooks and write clear paragraphs. Thus, the basic reason for children's failure in the middle grades may not be the difficulty of literacy but the problems associated with decontextualizing language use ... many of the experiences identified as contributing to preschool children's literacy development (such as being told stories, being read to, receiving help in constructing descriptions of past events, being asked tutorial questions) contribute more to their ability to use language in a decontextualized, even noncommunicative, way than to their literacy skills per se ... it may be that literacy skills are simple enough to be acquired at school, whereas the skill of using language in a decontextualized way relies more heavily on experiences only home can provide

(1983, pp. 186–7)

There are problems here with her definition of 'literacy skills'. For example she uses a relatively narrow description in comparison with the concept of literacy skill outlined here. Indeed, with the more encompassing definition of symbolic skill in the earlier chapters there is a blurring between her concept of decontextualized written language and the development of literacy skills in reading for meaning.

But the essential point of this research on the match or mismatch between homes and schools in language skill remains. Children can be well or poorly matched with school expectations in terms of language skills in which they have become competent. Similar arguments can be made for general knowledge, parental teaching styles and even knowledge of and attitudes at school (see McNaughton, 1986). What this means is that achievement at school can be related to a number of sources of influence. We have identified one major route that primarily relates to reading and writing at school. It can exist in varying combinations with the others or relatively independently of other sources of matching between home and school.

Some implications

From this analysis of the socializations of literacy skill it is possible to draw implications for educational policy. If, in a developed country such as my own, it is seen to be necessary to ensure that children become literate and in the easiest and most effective ways, then educational practice in at least three areas needs some modification. However, these three areas of change must be seen as weak responses to those social groups who are most likely to enter schools at a disadvantage to their peers from the dominant sociocultural groups.

The idea of schools

Schools as typically constructed in western societies are rather ineffective settings for individuals learning symbolic skills. One obvious implication of our analysis of socialization settings as contexts for development is that classrooms are inherently problematic. Nevertheless, some tinkering is possible to enable them to approximate more closely the ideal for primary and secondary developmental contexts.

Lowering class ratios so that children have greater access to their tutors is a small step. The ratio would have to be very small before it began to allow for the general development of productive one-to-one relationships. This is because the criterion suggeted by our analysis is the extent to which individualized instruction is made possible and groups with their inevitable contrast can be avoided.

But perhaps there is a more significant effect of reducing ratios. Small numbers of pupils might allow a teacher time and energy to muster other resources. For example within schools there are considerable opportunities for peer and parent participation in reading instruction at school. Peers and parents are demonstrably effective as tutors (Glynn and McNaughton, 1985; Limbrick, McNaughton and Glynn, 1985). The barriers that exist to their use are mostly to do with the time needed to set in motion and maintain the systems.

There are other weaknesses in the idea of schooling for literacy. Programmes, and setting events and interactions associated with those programmes, may restrict the opportunities for performance-directed regulation on meaningful tasks. Beginning classroom practices need to be so organized that children have many opportunities to engage in reading tasks at an appropriate level of difficulty. In these tasks they need to be able to be perturbed and learn from overcoming those perturbations. Moreover, they need to be stimulated to read playfully.

On making settings meet

Another area of educational practice has potential for increasing the effectiveness of classroom instruction. The relationship between home and school takes on a critical role in our model of socialization settings. Until very recently there has been considerable reluctance by some school authorities actively to encourage and nurture interconnections. Yet the potential for children's learning is enormous.

It is clearly not the case that most parents are uninterested in their children's adaptation to school (McNaughton, Glynn and Robinson, 1981). The existing evidence suggests considerable general interest but little knowledge of what might be done. We have already suggested that children themselves influence and modify the literacy-related experiences available at home as a consequence of going to school. However, this influence and the reaction it produced in parents to interact with their children could be considerably enhanced with information and resources supplied by their child's professional tutor.

The tutor's role here may be to fine tune setting events and interactions that can take place at home. Providing appropriate level texts, providing guidelines for, and feedback on how to set up supportive interactions, should be a part of the professional knowledge of educators. Classroom teachers could respond to the concern of parents, providing a means of expression to their power. In so doing, socialization for literacy at home would alter.

This is certainly the function that the school personnel had in the Haringey Project (Tizard, Schofield and Hewison, 1983). Reading achievement over the first years at school was considerably advanced when a collaborative home and school reading programme operated.

An early involvement

But the Haringey Project was based on earlier investigative correlational studies which Hewison and Tizard (1980) had carried out. These studies were described in Chapter 11; they showed that high reading achievement within the working-class population she studied was predicted by parental involvement in their children's reading. The major indicator variable was hearing a child read. What is significant about her data is the simple relationship between this involvement and reading achievement. The more regular that involvement was and the longer it lasted from entry to school, the higher the achievement.

These data are consistent with other longitudinal data which have been reviewed in earlier chapters. Not only does collaborative activity between home and school have considerable potential, but also if children have some knowledge and some strategies for simple tasks then the experience of schooling is potentially more understandable. It is likely then to be more productive as an environment for learning.

The implication is clear. Literacy-related experiences *before* school should be a focus of educational concern because they can have a significant effect on the transition to school. This means preschool facilities have an important role to play. In this book we have focused on homes and schools. But the availability of preschools introduces the possibility of a transitional setting.

Kindergartens and other forms of preschool which are available vary tremendously in their pedagogical assumptions. But what has become a traditional preschool view is a commitment to 'discovery' learning and 'readiness' to learn, and this is often interpreted to mean not directing or arousing a child's curiosity, or systematically attempting to influence a child's development. There is a confusion that can be detected in some preschool writing. The confusion is introduced because discovery learning is equated with the absence of teaching, and teaching is equated with immediate direct control over a child's interest.

But all environments set up setting events and interactions which influence skill learning, whether or not those responsible for the environment intend to do so. Discovery learning and readiness to learn are products of a set of experiences, a negotiation between active learner and active environment. Surely the benign yet systematic arrangement of setting events (for example repeated examples of reading and writing as salient adult and child activities), and interactions responsive to child intentions and curiosity are defensible educational provisions. They are essential if we want preschools to have a useful function in developing literacy skills.

Real changes

But these are tinkerings. From the earlier part of this chapter it would seem that the needs of sociocultural groups who have relatively little economic, social and political power can be met only with further changes. Of overriding concern is the response to the question of whether or not parents see it as both useful and possible to be skilled readers and writers: that is does having these skills enable more equitable social, economic and political functioning?

In the first instance the tinkerings we have outlined become more significant if control over them, and responsibility for them, comes from the sociocultural group. That means local parents have power in deciding on and controlling educational policy.

More than this, it means the school has to come to have believable local functions, to be recognizable as a potentially useful institution. Ways of being in the world, including strategies of learning, can be very different for some groups from those expected at school. Given the school changes, better matching between the two socialization settings is possible, with the benefits predicted by Bronfenbrenner. This means in a country like New Zealand, shifting at least to bilingual schools which take on significant aspects of the Tangata Whenua, the people of the land who are the victims of colonization. In order for the institution of schooling to be perceived and used differently wider economic, social and political changes are needed: the conclusion reached by Ogbu.

Literacy is not independent of political realities. Both Freire and Postman then are right. These writers, who were referred to at the beginning of this book, claimed both that becoming skilled and reading arose from acts of political domination (Postman), and that it was an act for political freedom (Freire). They are both right because teaching reading and learning to read can have both outcomes, depending on conditions of socialization.

Notes

Another account of learning to read?

1 The assumption made here, as in studies of error patterns made when reading prose (sometimes called miscue analysis), is that consistent patterns reflect the way in which a reader attempts to identify words.

2 Oliver in *As You Like It* (Act I, Scene I, line 175).

1 Strategies and feedback

1 Often when the term 'learning strategy' has been used it still refers to rule-bound performance. In these cases the task itself demands, sets criteria for and measures some learning product such as making a discrimination (e.g. Gholson, 1980) or identifying a concept (e.g. Bruner, Goodnow and Austin, 1956). To perform in accordance with the goals of the task a child must demonstrate some knowledge. While the strategy is associated with the acquisition of this knowledge (a solution to the problem the experimenter has set) the strategy itself is not the primary determinant of changes in performance capabilities.

2 The general description of self-correction in this section is based on research reported by Clay, 1968, 1979; Goodman and Burke, 1973; Weber, 1970.

3 The rate or mathematically equivalent proportion is calculated as

$$\frac{a}{a + b}$$

where a = selfcorrected errors and b = unselfcorrected errors. Thus the number of errors made (a + b) critically affects the ratio. For example:

$$\frac{2}{2 + 1} \text{ versus } \frac{2}{2 + 10}$$

4 Data showing self-corrections in language learning are provided by Karmiloff-Smith, 1979; Ng, 1979; Nelson, 1972; Weir, 1962. Sensori-motor examples can be found in Bower, 1977; Bruner, 1973.

2 Intending and knowing

1 See Bruner, 1973; Kelso and Wallace, 1978; and K.M. Newell, 1978. In these psychological analyses terms such as 'feedforward' and 'internal feedback' are used alongside physiological terms such as 'corollary discharge' to refer to a preparedness to act and receive feedback.

3 Being perturbed: Learning from problems

1 It could be argued that similar processes are associated with the 'word superiority effect' (e.g. Baron, 1978), or the finding that a syn-tactically well-formed sentence in the context of a meaningful story can be read more quickly than the component words could be identi-fied in isolation.
2 This is one observation from a series taken from personal diaries.
3 In three such studies this incidental learning about words in the course of solving them in context has been readily observable. The rate of learning to identify words in isolation varies in the studies between four and ten words after six sessions. The readers achieved this having encountered the words about three times in context and meeting about one unknown word in every ten words of text.
4 This claim can be found in a range of theoretical writings, such as those by Bruner (e.g. Bruner, Goodnow and Austin, 1956); Harlow, 1949; Kohler, 1927; and Simon (e.g. Langley and Simon, 1981).

4 Overcoming the general problem: Practice making perfect

1 The processes which are suggested as operating here are similar to E.J. Gibson's account of perceptual learning. For Gibson perceptual learning is achieved in strategic expressions of perceiving described as attending behaviour. She describes attending strategies in active yet behavioural terms and claims they are dependent on knowledge of goals, expectations and learner's needs. See Gibson and Rader, 1979, p. 3.
2 The argument here is that those descriptions show that children exhibit task-specific strategies (acts of integration) for generalizing behaviour. To support this there are experimental studies which demonstrate that child behaviours associated with generalization in complex skills are both strategic and modifiable, e.g. Goetz and Baer, 1973; Meichenbaum and Asarnow, 1979.

5 Dominance during instruction

1 The development of reading skills ordinarily entails a shift from a mixture of externally cued and self-initiated learning to complete independence from instruction. The major issue facing any analysis of learning processes therefore concerns how conditions can best be arranged for the development of independence.
2 Similar claims are made by Burton White for his concept of 'competence motivation' (White, 1959). Such claims are supported by observations that even neonates engage in rudimentary forms of performance-directed regulated learning, given the appropriate circumstances (Haith, 1980).
3 The authors whose ideas contributed to this section include Bruner, 1973; Donaldson, 1978; Hayes-Roth, Klahr and Mostow, 1981; Kaye, 1979; Kohler, 1927.
4 The authors whose ideas contributed to this section include Bornstein, 1981; Haith, 1980; Melzoff and Moore, 1979, and various articles in *Infant Behaviour and Development*, 1983; Rovee-Collier and Gekoski, 1979; J.S. Watson, 1979.

6 The conditions of learning

1 It is the same child who supplied the comments on p. 55. There are similar observations by Scollon and Scollon, 1982; and Heath, 1982b.
2 The term tutor will be used when referring to any more expert person who intentionally or unintentionally influences a child's learning.
3 This conceptualization is also present in Vygotsky's writings on development, e.g. Vygotsky, 1978.

7 Making interactions work: Setting events for learning

1 In the following analyses it is assumed that books rather than compartmentalized tasks such as letter identification exercises are the major vehicle for learning to read. The analysis therefore is limited to this vehicle.
2 The reasons why isolation produced fewer errors in Singer, Samuels and Spiroff's study result from the sequencing of training and test trials which for the isolation group set up appropriate conditions for transfer of training across trials, plus the limited nature of the context.
3 A more general perspective can be added to Bandura's. Early socialization, particularly the mode of interaction between care-givers and infants, have been claimed to influence a general motivational urge to become competent, or a general disposition to control the environment – see Kaye, 1979; Watson 1979; White, 1959.

9 Praise, conversation and putting it all together

1 In keeping with the previous section attention contingent on correct or appropriate performance will be referred to as positive feedback.

2 It is possible that Brophy's data, because of their non-developmental basis, simply reflect the operation of a very 'lean' and perhaps variable interval schedule of praise which in the initial stages approximated a high density (e.g. fixed ratio) schedule. But although not specifically developmental Brophy's review included first grade classrooms. In the first year of schooling the incidence of praise was still found to be low. Brophy cannot examine his data from a developmental shaping perspective but the indications are that the praise and approval are not clearly or predictably a specific component of interactions over time. They are more likely to be given for performing, so it often occurs at the end of an interactional sequence.

3 The rates that Brophy has obtained should not be seen as an ideal. Average doesn't necessarily equal best. In fact given the ideal of an enduring one-to-one relationship as described by Bronfenbrenner it could be predicted that rates of affectionate positive feedback are generally too low in classrooms. The point of the comment, however, relates to the function of positive feedback.

10 The early socializations of learning to read

1 There are compelling personal accounts of this concern and tentativeness in both Durkin and Clark.

2 Durkin asked, did you give 'the following kinds of help?', and listed a limited number of specific types.

3 It cannot be clearly established from Durkin's methodology that the later difference between early readers and non-early readers was attributable to early skills. As Coltheart (1979) has pointed out there are significant problems of matching and statistical analysis in the comparisons. The methodological weaknesses do not detract, however, from the conclusion that the early readers continued to be relatively high achievers as they progressed through school. All that is at issue is the source of the difference *between* early and non-early readers.

11 The transition: From home to school

1 This is a highly simplified model in that it shows the child's non-school experiences as occurring in only one social setting with one tutor. It also refers only to interactions and changes in interactions. Ideally setting events and their changes should also be represented in the model.

2 Unfortunately, the statistical evidence for this conclusion is not supplied in Cohen's published report.

3 For example these surveys contain information that teachers initiated more contact with parents in higher social classes. That contact was discriminatory as was the frequency of sending schoolwork home.

4 Contrary to what has also been argued in this book Hewison has claimed that setting events such as reading as a salient activity are very weak by comparison. Two points can be made. In her question-naire data parents who were given no standard for their judgements were categorized as either 'reads a lot of books' or doesn't. This is a very insensitive measure. Other surveys which ask more specific quantifiable questions yield higher correlations between number of books in the home and reading (Whitehead *et al.*, 1977). Secondly, in this book setting events are conceptualized as just that, influencing the probability of certain interactions which are the actual vehicles of learning.

12 Being schooled

1 It should be emphasized that these are average differences. There is a strong likelihood that these experiences will be part of low progress, but this may not be the experience of some low progress readers.

2 It has been pointed out that this may not in itself be entirely approp-riate. If low progress readers are to 'catch up' with their peers more time should be allocated (Allington, 1983).

3 Other studies report similar findings, and this sensitivity is also found in the interactions which involve some minority culture students (Cunningham, 1976; Neisser, 1986).

4 Allington (1983). But it must be noted that the direction of the prompt may differ across different programmes. Drake (1984) observed poor readers in a natural language programme. The great majority of teacher interruptions over an error directed children to contextual cues.

5 Reviews by Becker and Englemann, 1978; Becker and Carnine, 1980; Becker, Englemann, Carnine and Rhine, 1981, are used in the following discussion, with additional data supplied by Guthrie, Martuza and Siefert, 1979.

6 See papers in *Harvard Educational Review*, 1978, 48.

13 Becoming a skilled reader

1 The same implication is drawn from cross-cultural comparisons of experiences related to language learning; see Snow, 1979.

2 Holding a variable constant is a statistical technique whereby the separate influence of a variable on the results can be controlled for, thus showing how much it contributed to the finding.

Bibliography

Acland, H. (1980) 'Research as stage management: the case of the Plowden Committee', in M. Bulmer (ed.) *Social Research and Royal Commissions*, London, Allen & Unwin.

Adams, J.A. (1978) 'Theoretical issues for knowledge of results', in G.E. Stelmach (ed.) *Information Processing in Motor Control and Learning*, New York, Academic Press.

Allington, R.L. (1980) 'Teacher interruption behaviour during primary-grade oral reading', *Journal of Educational Psychology*, 72, 371–7.

Allington, R.L. (1983) 'The reading instruction provided readers of differing reading abilities', *Elementary School Journal*, 83, 548–59.

Anderson, A.B. and Stokes, S.J. (1984) 'Social and institutional influences on the development and practice of literacy', in H. Goelman, A. Oberg and F. Smith (eds) *Awakening to Literacy*, London, Heinemann.

Anderson, R.B., St Pierre, R.G., Proper, E.C. and Stebbins, L.B. (1978) 'Pardon us but what was the question again? A response to the critique of the Follow Through evaluation', *Harvard Educational Review*, 48, 161–70.

Arlin, M., Scott, M., and Webster, J. (1979) 'The effects of pictures on rate of learning sight words: a critique of the focal attention hypothesis', *Reading Research Quarterly*, 14, 645–7.

Asher, S.R. (1980) 'Topic interest and children's reading comprehension', in R.J. Sprio, B.C. Bruce and W.F. Brewer (eds) *Theoretical Issues in Reading Comprehension*, Hillsdale, NJ, Lawrence Erlbaum.

Ausubel, D.P. (1968) *Educational Psychology: A Cognitive View*, New York, Holt, Rinehart & Winston.

Bandura, A. (1982) 'Self-efficacy mechanism in human agency', *American Psychologist*, 37, 122–47.

Baron, J. (1977) 'Intelligence and general strategies', in G. Underwood (ed.) *Strategies in Information Processing*, New York, Academic Press.

Baron, J. (1978) 'The word superiority effect: perceptual learning from reading', in W.K. Estes (ed), *Handbook of Learning and Cognitive Processes*, vol. 6, Hillsdale, NJ, Lawrence Erlbaum.

Barr, R. (1972) The influence of instructional conditions on word recognition errors', *Reading Research Quarterly*, 7, 509–29.

Barr, R, (1974) 'The effect of instruction on pupil reading strategies', *Reading Research Quarterly*, 10, 555–82.

Becker, W. and Carnine, D. (1980) 'Direct instruction: an effective approach to educational intervention with the disadvantaged and low performers', in B.B. Lahey and A.E. Kazdin (eds) *Advances in Clinical Child Psychology*, vol. 3, 429–73.

Becker, W. and Engelmann, S. (1978) 'Systems for basic instruction: theory and applications', in A.C. Catania and T.A. Brigham (eds) *Handbook of Applied Behavior Analysis: Social and Instructional Processes*, New York, Wiley.

Becker, W., Engelmann, S. and Carnine, D. (1982) 'Direct Instruction technology: making learning happen', in P. Karolz and J.J. Steffen, (eds) *Advances in Child Behavior and Therapy*, vol. 2, New York, Gardner Press.

Becker, W., Engelmann, S., Carnine, D. and Rhine, W.R. (1981) 'Direct instructional model', in W.R. Rhine (ed.) *Making Schools More Effective: New Directions from Follow Through*, New York, Academic Press.

Berlin, I. (1953) *The Hedgehog and the Fox*, New York, Simon & Schuster.

Betts, E.A. (1946) *Foundations of Reading Instruction*, New York, American Book Company.

Bijou, S. and Baer, D. (1978) *Behavior Analysis of Child Development*, Englewood Cliffs, NJ, Prentice-Hall.

Bissex, G.L. (1980) *Gnys at Wrk*, Cambridge, Mass., Harvard University Press.

Bloom, B. (1984) 'The two-sigma problem: the search for methods of group instruction as effective as one-to-one tutoring', *Educational Researcher*, 13, 4–15.

Borger, R. and Seabourne, A.E.M (1982) *The Psychology of Learning* (2nd edn), Harmondsworth, Penguin.

Bornstein, M.H. (1981) 'Two kinds of perceptual organisation near the beginning of life', in W.A. Collins (ed.) *Aspects of the Development of Competence*, Hillsdale, NJ, Lawrence Erlbaum.

Bower, T.G.R. (1977) *A Primer of Infant Development*, San Francisco, CA, Freeman.

Bransford, J.D. (1979) *Human Cognition; Learning Understanding and Remembering*, Belmont, NJ, Wadsworth.

Bronfenbrenner, U. (1979) 'Contexts of child rearing: problems and prospects' *American Psychologist*, 34, 844–50.

Brophy, J. (1981) 'Teacher praise: a functional analysis', *Review of Educational Research*, 51, 5–32

Brown, R. and Hanlon, C. (1970) 'Derivational complexity and order of acquisition in child speech', in J.R. Hayes (ed.) *Cognition and the Development of Language*, New York, Wiley.

Bruner, J.S. (1971) *The Relevance of Education*, London, Allen & Unwin.

Bruner, J.S. (1973) *Beyond the Information Given: Studies in the Psychology of Knowing* (selected, edited and introduced by J.M. Anglin), New York, Norton.

Bruner, J.S. (1977) 'Early social interaction and language acquisition', in H.R. Schaffer (ed.) *Studies in Mother–Infant Interaction*, London, Academic Press.

Bruner, J.S., Goodnow, J.J. and Austin, G.A. (1956) *A Study of Thinking*, New York, Wiley.

Bruner, J.S., Wallach, M.A. and Galanter, E.H. (1959) 'The identification of recurrent regularity', *American Journal of Psychology*, 72, 200–9.

Bullock Report (1975) *A Language for Life*, Department of Education and Science, London, HMSO.

Calfee, R.C. and Piontkowski, D.C. (1981) 'The reading diary: acquisition of decoding', *Reading Research Quarterly*, 16, 346–73.

Campbell, R. (1981) 'An approach to analysing teacher verbal moves in hearing children read', *Journal of Research in Reading*, 4, 43–56.

Carnine, D. and Silbert, J. (1979) *Direct Instruction Reading*, Columbus, Ohio, Charles Merrill.

Cazden, C. (1979) 'Learning to read in clasroom interaction', in L.B. Resnick and R.A. Weaver (eds) *Theory and Practice of Early Reading*, vol. 3, Hillsdale, NJ, Lawrence Erlbaum.

Cazden, C. (1983) 'Ability grouping and differential instruction: what happens and some possible whys', paper presented at Wingspread Conference Centre, March.

Chall, J. (1967) *Learning to Read: The Great Debate*, New York, McGraw-Hill.

Chapin, M. and Dyck, D.G. (1976) 'Persistence in children's reading behaviour as a function of N length and attribution retraining', *Journal of Abnormal Psychology*, 85, 511–15.

Chazan, M., Laing, A. and Jackson, S. (1971) *Just Before School*, Oxford, Basil Blackwell.

Chazan, M., Laing, A., Cox, T., Jackson, S. and Lloyd, G. (1977) *Studies of Infant School Children 1. Deprivation and School Progress*, Oxford, Basil Blackwell.

Chomsky, C. (1972) 'Stages in language development and reading exposure', *Harvard Educational Review*, 42, 1–33.

Clark, M.M. (1976) *Young Fluent Readers*, London, Heinemann.

Clarke-Stewart, K.A. (1978) 'Popular primers for parents', *American Psychologist*, 33, 359–69.

Clay, M.M. (1966) 'Emergent reading behaviour', unpublished Ph.D thesis, University of Auckland.

Clay, M.M. (1968) 'A syntactic analysis of reading errors', *Journal of Verbal Learning and Verbal Behavior*, 7, 434–8.

Clay, M.M. (1979) *Reading: The Patterning of Complex Behaviour* (2nd edn), Auckland, Heinemann.

Clay, M.M. (1980) 'Early writing and reading: reciprocal gains', in M.M. Clark and T Glynn (eds) *Reading and Writing for the Child with Difficulty*, Educational Review, Ocasional Publications no. 8, University of Birmingham.

Cohen, A.S. (1975) 'Oral reading errors of first grade children taught by a code emphasis approach', *Reading Research Quarterly*, 10, 616–50.

Cohen, J. (1979) 'Patterns of parent help', *Educational Research*, 21, 186–93.

Coleman, J.S., Campbell, E., Hobson, C.J., McPartland, J., Mood, A.M., Weinfeld, F. and York, R.L. (1966) *Equality of Educational Opportunity*, Washington, DC, US Government Printing Office.

Coltheart, M. (1979) 'When can children learn to read – and when should they be taught?, in T.G. Waller and G.E. Mackinnon (eds) *Reading Research: Advances in Theory and Practice*, vol. 1, New York, Academic Press.

Cox, T. (1977) 'School progress and adjustment in urban areas', in M. Chazan, A. Laing, T. Cox, S. Jackson and G. Lloyd, *Studies of Infant School Children 1. Deprivation and School Progress*, Oxford, Basil Blackwell.

Cunningham, P.M. (1976) 'Teacher's correction responses to black dialect miscues which are non meaning changing', *Reading Research Quarterly*, 12, 637–53.

Curie, E. (1938) *Madame Curie*, London, Heinemann.

d'Ydewalle, G. and Buchwald, A.M. (1976) 'Effects of "right" and "wrong" as a function of recalling either the response or the outcome', *Journal of Experimental Psychology: Human Learning and Memory*, 2, 728–38.

Davie, R., Butler, N. and Goldstein, H. (1972) *From Birth to Seven: The Second Report of the National Child Development Study*, London, Longman.

Donald, D.R. (1979) 'Effects of illustrations on early oral reading accuracy, strategies and comprehension', *British Journal of Educational Psychology*, 49, 282–9.

Donaldson, M. (1978) *Children's Minds*, Glasgow, Fontana.

Douglas, J.W.B. (1964) *The Home and the School*, London, MacGibbon & Kee.

Downing, J. (1970) 'Children's concepts of language in learning to read', *Educational Research*, 12, 106–12.

Downing, J. and Leong, C.K. (1982) *Psychology of Reading*, New York, Macmillan.

Drake, J. (1984) 'The development of interactions between a teacher and high and low progress readers', unpublished MA thesis, University of Auckland.

Durkin, D. (1966) *Children Who Read Early*, New York, Teachers College Press.

Durkin, D. (1978) 'What classroom observations reveal about reading comprehension instruction', *Reading Research Quarterly*, 14, 481–533.

Eder, D (1982) 'Differences in communicative styles across ability groups', in L.C. Wilkinson (ed.), *Communicating in the Classroom*, New York, Academic Press.

Ehri, L.C. and Wilce, L.S. (1979) 'Do beginners learn to read function words better in sentences or in lists?' *Reading Research Quarterly*, 14, 451–76.

Elley, W.B. (1966) 'The role of errors in learning with feedback', *British Journal of Educational Psychology*, 36, 296–300.

Finkelstein, N.W. and Ramey, C.T. (1977) 'Learning to control the environment in infancy', *Child Development*, 48, 806–19.

Flower, R.D.K. (1983) 'Factors influencing on-task behaviours during reading instruction', unpublished MA thesis, University of Auckland.

Francis, H. (1982) *Learning to Read*, London, Allen & Unwin.

Fraser, E. (1959) *Home Environment and the School*, London, University of London Press.

Freire, P. (1972) *Pedagogy of the Oppressed*, Harmondsworth, Penguin.

Gallistel, C.R. (1980) *The Organisation of Action: A New Synthesis*, Hillsdale, NJ, Lawrence Erlbaum.

Gambrell, L.B., Wilson, R.M. and Gantt, W.N. (1981) 'Classroom observations of task-attending behaviors of good and poor readers', *Journal of Educational Research*, 17, 400–4.

Gholson, B. (1980) *The Cognitive-developmental Basis of Human Learning: Studies in Hypothesis Testing*, New York, Academic Press.

Gibson, E.J. and Rader, N. (1979) 'Attention: the perceiver as performer', in G.A. Hale and M. Lewis (eds) *Attention and Cognitive Development*, New York, Plenum.

Glynn, T. (1982) 'Antecedent control of behaviour in educational contexts', *Educational Psychology*, 2, 214–29.

Glynn, T. and McNaughton, S. (1985) 'The Mangere Home and School Remedial Reading procedures: continuing research on their effectiveness', *New Zealand Journal of Psychology*, 14, 66–77.

Goetz, E.M. and Baer, D. (1973) 'Social control of form diversity and the emergence of new forms in children's block building', *Journal of Applied Behavior Analysis*, 6, 209–17.

Gombrich, E. (1979) *Art and Illusion: A Study in the Psychology of Pictorial Representation*, Oxford, Phaidon.

Goodman, K. and Burke, C. (1973) 'Theoretically based studies of patterns of miscues in oral reading performance', Report on Project 9–0375, US Office of Education Bureau of Research, 786.

Goodman, K. and Gollasch, F.V. (1981) 'Word omissions: deliberate and non-deliberate', *Reading Research Quarterly*, 16, 6–31.

Grass, G. (1965) *The Tin Drum*, Harmondsworth, Penguin.

Guthrie, J. (1982) 'Reading in New Zealand: achievement and volume', *Reading Research Quarterly*, 17, 6–27.

Guthrie, J., Martuza, V. and Siefert, M. (1979) 'Impact of instructional time in reading', in L.B. Resnick and R.A. Weaver (eds) *Theory and Practice of Early Reading*, vol. 3, Hillsdale, NJ, Lawrence Erlbaum.

Haith, M.M. (1980) *Rules that Bagies Look by: The Organisation of Newborn Visual Activity*, Hillsdale, Lawrence Erlbaum.

Hale, G.A. (1979) 'Development of children's attention to stimulus components', in G.A. Hale and M. Lewis (eds) *Attention and Cognitive Development*, New York, Plenum.

Hansen, C.L. and Eaton, M.D. (1978) 'Reading' in H.G. Haring, T.C. Lovitt, M.D. Eaton and C.L. Hansen (eds) *The Fourth R: Research in the Classroom*, Columbus, Ohio, Merrill.

Harlow, H.F. (1949) 'The formation of learning sets', *Psychological Review*, 56, 51–65.

Hart, B. and Risley, T.R. (1980) 'In vivo language intervention: unanticipated general effects', *Journal of Applied Behaviour Analysis*, 13, 407–32.

Hayes-Roth, F., Klahr, P. and Mostow, P. (1981) 'Advice taking and knowledge refinement: an iterative view of skill development', in J.R. Anderson (ed.) *Cognitive Skills and their Acquisition*, Hillsdale, NJ, Lawrence Erlbaum.

Heath, S.B. (1982a) 'Questioning at home and at school: a comparative study', in G. Spindler (ed.) *Doing the ethnography of schooling*, New York, Holt, Rinehart & Winston.

Heath, S.B. (1982b) *Ways with Words*, Cambridge, Cambridge University Press.

Held, R. and Hein, A (1963) 'Movement produced stimulation in the development of visually guided behaviour', *Journal of Comparative and Physiological Psychology*, 56, 872–6.

Hess, R.D. and Holloway, S.D. (1984) 'Family and school as educational institutions', in R.D. Parke (ed.) *Review of Child Development Research*, vol. 7, Chicago, Ill., Chicago University Press.

Hewison, J. and Tizard, J. (1980) 'Parental involvement and reading attainment', *British Journal of Educational Psychology*, 50, 209–15.

Heyns, B. (1978) *Summer Learning and the Effects of Schooling*, New York, Academic Press.

Holland, J.G. (1979) 'Analysis of behaviour in reading instruction', in L.B. Resnick and P.A. Weaver (eds) *Theory and Practice of Early Reading Instruction*, vol. 1, Hillsdale, NJ, Lawrence Erlbaum.

Hulse, S.W., Deese, J. and Egeth, H. (1975) *The Psychology of Learning* (4th edn), New York, McGraw-Hill.

Illich, I. (1973) *Deschooling Society*, Harmondsworth, Penguin.

Jencks, C., Smith, M.S., Acland, H., Bane, M.J., Cohen, D., Gintis, H., Heyns, B. and Michelson, S. (1972) *Inequality: A Reassessment of the Effect of Family and Schooling in America*, New York, Basic Books.

John-Steiner, V. and Roth, N. (1984) 'Study of children's writings in non-instructional settings', in J. Sloboda (ed.) *The Acquisition of Symbolic Skill*, London, Plenum.

Kagan, J., Kearsley, R. and Zelazo, P. (1978) *Infancy: Its Place in Human Development*, Cambridge, Mass., Harvard University Press.

Karmiloff-Smith, A. (1979) *A Functional Approach to Child Language: A Study of Determiners and Reference*, Cambridge, Cambridge University Press.

Kaye, K. (1979) 'The development of skills', in G.J. Whitehurst and B.J. Immerman (eds) *The Functions of Language and Cognition*, New York, Academic Press.

Kelso, J.A. and Wallace, S.A. (1978) 'Conscious mechanisms in movement', in G.E. Stelmach (ed.) *Information Processing in Motor Control and Learning*, New York, Academic Press.

Klein, G. (1976) 'Effect of attentional demands on context utilization', *Journal of Educational Psychology*, 68, 25–31.

Kohler, W. (1927) *The Mentality of Apes*, London, Routledge & Kegan Paul.

Krantz, P.J. and Risley, T. (1977) 'Behavioural ecology in the classroom', in K.D. O'Leary (ed.) *Classroom Management: The Successful Use of Behavior Modification* (2nd edn), New York, Pergamon.

Kulhavy, R.W. (1977) 'Feedback in written instruction', *Review of Educational Research*, 47, 211–32.

Langley, P. and Simon, H. (1981) 'The central role of learning in cognition', in J.R. Anderson (ed.) *Cognitive Skills and their Acquisition*, Hillsdale, NJ, Lawrence Erlbaum.

Laosa, L. (1982) 'Maternal behavior: sociocultural diversity in modes of family interaction', in R.W. Henderson (ed.) *Parent–Child Interaction: Theory, Research and Prospects*, New York, Academic Press.

Leinhardt, G., Zigmond, N. and Cooley, W. (1981) 'Reading instructions and its effects', *American Educational Research Journal*, 18, 343–61.

Lepper, M.R. (1981) 'Intrinsic and extrinsic motivation in children: detrimental effects of superfluous social controls', in W.A. Collins (ed.) *Aspects of the Development of Competence*, Hillsdale, NJ, Lawrence Erlbaum.

Limbrick, E., McNaughton, S. and Glynn, T. (1985) 'Reading gains for underachieving tutors and tutees in a cross-age peer tutoring programme', *Journal of Child Psychology and Psychiatry*, 26, 939–53.

Lorenz, K. (1977) *Behind the Mirror: A Search for a Natural History of Human Knowledge*, New York, Harcourt, Brace & Jovanovich.

Lovitt, T. (1976) 'Applied behavior analysis techniques and curriculum research: implications for instruction', in N.G. Haring and R.L. Schiefelbusch (eds) *Teaching Special Children*, New York, McGraw-Hill.

Luria, A.R. (1973) *The Working Brain: An Introduction to Neuropsychology*, Harmondsworth, Penguin.

McNaughton, S. (1981a) 'Becoming an independent reader: problem solving during oral reading', *New Zealand Journal of Educational Studies*, 16, 177–85.

McNaughton, S. (1981b) 'Low progress readers and teacher instructional behaviour during oral reading: the risk of maintaining instructional dependence', *The Exceptional Child*, 28, 167–76.

McNaughton, S. (1981c) 'The influence of immediate teacher correction on self-corrections and proficient oral reading', *Journal of Reading Behaviour*, 13, 367–71.

McNaughton, S. (1983a) 'How effective are proficient six-year-olds at solving words in context?', *New Zealand Journal of Educational Studies*, 18, 59–68.

McNaughton, S. (1983b) 'The development of independence in learning to read: progress across age levels and classroom instruction', Research Report 55/2/104, Wellington, Department of Education.

McNaughton, S. (1984) 'Finding solutions: the development of independent problem solving during oral reading', paper presented at the NZ Association for Research in Education Annual Conference, University of Otago, Dunedin.

McNaughton, S. (1986) 'Transitions from home to school and learning to read: explaining differences in classroom interaction in the New Zealand context', paper presented at the 21st Regional Language Centre Seminar, Singapore.

McNaughton, S. and Delquadri, J. (1978) 'Error attention tutoring in oral reading', in T. Glynn and S. McNaughton (eds) *Applied Behaviour Analysis in New Zealand, 1978*, Auckland, University of Auckland Education Department.

McNaughton, S. and Glynn, T. (1981) 'Delayed versus immediate attention to oral reading errors: effects on accuracy and self-correction', *Educational Psychology*, 1, 57–65.

McNaughton, S., Glynn, T. and Robinson, V. (1981) *Parents as Remedial Reading Tutors: Issues for Home and School*, Wellington, New Zealand Council for Educational Research.

Marks, C.B., Doctorow, M.J. and Wittrock, M.C. (1974) 'Word frequency and reading comprehension', *Journal of Educational Research*, 67, 259–62.

Meichenbaum, D. and Asarnow, J. (1979) 'Cognitive-behavioural modification and metacognitive development: implications for the classroom', in P.C. Kendall and S.D. Hollon (eds) *Cognitive Behavioural Interventions: Theory, Research and Procedures*, New York, Academic Press.

Melzoff, A.N. and Moore, M.K. (1979) 'Imitation of facial and manual gestures in human neonates', *Science*, 198, 75–8.

Moon, C. and Wells, G. (1979) 'The influence of home on learning to read', *Journal of Research in Reading*, 2, 53–62.

Moore, T. (1968) 'Language and intelligence: a longitudinal study of the first eight years', *Human Development*, 11, 1–24.

National Assessment of Educational Progress (NAEP) (1985) *The Reading Report Card: Progress Towards Excellence in our Schools*, Princeton, NJ. Educational Testing Service.

Neisser, U. (1976) *Cognition and Reality*, San Francisco, Calif., Freeman.

Neisser, U. (1986) *The School Achievement of Minority Children: New Perspectives*, Hillsdale, NJ, Lawrence Erlbaum.

Nelson, K. (1972) 'Structure and strategy in learning to talk', *Monographs of the Society for Research in Child Development*, 38.

Newell, A. and Simon, H.A. (1972) *Human Problem Solving*, Englewood Cliffs, NJ, Prentice-Hall.

Newell, A. and Rosenbloom, P.S. (1982) 'Mechanisms of skill acquisition and the law of practice', in J.R. Anderson (ed.) *Cognitive Skills and their Acquisition*, Hillsdale, NJ, Lawrence Erlbaum.

Newell, K.M. (1978) 'Some issues on action plans', in G.E. Stelmach (ed.) *Information Processing in Motor Control and Learning*, New York, Academic Press.

Newson, J. and Newson, E. (1977) *Perspectives on School at Seven Years Old*, London, Allen & Unwin.

Ng, S.M. (1979) 'Error behaviour and self-correction in reading and oral language', unpublished Ph.D thesis, University of Auckland.

Nitsch, K.E. (1977) 'Structuring decontextualised forms of knowledge', paper cited in J.D. Bransford, *Human Cognition: Learning, Understanding and Remembering*, Belmont, Wadsworth.

Ogbu, J.U. (1981) 'Origins of human competence: a cultural ecological perspective', *Child Development*, 52, 413–29.

Olton, D.S. (1979) 'Mazes, maps and memory', *American Psychologist*, 34, 583–96.

Pearson, P.D. (1974) 'The effects of grammatical complexity on children's comprehension recall and conception of certain semantic relations', *Reading Research Quarterly*, 10, 92–115.

Pepler, D.J. and Rubin, K.H. (1982) *The Play of Children: Current Theory and Research*, Geneva, Karger AG.

Plowden Report (1967) *Children and their Primary Schools*, Department of Education and Science, London, HMSO.

Pluck, M.L., Ghafari, E., Glynn, T. and McNaughton, S. (1984) 'Teacher and parent modelling of recreational reading', *New Zealand Journal of Educational Studies*, 19, 114–23.

Pohl, H. and McNaughton, S. (1985) 'After eight years at school: high and low progress readers on entry to secondary school', *New Zealand Journal of Educational Studies*, 20, 140–50.

Postman, N. (1970) 'The politics of reading', *Harvard Educational Review*, 40, 244–52.

Reid, J.F. (1966) 'Learning to think about reading', *Educational Research*, 9, 56–62.

Resnick, L.B. (1979) 'Theories and prescriptions for early reading instruction', in L.B. Resnick and P.A. Weaver (eds) *Theory and Practice of Early Reading*, vol. 2, Hillsdale, NJ, Lawrence Erlbaum.

Resnick, L.B. (1980) 'The role of invention in the development of mathematical competence', in R.H. Kluwe and H. Spada (eds) *Developmental Models of Thinking*, New York, Academic Press.

Rosenshine, B.U. and Berliner, D.C. (1978) 'Academic engaged time', *British Journal of Teacher Education*, 4, 3–16.

Rovee-Collier, C.K. and Gekowski, M.J. (1979) 'The economics of infancy: a review of conjugate reinforcement', in H.W. Reese and L.P. Lipsitt (eds) *Advances in Child Development and Behaviour*, vol. 13, New York, Academic Press.

Schmidt, E. (1981) 'Early learnings about written language: a comparison of United States and Danish children', paper presented at the Second European Conference on Reading, Joensuu, Finland.

Schunk, D.H. (1982) 'Effect of effort attributional feedback on children's perceived self-efficacy and achievement', *Journal of Educational Psychology*, 74, 548–56.

Scollon, R. and Scollon, S. (1982) *Narrative, Literacy and Face in Interethnic Communication*, Norwood, NJ, Ablex.

Searle, J.R. (1980) 'The unintentionality of intention and action', *Cognitive Science*, 4, 47-70.

Shiffrin, R.M. and Dumais, S.T. (1981) 'The development of automatism', in J.R. Anderson, *Cognitive Skills and their Acquisition*, Hillsdale, NJ, Lawrence Erlbaum.

Sidman, M. and Wilson-Morris, M. (1974) 'Testing reading comprehension: a brief report on stimulus control', *Journal of Applied Behavior Analysis*, 7, 327–32.

Siegler, R.S. (1981) 'Development sequences within and between concepts', *Monographs of the Society for Research in Child Development*, 189, vol. 46.

Siegler, R.S. and Klahr, D. (1982) 'When do children learn? The relationship between existing knowledge and the acquisition of new knowledge', in R. Glaser (ed.) *Advances in Instructional Psychology*, vol. 2, Hillsdale, NJ, Lawrence Erlbaum.

Simons, H.D. (1979) 'Black dialect, reading interference and classroom interaction', in L.B. Resnick and P.A. Weaver (eds) *Theory and Practice of Early Reading*, vol. 3, Hillsdale, NJ, Lawrence Erlbaum.

Singer, H., Samuels, S.J. and Spiroff, J. (1973) 'The effect of pictures and contextual conditions on learning response to printed words', *Reading Research Quarterly*, 9, 555–67.

Singh, N., Winton, A.S.W. and Singh, J. (1984) 'Effects of delayed versus immediate attention to oral reading errors on the reading proficiency of mentally retarded children', *Applied Research in Mental Retardation*, 5, 295–305.

Skinner, B.F. (1968) *The Technology of Teaching*, New York, Appleton Century Crofts.

Smith, F. (1978) *Understanding Reading* (2nd edn), New York, Holt, Rinehart & Winston.

Snow, C. (1979) 'The role of social interaction in language acquisition', in W.A. Collins (ed.) *Children's Language and Communication*, Hillsdale, NJ, Lawrence Erlbaum.

Snow, C. (1983) 'Literacy and language: relationships during the preschool years', *Harvard Educational Review*, 55, 165–89.

Soderbergh, R. (1971) *Reading in Early Childhood*, Stockholm, Almquist & Wiksell.

Southgate, V. Arnold, H. and Johnson, S. (1981) *Extending Beginning Reading*, London, Heinemann Educational.

Steinert, Y.E., Campbell, S.B. and Kiely, M.C. (1981) 'A comparison of maternal and remedial teacher teaching styles with good and poor readers', *Journal of Learning Disabilities*, 14, 38–42.

Terman, L.M. (1925) *Genetic Studies of Genius*, vol. 1, Stanford, Calif., Stanford University Press.

Terrace, H.S. (1966) 'Stimulus control', in W.K. Honig (ed.) *Operant Behavior: Areas of Research and Application*, New York, Appleton Century Crofts.

Thompson, G.B. (1981) 'Individual differences attributed to self-corrections in reading', *British Journal of Educational Psychology*, 51, 228–9.

Tizard, J., Schofield, J. and Hewison, J. (1983) 'Collaboration between teachers and parents in assisting children's reading', *British Journal of Educational Psychology*, 52, 1–15.

Torrey, J. (1979) 'Reading that comes naturally: the early reader', in T.G. Waller and G.E. Mackinnon (eds), *Reading Research in Theory and Practice*, New York, Academic Press.

Vanderbilt, B.M. (1971) *Thomas Edison, Chemist*, Washington, DC, American Chemical Society.

von Wright, J.M. (1957) 'A note on the role of "guidance" in learning', *British Journal of Psychology*, 48, 133–7.

Vygotsky, L.S. (1962) *Thought and Language*, Cambridge, Mass., MIT Press.

Vygotsky, L.S. (1978) *Mind in Society: The Development of Higher Psychological Processes*, Cambridge, Mass., Harvard University Press, edited by M. Cole, V. John-Steiner, S. Scribner and E. Souberman.

Wade, T.A. (1978) 'Promotion patterns in the junior school', unpublished Diploma of Education dissertation, University of Auckland.

Watson, B. (1980) 'Teaching reading to new entrant children: an observational study', unpublished MA thesis, University of Auckland.

Watson, J.S. (1979) 'Perception of contingency as a determinant of social responsiveness', in E.G. Thoman (ed.) *Origins of the Infant's Social Responsiveness*, Hillsdale, NJ, Lawrence Erlbaum.

Weber, R.M. (1970) 'First-grader's use of grammatical context in reading', in H. Levin and J.P. Williams (eds) *Basic Studies on Reading*, New York, Basic Books.

Weinstein, R.S. (1976) 'Reading group membership in the first grade: teacher behaviours and pupil experience over time', *Journal of Educational Psychology*, 88, 103–16.

Weir, R.H. (1962) *Language in the Crib*, The Hague, Mouton.

Wells, G. (1979) 'Influences of the home on language development', *Bristol Working Papers in Language*, 1, 52–70.

Wells, G. (1981) *Learning through Interactions*, Cambridge, Cambridge University Press.

Wertsch, J.V. (ed.) (1984) *Culture, Communication and Cognition*, Cambridge, Cambridge University Press.

Wheldall, K. (1981) 'Behavioural pedagogy or behavioural overkill', *Educational Psychology*, 2, 181–4.

White, R.W. (1959) 'Motivation reconsidered: the concept of competence', *Psychological Review*, 66, 297–333.

White, B.L. and Held, R. (1966) 'Plasticity of sensorimotor development in the human infant', in J.F. Rosenblith and W. Allinsmith (eds) *The Causes of Behavior: Readings in Child Development and Educational Psychology*, Boston, Allyn & Bacon.

Whitehead, F., Capey, A.C., Maddren, W. and Wellings, A. (1977) *Children and their Books*, London, Macmillan.

Wildman, D.M. and Kling, M. (1979) 'Semantic, syntactic and spatial anticipation in reading', *Reading Research Quarterly*, 14, 128–64.

Wilkinson, L.C. (ed.) (1982) *Communicating in the Classroom*, New York, Academic Press.

Williams, J.P. (1970) 'From basic research on reading to educational practice', in H. Levin and J.P. Williams (eds) *Basic Studies on Reading*, New York, Basic Books.

Willows, D.M. (1978) 'Individual differences in distraction by pictures in a reading situation', *Journal of Educational Psychology*, 70, 837–47.

Wilson, M. and McNaughton, S. (1983) 'Removing the scaffolding: a developmental study of teacher–reader interactions during oral reading sessions', paper presented at NZ Psychological Society Annual Conference, Auckland.

Wolwhill, J. (1970) 'The age variable in psychological research', *Psychological Review*, 77, 49–64.

Wong, P. and McNaughton, S. (1981) 'The effects of prior provision of context on the oral reading proficiency of a low progress reader', *New Zealand Journal of Educational Studies*, 15, 169–75.

Wood, D. (1978) 'Problem solving – the nature and development of strategies', in G. Underwood (ed.) *Strategies of Information Processing*, New York, Academic Press.

Wood, D., Bruner, J.S. and Ross, G. (1976) 'The role of tutoring in problem solving', *Journal of Child Psychology and Psychiatry*, 17, 87–100.

Zelazo, P.R., Zelazo, N.A. and Kolb, S. (1971) 'Walking in the newborn', *Science*, 176, 314–15.

Name index

Subject index